BLOND'S® CRIMINAL LAW

Fourth Edition

Sulzburger & Graham Publishing, Ltd.

New York

ALSO AVAILABLE IN THIS SERIES:

Blond's Administrative Law
Blond's Civil Procedure
Blond's Commercial Law
Blond's Constitutional Law
Blond's Contracts
Blond's Corporate Tax
Blond's Corporations
Blond's Criminal Law
Blond's Criminal Procedure
Blond's Essay Questions — Contracts
Blond's Essay Questions — Torts
Blond's Evidence
Blond's Family Law
Blond's Income Tax
Blond's International Law
Blond's Multistate Questions
Blond's Property
Blond's Torts

© 1995 SULZBURGER & GRAHAM PUBLISHING, LTD.

ISBN 0-945819-83-8

PRINTED IN THE UNITED STATES OF AMERICA

BLOND'S®
CRIMINAL LAW

Neil C. Blond
Elliot Felig
Amy Johannesen
Peter J.W. Sherwin

Fourth Edition
Revised by
Kevin L. Kite
Adam Rappaport
Craig A. Sperling

Abbreviations used in this book

D   Defendant
MPC   Model Penal Code
FRE   Federal Rules of Evidence
S.Ct. United States Supreme Court

KS   Kadish & Schulhofer, Criminal Law and Its Processes, Cases and Materials

L   LaFave, Modern Criminal Law, Cases, Comments and Questions

KW   Kaplan & Weisberg, Criminal Law, Cases and Materials

W   Weinreb, Criminal Law, Cases, Comment, Questions

DS   Dix & Sharlot, Criminal Law, Cases and Materials

J   Johnson, Criminal Law, Cases, Materials and Text

MIB   Moenssens, Inbau & Bacigal, Criminal Law, Cases and Comments

Blond's Criminal Law	Kadish Schulhofer	LaFave	Kaplan Weisberg	Weinreb
Chapter 1 Criminal Justice System	1-96	1-22		1-69
Chapter 2 Punishment	97-170 282-314	23-95	1-51 953-1024	410-434 803-900
Chapter 3 Actus Reus and Mens Rea	171-314	96-237	51-186	349-369 710-731
Chapter 4 Crimes Against the Person	315-384	590-593	1071-1119	521-592
Chapter 5 Homicide	385-546	238-315 334-353	187-460	69-220 310-348
Chapter 6 Causation and Attempt	547-640	315-334 540-595 696-703	461-567	370-391 732-756
Chapter 7 Group Criminality	641-800	596-696 704-807	567-762	756-802
Chapter 8 Justification and Excuse	801-1038	354-539	763-952	221-309 593-709
Chapter 9 Theft Offenses	1034-1125	593-595	1025-1070	435-520

Blond's Criminal Law	Dix Sharlot	Johnson	Inbau Moenssens Thompson
Chapter 1 Criminal Justice System	1-64	97-121 494-558	1-20 116-135
Chapter 2 Punishment	65-153	75-97 121-170	21-74 289-350 775-960
Chapter 3 Actus Reus and Mens Rea	154-186 242-344	1-74	626-667
Chapter 4 Crimes Against Person	230-242 496-540		273-289
Chapter 5 Homicide	377-466	171-307	75-197 228-272
Chapter 6 Causation and Attempt	467-495 541-581	559-600	462-488
Chapter 7 Group Criminality	581-714	600-675	488-584
Chapter 8 Justification and Excuse	344-376 715-837	308-493	198-228 585-625 668-774
Chapter 9 Theft Offenses	187-230 294-307	676-754	351-461

How To Use This Book
"You teach yourself the law, we teach you how to think"
— Professor Kingsfield, The Paper Chase

Law school is very different from your previous educational experiences. In the past, course material was presented in a straightforward manner both in lectures and texts. You did well by memorizing and regurgitating. In law school, your fat casebooks are stuffed with material, most of which will be useless when finals arrive. Your professors ask a lot of questions but don't seem to be teaching you either the law or how to think. Sifting through voluminous material seeking out the important concepts is a hard, time-consuming chore. We've done that job for you. This book will help you study effectively. We hope to teach you the law and how to think.

Preparing for class
Most students start their first year by reading and briefing all their cases. They spend too much time copying unimportant details. After finals they realize they wasted time on facts that were useless on the exam.

Case Clips
This book contains a case clip of every major case covered in your casebook. Case Clips help you focus on what your professor wants you to get out of your cases. Case Clips are written in a way that should provide a tremendous amount of understanding in a relatively short period of time. Facts, Issues, and Rules are carefully and succinctly stated. Left out are details irrelevant to what you need to learn from the case. In general, we skip procedural matters in lower courts. We don't care which party is the appellant or petitioner because the trivia is not relevant to the law. Case Clips should be read before you read the actual case. You will have a good idea what to look for in the case, and appreciate the significance of what you are reading. Inevitably you will not have time to read all your cases before class. Case Clips allow you to prepare for class in about five minutes. You will be able to follow the discussion and listen without fear of being called upon.

Hanau Charts
When asked how he managed to graduate in the top ten percent of his class at one of the ten most prestigious law schools in the land, Paul Hanau introduced his system of flow charts now known as Hanau Charts.

A very common complaint among first year students is that they "can't put it all together." When you are reading 400 pages a week it is difficult to remember how the last case relates to the first and how November's readings relate to September's. It's hard to understand the relationship between different torts topics when you have read cases for three or four other classes in between. Hanau Charts will help you put the whole course together. They are designed to help you memorize fundamentals. They reinforce your learning by showing you the material from another perspective.

Outlines

More than one hundred lawyers and law students were interviewed as part of the development of this series. Most complained that their casebooks did not teach them the law and were far too voluminous to be useful before an exam. They also told us that the commercial outlines they purchased were excellent when used as hornbooks to explain the law, but were too wordy and redundant to be effective during the weeks before finals. Few students can read four 500-page outlines during the last month of classes. It is virtually impossible to memorize that much material and even harder to decide what is important. Almost every student interviewed said he or she studied from homemade outlines. We've written the outline you should use to study.

"But writing my own outline will be a learning experience."

True, but unfortunately many students spend so much time outlining they don't leave time to learn and memorize. Many students told us they spent six weeks outlining, and only one day studying before each final!

Mnemonics

Most law students spend too much time reading, and not enough time memorizing. Mnemonics are included to help you organize your essays and spot issues. They highlight what is important and which areas deserve your time.

TABLE OF CONTENTS

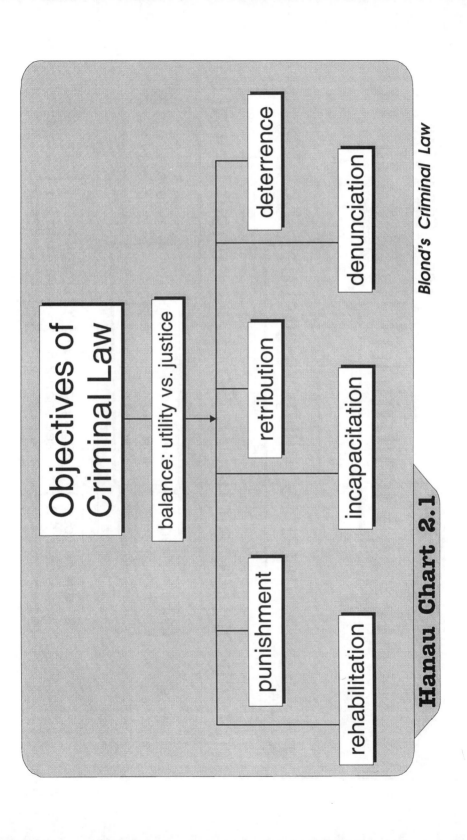

Objectives of Criminal Law

balance: utility vs. justice

punishment

retribution

deterrence

rehabilitation

incapacitation

denunciation

Blond's Criminal Law

Hanau Chart 2.1

Hanau Chart 2.2

Blond's Criminal Law

Limitations

theoretical

balance: utility vs. justice

practical (*DIC*tatorial *DoDo*)

constitutional

diversion of police power

ineffectiveness of deterrents

corruption enforcement officials

discrimination against minorities

deterioration in respect for law

due process see chart 2.3

equal protection see chart 2.5

proportionality see chart 2.6

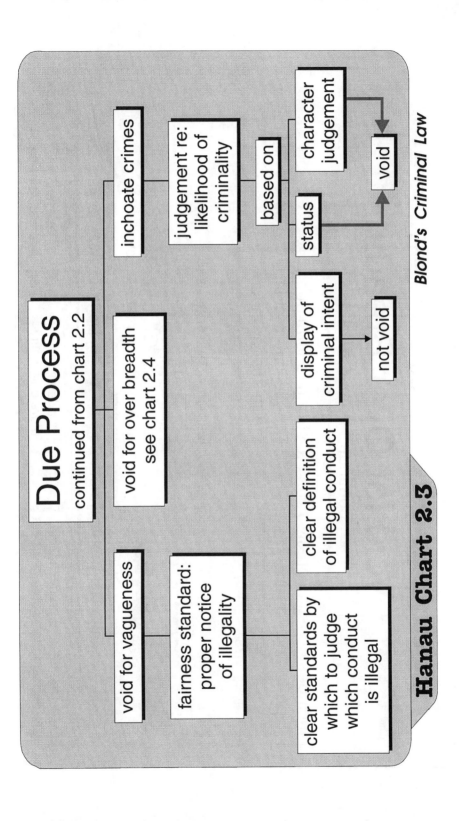

Due Process
continued from chart 2.2

void for vagueness

- fairness standard: proper notice of illegality
  - clear standards by which to judge which conduct is illegal
  - clear definition of illegal conduct

void for over breadth
see chart 2.4

- display of criminal intent → not void

inchoate crimes

- judgement re: likelihood of criminality
  - based on
    - status → void
    - character judgement → void

Blond's Criminal Law

Hanau Chart 2.3

Hanau Chart 2.4

Void for Over Breadth

continued from chart 2.3

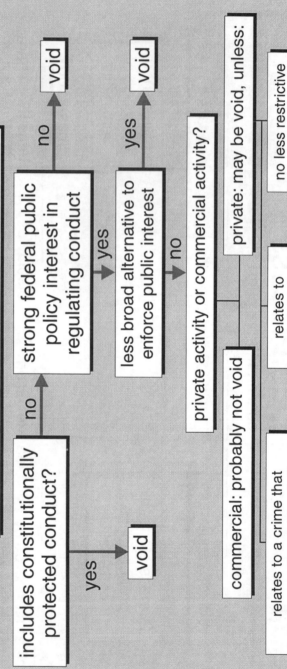

includes constitutionally protected conduct?

yes → void

no → strong federal public policy interest in regulating conduct

no → void

yes → less broad alternative to enforce public interest

yes → void

no → private activity or commercial activity?

commercial: probably not void

- relates to a crime that infringes on the rights of others
- relates to future criminality

private: may be void, unless:

- no less restrictive alternative exists

Equal Protection

continued from chart 2.2

statute must not arbitrarily classify
the kind of people to whom it applies

classification

all individuals who are similarly situated
are required to conform to same standard

fair and substantial relation
to conduct prohibited

classification furthers
the purpose of the act

no nondiscriminative
alternative exists

classification
makes enforcement
more effective

discrimination
is not
intended result

Blond's Criminal Law

Hanau Chart 2.5

Hanau Chart 2.6

Proportionality
continued from chart 2.2

theoretical standards

- severe enough to outweigh the profit of the offense
- increases proportionally with the severity of the crime
- increases proportionally with the likelihood of the success of the crime

constitutional standards
continued on chart 2.7

- not more severe than necessary to deter

Constitutional Standards

continued from chart 2.6

balance →

nature of crime
vs.
severity of punishment

deference to legislature

evolving standards of decency

punishment for similar crimes
in different jurisdictions

less severe alternative

punishment for more severe
crimes in the same jurisdiction

Blond's Criminal Law

Hanau Chart 2.7

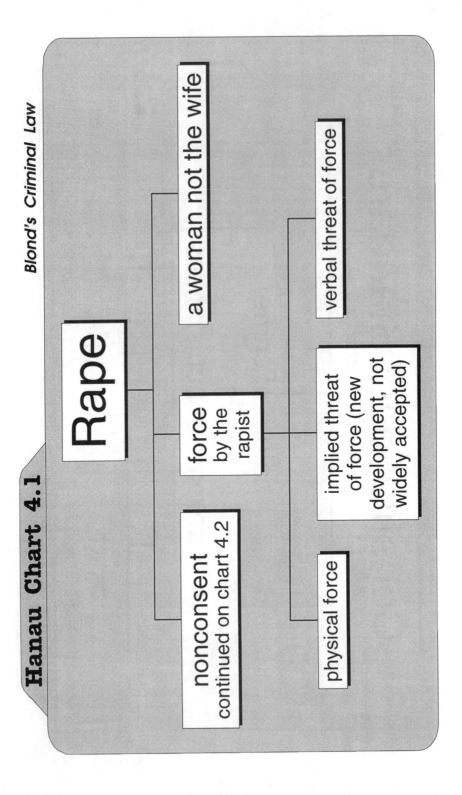

Hanau Chart 4.1

Rape

a woman not the wife

nonconsent
continued on chart 4.2

force
by the
rapist

physical force

implied threat
of force (new
development, not
widely accepted)

verbal threat of force

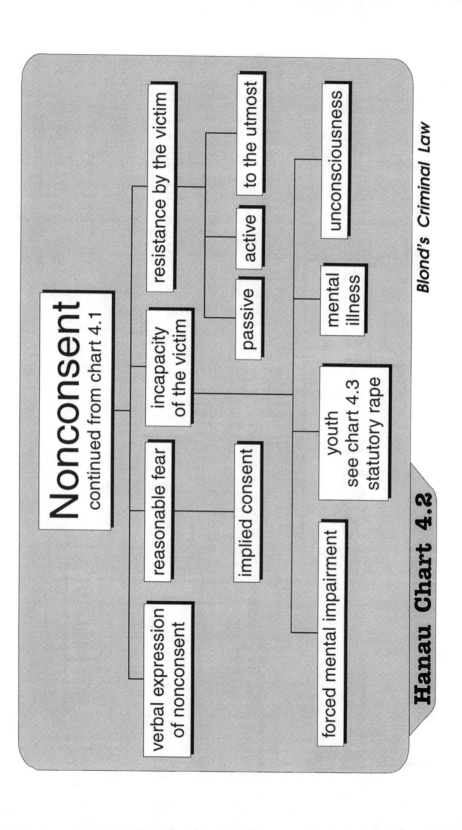

Nonconsent
continued from chart 4.1

- verbal expression of nonconsent
- reasonable fear
  - implied consent
- incapacity of the victim
  - youth
    see chart 4.3
    statutory rape
  - forced mental impairment
  - mental illness
  - unconsciousness
- resistance by the victim
  - passive
  - active
  - to the utmost

Blond's Criminal Law

Hanau Chart 4.2

Statutory Rape

from chart 4.2

age of consent

strict liability → no mistake of fact as to age

intent → not required

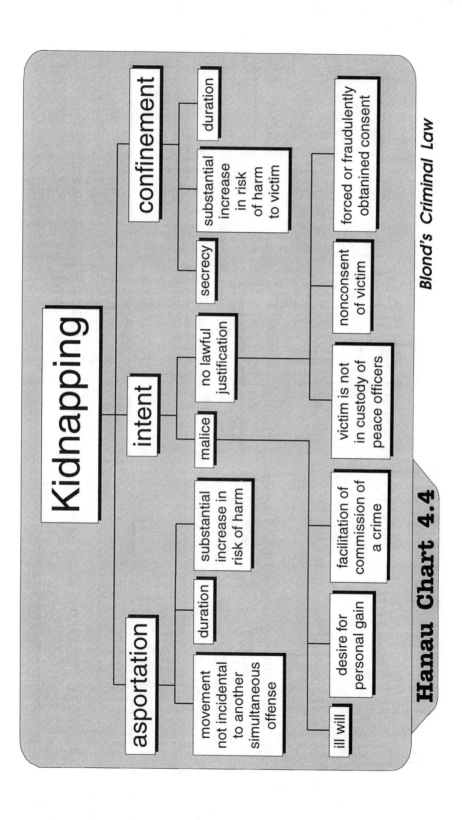

Kidnapping

- **asportation**
  - duration
    - movement not incidental to another simultaneous offense
  - substantial increase in risk of harm
- **intent**
  - malice
    - ill will
    - desire for personal gain
    - facilitation of commission of a crime
  - no lawful justification
    - victim is not in custody of peace officers
    - nonconsent of victim
      - forced or fraudulently obtained consent
- **confinement**
  - secrecy
  - substantial increase in risk of harm to victim
  - duration

Blond's Criminal Law

Hanau Chart 4.4

Hanau Chart 4.5

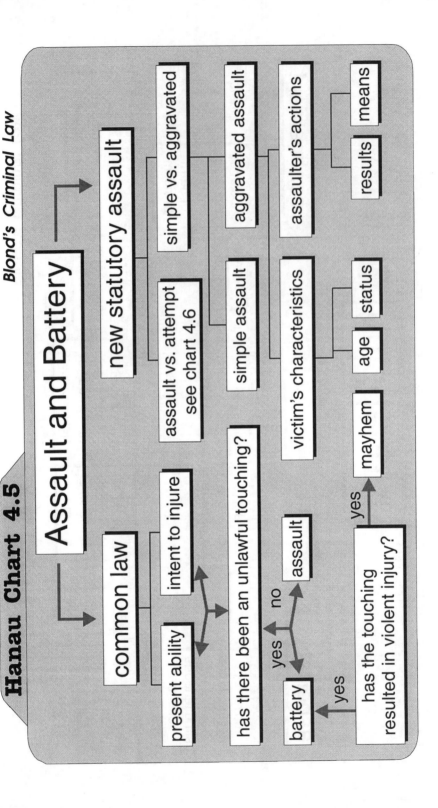

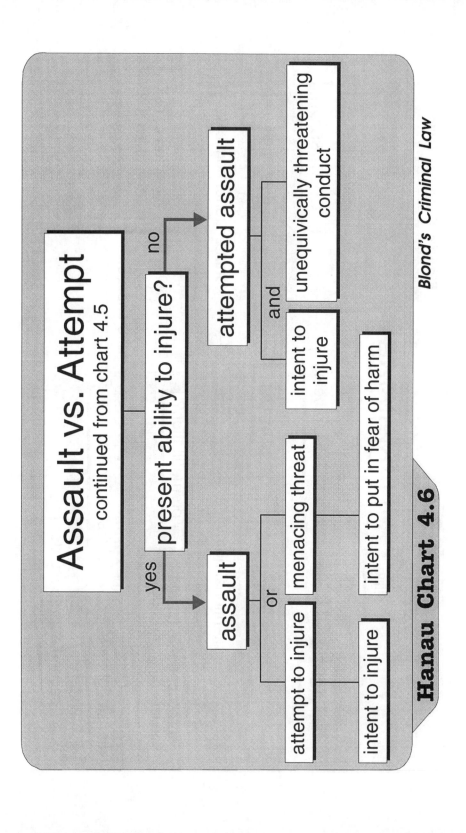

Assault vs. Attempt

continued from chart 4.5

present ability to injure?

yes → assault

no → attempted assault

assault

or

- attempt to injure
  - intent to injure
- menacing threat
  - intent to put in fear of harm

attempted assault

and

- intent to injure
- unequivically threatening conduct

Blond's Criminal Law

Hanau Chart 4.6

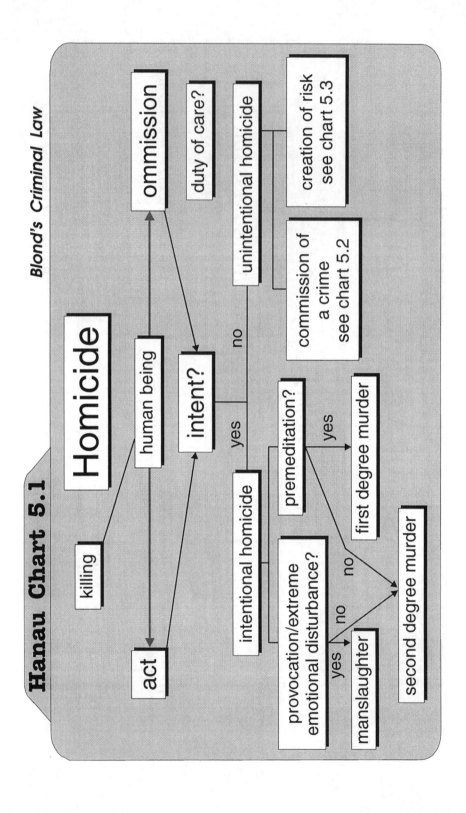

Hanau Chart 5.1

Blond's Criminal Law

Homicide

killing

human being

act ⟷ ommission

duty of care?

intent?

no → unintentional homicide

commission of a crime see chart 5.2

creation of risk see chart 5.3

yes → intentional homicide

premeditation?

yes → first degree murder

no → second degree murder

provocation/extreme emotional disturbance?

yes → manslaughter

no → second degree murder

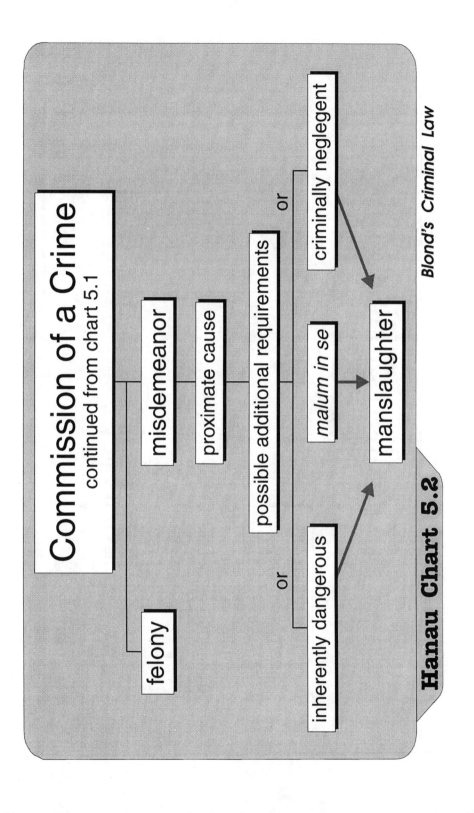

Commission of a Crime
continued from chart 5.1

felony

misdemeanor

proximate cause

possible additional requirements

or

malum in se → manslaughter

inherently dangerous → manslaughter

or

criminally neglegent

Hanau Chart 5.2

Blond's Criminal Law

Creation of Risk
continued from chart 5.1

recklessness

inherently dangerous instrumentality

extreme indifference to human life?

gross negligence

simple negligence

yes → second degree murder

no → reasonably foreseeable risk of death?

reasonably foreseeable risk of death? → manslaughter

simple negligence → manslaughter

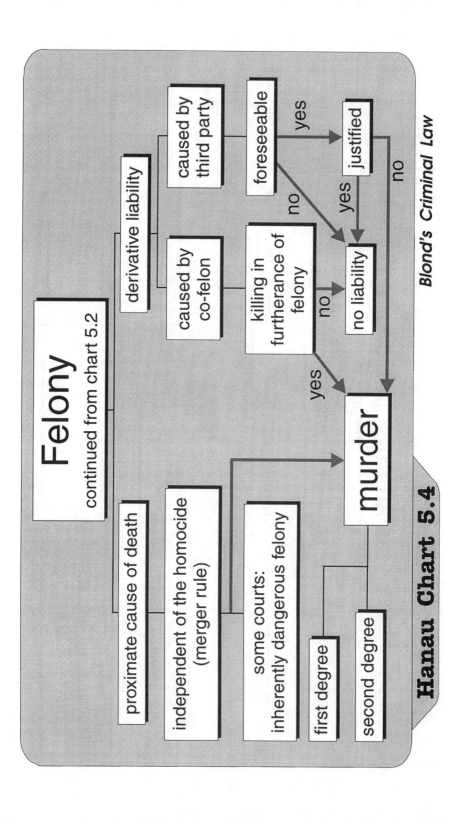

Felony

continued from chart 5.2

- proximate cause of death
- derivative liability

derivative liability

- caused by co-felon
- caused by third party
  - foreseeable
    - yes → justified
    - no → no liability

caused by co-felon

- killing in furtherance of felony
  - yes → murder
  - no → no liability

justified

- yes → no liability
- no → murder

proximate cause of death

- independent of the homocide (merger rule)
- some courts: inherently dangerous felony

→ murder

murder

- first degree
- second degree

Hanau Chart 5.4

Blond's Criminal Law

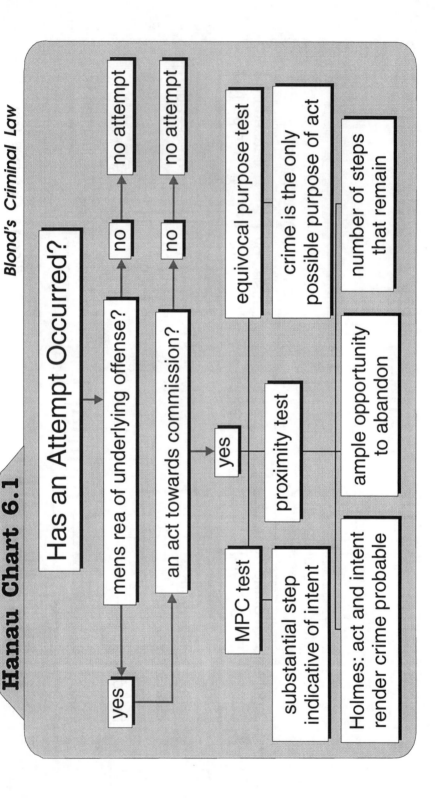

Hanau Chart 6.1

Blond's Criminal Law

Has an Attempt Occurred?

mens rea of underlying offense? → no → no attempt

an act towards commission? → no → no attempt

yes

yes

equivocal purpose test

crime is the only possible purpose of act

number of steps that remain

proximity test

ample opportunity to abandon

MPC test

substantial step indicative of intent

Holmes: act and intent render crime probable

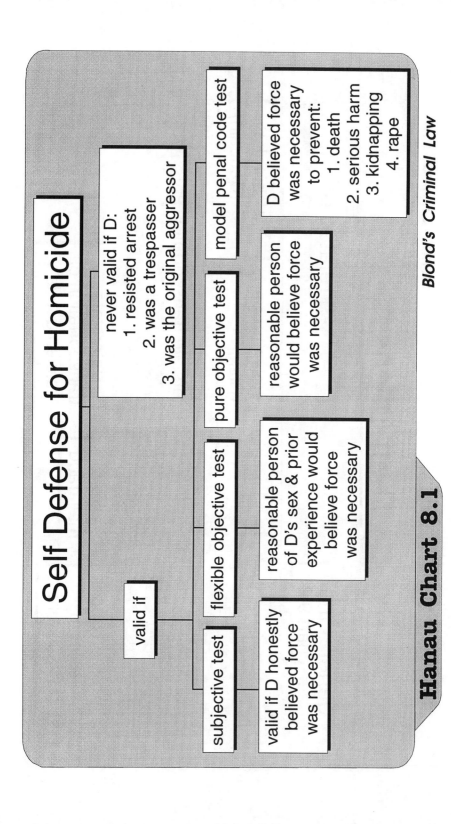

Self Defense for Homicide

valid if

never valid if D:
1. resisted arrest
2. was a trespasser
3. was the original aggressor

subjective test
valid if D honestly believed force was necessary

flexible objective test
reasonable person of D's sex & prior experience would believe force was necessary

pure objective test
reasonable person would believe force was necessary

model penal code test
D believed force was necessary to prevent:
1. death
2. serious harm
3. kidnapping
4. rape

Blond's Criminal Law

Hanau Chart 8.1

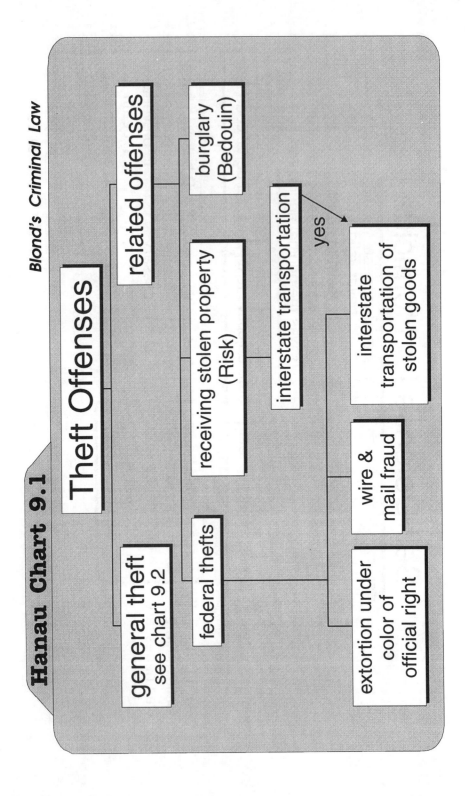

Theft Offenses

general theft
see chart 9.2

related offenses

federal thefts

receiving stolen property
(Risk)

burglary
(Bedouin)

interstate transportation

yes

extortion under
color of
official right

wire &
mail fraud

interstate
transportation of
stolen goods

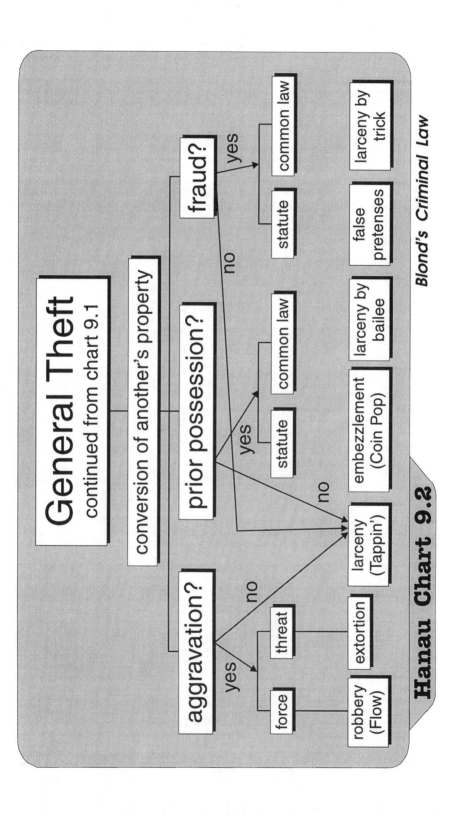

General Theft
continued from chart 9.1

conversion of another's property

aggravation?

yes → force → robbery (Flow)
threat → extortion

no → larceny (Tappin')

prior possession?

yes → statute / common law

no → embezzlement (Coin Pop)
larceny by bailee

fraud?

yes → statute / common law

false pretenses
larceny by trick

Blond's Criminal Law

Hanau Chart 9.2

Chapter 1

THE CRIMINAL JUSTICE SYSTEM

I. STRUCTURE OF THE SYSTEM

The criminal justice system enforces the standards of conduct that a community considers important and necessary. This is accomplished by punishing, reforming, and/or removing from society those who engage in undesirable conduct. In designing a criminal justice system, society must balance the efficiency and effectiveness of enforcement against the protection of individual autonomy and rights.

A. Police
Police make up the largest group of administrators of the law. The majority of police are local and are concentrated in cities and towns. As part of their role as investigators, police control the early weeding out of criminal conduct. They decide when undesirable conduct reaches a level that is criminally punishable and which cases are more properly excepted from punishment.

B. Prosecutors
Prosecutors control the pretrial process. Their discretion determines which charges are brought at a pretrial hearing and whether a defendant will be brought to trial. Local prosecutors generally work for the government and are assigned by district. Federal prosecution is done through the United States Attorney, who is a member of the executive branch and is appointed by the President.

C. Public Defenders

1. Indigent Defendants
The majority of felony defendants cannot afford counsel. All indigent defendants are constitutionally entitled to free counsel for the initial defense and first appeal of any indictment for a crime punishable by at least six months imprisonment. Any counsel that is competent and has no conflict of interest with an indigent may be appointed to represent him. On appeal, counsel may not refuse to represent an indigent defendant unless counsel submits a written

brief showing that there are no legal points that are arguable on the merits.

2. Types of Public Defenders
In most jurisdictions, an assigned counsel system requires private practice attorneys to represent a certain percentage of indigent defendants per year. In larger jurisdictions, public defender agencies represent indigent clients. Most of these agencies are governmental, although some are nonprofit organizations.

D.   Courts

1. Magistrate Courts
Also called municipal courts or justice of the peace courts, magistrate courts are courts of first instance. All cases go initially to a magistrate court that determines whether the evidence merits a trial. Magistrate courts have jurisdiction over all lower level cases; these are generally misdemeanors or the less severe misdemeanors.

2. General Jurisdiction Trial Courts
The same courts that try civil cases also have jurisdiction to hear felonies and the more severe misdemeanors.

3. Appellate Courts
Appellate courts hear a defendant's appeal. In states that have no intermediary appellate court, an appeal goes directly to the state supreme court.

E.   Judges
Judges monitor the justice of the system by supervising and reviewing trial. Judges decide questions of law and instruct a jury on the law applicable to a case. This power of instruction is limited; in the federal system and in most states the use of special verdicts to put undue pressure on a jury to reach a certain conclusion is not allowed. Judges also review the fairness of a jury decision in light of the special circumstances of a case.

F.   Jury
A jury is an impartial body of a defendant's peers that decides questions of fact.

1. Power of Nullification
A jury has the power to nullify standing laws by returning a verdict contrary to the law as it stands. This avoids the unfairness that may result from strict adherence to the law or to the instructions of a biased judge. However, federal courts and most state courts do not permit a judge to inform a jury of its nullification power fearing that this might transfer the law-making role to the jury.

2. Constitutional Requirements

a. Jury Trial
A jury trial is constitutionally required for any offense carrying a penalty of more than six months imprisonment.

b. Number of Peers
Although a jury was traditionally composed of twelve of the defendant's peers, the Supreme Court has ruled that a jury may be composed of as few as six people.

c. Unanimity
Most states require unanimous jury verdicts. However, the Supreme Court has ruled that a verdict by a substantial majority is sufficient for a valid verdict in state criminal trials.

G.   Corrections
The emphasis of the corrections system is on custody rather than on rehabilitation of criminals. Although most defendants are not incarcerated, a larger amount of money is spent on prisons than on treatment programs.

II.   CRIMINAL PROCEDURE

A.   Discovery of the Crime
Crimes are discovered by police observation or through reports from members of the public. The majority of reported crimes involve the taking or destruction of property. The second largest group of reported crimes is assault, followed by drug-related crimes. Violent crimes are a very small minority of the total.

B.   Investigation
If police observe behavior that is merely suspicious, or do not witness the actual commission of a crime, they must investigate to determine if:

1. Commission
A crime has actually been committed, and

2. Probable Cause
There is a suspect with apparent guilt of a sufficient magnitude to warrant arrest, and

3. Evidence
There is enough evidence of the suspect's guilt to sustain a conviction.

Investigation is accomplished by interviewing the suspect and witnesses, and examining the scene of the crime.

C.   Arrest
Most arrests are for misdemeanors and are made merely on a showing of probable cause, rather than with a warrant.

D.   Booking
Subsequent to arrest, suspects are taken to a central holding facility for booking. Here their names and addresses and the particulars of the crime are recorded, and suspects are fingerprinted and photographed. If arrested for a minor crime, a suspect may obtain release by posting bail or promising to appear before a magistrate. Otherwise, suspects are placed in a holding cell until they can appear before a magistrate.

E.   Questioning
A more thorough investigation is now conducted. A suspect is questioned, interviewed by witnesses, and made to appear in a lineup.

F.   Charge

   1. Review of Decision to Charge
The decision to charge a suspect with a crime, which is usually made by a high ranking police officer, is based on the severity of the offense and strength of the evidence as it appears in the police report. Some jurisdictions allow a prosecutor to review the decision to charge at this time. In others, this is done after appearance before a magistrate, thereby allowing more time for the gathering of evidence.

   2. Evidence
If evidence seems sufficient to support a conviction, a charge is brought; if not, the suspect is released or a lesser charge is brought. Due to understaffing and case overload, most jurisdictions have a case drop program whereby certain classes of cases, such as all first time offenses, are reduced to a lesser charge or dropped entirely.

   3. Habeas Corpus
A suspect has a constitutional right to the filing of a charge without unnecessary delay. If a suspect is detained without being charged, he may file a writ of habeas corpus, which secures release unless a charge is immediately filed.

G.   Filing
Charges are filed with a magistrate, which is the lowest level court.

   1. Ex Parte Review
A magistrate reviews a case in chambers to determine whether the evidence supports probable cause of guilt.

2. First Appearance
A suspect appears before the magistrate who makes certain that he is indeed the individual suspected of the crime charged, informs the suspect of his rights, and sets bail.

3. Bail
Originally, bail was determined by the type of offense charged. Because this did not account for the suspect's wealth, release was based not on propensity to appear for trial or on danger posed to society, but rather on economic circumstances. Indigent suspects were forced to resort to bail posting agencies which charged a fee of approximately ten percent, and tended to be corrupt. Today, many states have release programs which identify defendants who can be released on their own recognizance (promise to appear for trial), or on only ten percent of the bail amount.

H.   Pretrial Hearings

1. Misdemeanors
Misdemeanors are tried before a magistrate without further pretrial hearings.

2. Preliminary Hearings
If a crime is a felony, many states allow a preliminary hearing during which counsel may argue whether there is probable cause. A judge may not make a determination of probable cause until both sides have presented their arguments. However, a defendant may waive this hearing.

3. Indictment
The federal system and a minority of states require indictment by a grand jury for a felony. This group of impartial peers determines whether there is probable cause to believe that the evidence will support a conviction at trial. Indictment protects against unfounded prosecution. The U.S. Attorney has the discretionary power to determine if an indictment is valid.

I.   Arraignment

    1. Procedure
    The defendant is brought before the trial court to enter his plea of guilty, not guilty, or *nolo contendere. Nolo contendere* is an admission of the facts pleaded in the indictment, but not of guilt. The majority of cases that reach arraignment are disposed of by a guilty plea or by dismissal.

    2. Plea Bargaining
    Plea bargaining takes place at this stage.

J.   Jury Selection

    1. Voir Dire
    A group of potential jurors (a venire) is questioned either by counsel for each side or by the judge in order to determine which jurors must be disqualified due to potential prejudice.

    2. Peremptory Challenges
    Counsel for each party may disqualify a certain number of potential jurors without explanation.

K.   Trial Requirements

    1. Standard of Proof
    Every fact necessary to establish the crime charged against a defendant must be established beyond a reasonable doubt.

      a. Persuasion
      The prosecution always has the burden of persuading the trier of fact that an element of a crime is established beyond a reasonable doubt. A defendant can only have the burden of persuasion for affirmative defenses that are not constitutionally mandated.

      b. Production
      The prosecution has the burden of showing by production of evidence that there is an issue regarding every material element

of the case. However, some states require a defendant to produce evidence tending to show that he is not guilty before the prosecution must prove guilt beyond a reasonable doubt.

2. Presumption of Innocence
A defendant's innocence is presumed until the prosecution has proven guilt beyond a reasonable doubt.

3. Other Presumptions

   a. Presumption of Sanity
   Defendants are presumed sane until introduction of evidence to the contrary.

   b. Inference
   Inference of a fact or of intent from proof of another fact may be required or permitted. When inference is required, the likelihood that the presumed fact will flow from the proven fact must be beyond a reasonable doubt. When inference is merely permitted, the standard is reduced to "more likely than not."

4. Right Not to Take the Stand
The Fifth Amendment guarantees a criminal defendant the right to abstain from conduct that could result in self-incrimination. This includes the right not to testify against oneself.

5. Standard of Evidence

   a. Relevance
   Only relevant evidence is admissible. Relevant evidence is both:

      i. Probative
      The evidence increases the likelihood that the pleadings are true, and

    ii. Material
        The evidence affects the outcome of the case under the applicable law.

  b. Privilege
     Defendants have the right to withhold privileged testimony, such as any testimony that would incriminate him or a family member.

  c. Prejudice
     Evidence is inadmissible if it tends to cause a jury to draw unjustifiable inferences about a defendant without regard to the facts. For example, evidence of a defendant's character is not admissible unless the defendant puts his character at issue.

  d. Circumstantial
     Circumstantial evidence may be used to prove the commission of a crime.

L.   Trial Procedure

  1. Opening Statement
     During its opening statement, the prosecution explains the circumstances of the crime to the jury, as well as what will be proven. The defense may also make an opening statement.

  2. Presentation of Witnesses by the Prosecution
     The prosecution attempts to show beyond a reasonable doubt that the defendant has committed the crime by presenting the testimony of witnesses. The defense may cross-examine witnesses in order to impeach their testimony.

  3. Defense Options:

    a. Standing On The Presumption of Innocence
       The defense may move for an acquittal on the ground that the prosecution has not presented evidence proving guilt beyond a reasonable doubt and/or;

    b. Presentation of Evidence
    The defense may rebut the prosecution's evidence and establish affirmative defenses.

4. Jury Instruction
The judge instructs the jury as to which points of law are relevant to the case.

5. Jury Deliberation
The jury decides the defendant's guilt or innocence in light of its assessment of the veracity of the testimony.

    a. Verdict of Not Guilty
    No appeal or review of a verdict of not guilty is allowed.

    b. Verdict of Guilty
    A defendant may appeal a guilty verdict.

    c. Mistrial
    If a jury is unable to return a verdict supported by the requisite majority, the judge declares a mistrial, and the defendant may be retried at the prosecutor's discretion.

M. Sentencing
A separate hearing is held for sentencing, but it may be before the same jury.

1. Misdemeanors
The judge has the discretion to set a fine, a jail term or a period of probation for a misdemeanor.

2. Imprisonment
If the defendant is sentenced to a prison term, the judge will usually set a maximum and minimum sentence, with the actual length of time served to be determined by a parole board. Most state laws set the high and low extreme penalties for each class of offense. Some states also impose sentencing guidelines.

N.   Appeal
Nearly all trials that result in convictions are appealed. Felony appeals go to the appellate court, or in the absence thereof, to the supreme court. Appeals from a conviction for a misdemeanor are generally heard de novo in trial court.

III.   TRIAL ETHICS

A.   Defense Counsel

1. Knowledge of all Relevant Evidence
Counsel must discover all facts relevant to his client's defense.

2. Confidence
Counsel must hold all disclosures made by his client in strictest confidence.

3. Perjury
Counsel must not present facts as true if he knows they are perjured. The Supreme Court requires a defense attorney to disclose perjury to the court. However, critics have argued that a criminal defendant is entitled to a trial where credibility is evaluated by jury.

B.   Prosecution
The American Bar Association Code of Professional Responsibility asserts that in the case of criminal prosecution, the duty to convict is less important than the duty to seek justice.

1. Use of Perjured Testimony
The Supreme Court has declared that the knowing use of perjured testimony by a prosecutor is not only unethical, but unconstitutional.

2. Failure to Correct False Testimony
Failure to correct false testimony violates due process.

3. Exculpatory Evidence
A prosecutor's suppression of exculpatory evidence which is material to the mitigation of guilt or punishment violates due process.

CASE CLIPS

People v. Zackowitz (1930) KS
Facts: Some young men who were working on a car insulted a woman passerby. D, the passerby's husband, became enraged and shot one of the young men during an ensuing fight.
Issue: Is evidence of a defendant's character admissible at criminal trial?
Rule: Evidence of a defendant's character is not admissible at criminal trial unless the defendant puts his character at issue.
Dissent: Possession of dangerous weapons should be admissible whether a defendant stores them at his house or on his person.

Patterson v. New York (Sup. Ct. 1977) KS, DS, MIB
Facts: D brought a shotgun to the home of his estranged wife, where D saw his wife standing naked in front of her lover. D killed the lover, and later pled extreme emotional disturbance.
Issue: Is it a violation of due process to require a defendant to prove an affirmative defense beyond a reasonable doubt?
Rule: Requiring a defendant to prove an affirmative defense beyond a reasonable doubt does not violate due process. As long as the prosecution must prove all elements of the crime beyond a reasonable doubt, due process has been satisfied. The state cannot be required to rebut in advance every possible affirmative defense.
Dissent: This is the same as presuming guilt until proof of innocence. The burden of persuasion of an integral element of the offense is shifted onto the defendant by not mentioning in the definition of the crime that its nonexistence is necessary.

Duncan v. Louisiana (S.Ct. 1968) KS, J
Facts: A white boy claimed that D, a black man, slapped him on the elbow. D was convicted of simple assault, a misdemeanor.

Issue: Does denial of a jury trial right for an offense that does not involve severe punishment violate the Sixth and Fourteenth Amendments?

Rule: (White, J.) The Constitution guarantees the right to a trial by jury for any crime that is punishable by imprisonment.

Dissent: (Harlan, J.) The effectiveness and burden of jury trials are unique to each state; therefore the decision to allow jury trials should be left to the states.

United States v. Dougherty (1972) KS, J

Facts: Ds broke into the Dow Chemical company and destroyed property therein.

Issue: Must a jury be instructed as to its right to return a verdict contrary to the standing law?

Rule: A jury need not be informed of its right to nullification. A jury is well aware that its verdict choices are not limited to the judge's formal instructions on the law.

Concurrence/Dissent: The purpose of nullification is to counter biased judges and unconscionable laws. To allow a judge to conceal this right from the jury is contrary to this purpose.

Nix v. Whiteside (S.Ct. 1986) KS

Facts: D went to a man's apartment to buy marijuana. D got into an argument with the man, and stabbed him.

Issue: Does an attorney deny a client the right to effective assistance of counsel by advising the client not to commit perjury and stating that any perjury committed would necessarily be reported?

Rule: An attorney does not deny a client the right to effective counsel by advising the client not to commit perjury, or by stating that any known perjury will be reported. The Code of Professional Responsibility forbids an attorney from knowingly using or assisting in the use of fraudulent testimony.

Concurrence: The court has no constitutional authority to establish rules of conduct for lawyers.

Concurrence: The states should decide how attorneys must conduct themselves.

Concurrence: This does not provide limits as to when a lawyer may decide that a client is committing perjury.

People v. Chavez (1947) W

Facts: D gave birth into a toilet bowl, and thinking the baby drowned, wrapped it in newspaper and hid it under the bathtub.

Issue: Does a parent's failure to provide reasonable care for a viable newborn constitute manslaughter?

Rule: When there is a duty of care, the failure to exercise reasonable care in the treatment of a viable child constitutes manslaughter if death results.

Singleton v. State (1948) W

Facts: D, a poor mother of two, disposed of the body of her newborn infant on the grounds of a cemetery.

Issue: Does a mother's failure to act in her baby's best interests during childbirth constitute a criminal act sufficient to sustain a conviction for homicide if it results in death?

Rule: A mother's failure during childbirth to protect the best interests of her newborn baby is insufficient to sustain an inference of criminal intent, especially if the mother is uneducated and unattended at the time of childbirth.

Regina v. Onufrejczyk (1955) W

Facts: D's business partner disappeared without a trace. D was indicted for his murder.

Issue: May circumstantial evidence be used to prove the existence of a *corpus delicti* (a body of facts evincing the commission of a crime)?

Rule: Circumstantial evidence may establish the *corpus delicti* if the only conclusion the evidence allows is that a crime has certainly been committed.

United States v. Cox (1965) J

Facts: A federal grand jury wanted to indict two persons for perjury, but the U.S. Attorney refused to prepare the indictments.

Issue: Does the constitutional requirement of an indictment by a jury as a predicate for the prosecution of capital or infamous crimes allow a jury to enforce an indictment as valid?

Rule: Only the executive branch, embodied in the U.S. Attorney, has the power to determine if an indictment is valid. The role of the grand jury is limited to safeguarding against unfounded prosecutions.

Concurrence/Dissent: The U.S. Attorney's discretion in refusing to accept an indictment should be limited to cases where there has been a rational basis for dismissal such as a showing of bad faith.

Myers v. Commonwealth (1973) J

Facts: At a hearing to determine probable cause on rape charges, the judge found probable cause and terminated the proceedings before defense counsel finished cross examining the complaining witness.

Issue: Does a finding of probable cause made without allowing defense counsel to complete cross-examination of a complaining witness or to present his own witnesses violate due process?

Rule: Probable cause cannot be determined on a prima facie showing that the law has been breached. A defendant must be allowed to raise a conflict as to the credibility of the prosecution.

Bordenkircher v. Hayes (S.Ct. 1978) J

Facts: D was indicted for uttering a forged check. The prosecutor threatened that if D did not accept a plea bargain and plead guilty, the prosecutor would seek an indictment under a recidivist statute, subjecting D to mandatory life imprisonment due to his prior felonies.

Issue: Does a prosecutor's threat during plea bargain negotiations to seek a heavier but valid sentence amount to a vindictive exercise of the prosecutor's discretion prohibited by the Due Process Clause?

Rule: (Stewart, J) A prosecutor can threaten the risk of more severe but valid punishment during a plea bargain negotiation.

Dissent: (Powell, J) If the prosecutor's purpose in threatening is solely to discourage and penalize with unique severity the exercise of a defendant's constitutional right against compulsory self incrimination, an escalation of the charge against a defendant should not be allowed.

Gideon v. Wainright (S.Ct. 1963) J

Facts: D was indicted for breaking and entering with intent to commit a misdemeanor, which was a felony under Florida law. He requested that he be appointed counsel. State law allowed for the appointment of counsel only for capital offenses. D was forced to represent himself in court.

Issue: Does the Fourteenth Amendment extend to the states the Sixth Amendment right of criminal defendants to the assistance of counsel?

Rule: (Black, J) The constitutional guarantee of the assistance of counsel is a fundamental right which applies to all criminal defendants both federal and state, irrespective of the severity of their offense.

Douglas v. California (S.Ct. 1963) J

Facts: The state denied D, an indigent, the appointment of counsel on appeal, having determined that appointing counsel would aid neither D nor the court.

Issue: Does the Sixth Amendment allow a state to determine whether or not an indigent deserves the assistance of counsel on first appeal?

Rule: (Douglas, J.) A state cannot deny appointment of counsel to an indigent on a first appeal. This would be invidious discrimination against the poor.

Dissent: (Harlan, J.) The Equal Protection Clause does not impose an affirmative duty on the states to redress economic inequalities.

Anders v. California (S.Ct. 1967) J

Facts: D was convicted of felony possession of marijuana. Counsel was appointed to represent him at his appeal. The attorney determined that there was no merit to the appeal.

Issue: Does the Sixth Amendment require that an indigent be provided counsel for an appeal even after the counsel appointed determines that the appeal has no merit?

Rule: (Clark, J.) Counsel must represent an indigent unless it files a brief showing that there are no legal points that are arguable on their merits, and the defendant is given an opportunity to respond to it.

Dissent: (Stewart, J.) The filing of a no-merit letter should be sufficient to show that an appeal is wholly frivolous.

United States v. Ely (1983) J

Facts: The judge granted D's request for counsel, but refused to replace the appointee with an equally qualified who D preferred.

Issue: Does the Sixth Amendment require that indigent defendants be given their choice of counsel?

Rule: The Sixth Amendment does not require that an indigent defendant be appointed the counsel of his choice but merely counsel that is competent and does not have a conflict of interest with the defendant.

United States v. Childress (1983) J

Facts: D, a black man, was convicted by an all-white jury. The government used peremptory challenges to remove all prospective black jurors from the jury panel.

Issue: Does the Sixth Amendment prohibit the use of peremptory challenges to exclude potential jurors on the basis of race?
Rule: The Sixth Amendment bars the use of peremptory challenges for systematic exclusion based on race. The Sixth Amendment does not require that each jury exactly reflect a cross section of the community.

Mullaney v. Wilbur (S.Ct. 1975) J
Facts: D killed a man, claiming that he attacked the man in a frenzy provoked by the man's homosexual advance.
Issue: Does the Due Process Clause proscribe the requirement that a defendant must prove provocation in order to reduce the degree of the offense?
Rule: (Powell, J.) It is a violation of due process to require a defendant to prove provocation. The prosecution must prove its absence beyond a reasonable doubt, because this absence is an essential element of the offense.
Concurrence: (Rehnquist, J.) A defendant may still be required to prove insanity.

Sandstrom v. Montana (S.Ct. 1979) J, MIB
Facts: D killed a girl, but claimed the act was neither purposeful nor knowing because he was under the influence of a mental disorder that had been aggravated by alcohol consumption. The judge gave the instruction, "The law presumes that a person intends the ordinary consequences of his voluntary acts."
Issue: Does a jury instruction that the consequences of voluntary acts may be inferred to be intended violate the Fourteenth Amendment where intent is an element of the crime charged?
Rule: (Brennan, J.) A jury instruction that requires a jury to infer intent to cause the consequences of voluntary actions violates due process because it shifts the burden of proof onto the defendant.
Concurrence: (Rehnquist, J.) A single instruction to a jury must be viewed in the context of the overall charge to the jury.

Pointer v. Texas (S.Ct. 1965) J
Facts: Ds represented themselves at a preliminary hearing. The transcript of Ds' statements was used to convict them at trial.
Issue: Is the Sixth Amendment right to confront prosecuting witnesses applicable to states by the Fourteenth Amendment?

Rule: (Black, J.) A defendant's Sixth Amendment right to confront the witnesses against him through cross examination is applicable to the states through the Fourteenth Amendment.

Malloy v. Hogan (S.Ct. 1964) J

Facts: D was ordered to testify at an inquiry into alleged gambling, but refused on self-incrimination grounds. D was held in contempt.

Issue: Is Fifth Amendment protection against self incrimination applicable to the States through the Fourteenth Amendment?

Rule: (Brennan, J.) The Fourteenth Amendment requires states to apply the same guarantee against coerced self incrimination that the Sixth Amendment requires of the federal courts.

Griffin v. California (S.Ct. 1965) J

Facts: D was convicted of first degree murder of a woman in an alley. D did not testify at trial on the issue of his guilt.

Issue: Does an instruction that encourages a jury to draw unfavorable inferences about a defendant because of a refusal to testify violate the Fifth Amendment guarantee against self incrimination?

Rule: (Douglas, J.) An instruction that encourages unfavorable inferences from a refusal to testify amounts to a court-imposed penalty for the exercise of a constitutional privilege. This violates the Fifth Amendment.

Dissent: (Stewart, J.) A jury is more likely to draw unfavorable inferences from a defendant's refusal to testify if left on its own, than under an instruction that reminds the jury of the prosecution's burden of persuasion.

State v. Leverett (1990) MIB

Facts: Leverett was involved in a car accident, at which time a breath test registered his blood alcohol content at .121. The district court instructed the jury that a blood alcohol level greater that .10 raised a mandatory rebuttable presumption that the defendant was under the influence of alcohol. Leverett was convicted, and appealed on the ground that the instruction violated due process rights.

Issue: Is a jury instruction which contains an evidentiary presumption in a criminal case a violation of a defendant's due process rights?

Rule: An evidentiary presumption violates a criminal defendant's rights to due process only if the presumption goes to an element of the crime charged and a reasonable juror could read the presumption as mandatory. To avoid due process problems, presumptions must be made unambiguously permissive to the jury.

In Re Winship (S.Ct. 1970) MIB

Facts: (Not provided).

Issue: Does due process require that criminal guilt be proven beyond a reasonable doubt?

Rule: Due process requires that the guilt of a criminal defendant be proven beyond a reasonable doubt. The public must not fear that the criminal justice system will condemn the innocent.

Concurrence: It is far worse to convict an innocent man than to let a guilty man go free.

Chapter 2

CONCEPTS OF PUNISHMENT

I. JUSTIFICATION OF PUNISHMENT

Most courts have held that the main goal of the criminal law is punishment. Deterrence, rehabilitation and retribution are secondary goals.

A. Purposes of Punishment
(See also, MPC § 1.02)

Mnemonic: **PURE DRINk DElight**

1. **Pu**nishment
Because of his crime, an offender deserves to suffer. Punishment purges the criminal of his guilt by making him suffer, and it prevents him from benefitting from his crime.

2. **Re**tribution
The aim of retributory punishment is to satisfy society's desire for:

a. Revenge for the crime committed, so that the individuals who were harmed do not feel the need to resort to vigilantism.

b. Atonement to cancel out the offense since restitution often cannot be exacted by the victim of a crime.

Note: Most courts have held that punishment must be proportional to the crime, irrespective of public outcry.

3. **D**eterrence
Another goal of punishment is to discourage future offenses. Crimes are made less profitable by increasing the severity of the

punishment proportionally as the severity of the crime or the likelihood of its success increase.

    a. General Deterrence
      General Deterrence seeks to discourage other future offenders, and does not necessarily take the defendant's blameworthiness into account. General deterrence allows sacrifices in individual cases whenever this can be shown to improve the aggregate welfare. The logical extreme of general deterrence would be to impose a penalty of death on the offender and his family for even the most harmless crimes.

    b. Special Deterrence
      Special Deterrence is aimed at discouraging the particular defendant from repeating his crime, and therefore takes the circumstances of the crime and the criminal's propensity to commit a similar crime into account.

4. **R**ehabilitation
Rehabilitation seeks to strengthen the criminal's ability to stay within the law by changing his character and habits through therapy. It focuses on the criminal's background, rather than the severity of his crime.

5. **I**ncapacitation
Incapacitation deprives the criminal of his liberty in order to protect the public from his future criminality. Punishment may be prescribed:

    a. Collectively
      By basing the length of sentence on the type of crime committed, or

    b. Selectively
      By individualizing the length of the sentence depending on the particular circumstances of the crime and the propensity of the particular defendant for future criminality.

6. **De**nunciation
Denunciation addresses the fear that a lesser penalty would depreciate the seriousness of the crime and thereby foster imitation. It seeks to reaffirm society's moral standards and the view that the offense is not tolerated.

B.   Practical Limitations on Punishment

Mnemonic: **DICtatorial DoDo**

1. **D**iversion of Police Power and Judicial Resources
There is a finite amount of resources that must be used wisely in order to maximize the amount of illegal conduct curtailed.

2. **I**neffectiveness
Not all methods of punishment effectively deter future criminal conduct.

3. **C**orruption
With any system of punishment there is a tendency toward corruption amongst enforcement officials.

4. **D**iscrimination
The criminal system must have safeguards to protect against domination by the empowered majority over the disenfranchised, underprivileged, or adherents to minority viewpoints.

5. **D**eterioration of Respect for the Law
Harsh, arbitrary, or discriminatory punishment may lead to rebellion.

C.   Theoretical Limitations and Justifications For Punishment

1. The many different theories that justify punishment illustrate the tension between the desire for utility and justice.

    a. Utility
    The utilitarian goal is to discourage criminality in the most efficient and least costly way possible. The severity of the

punishment is justified by the beneficial consequences resulting from observance of the laws that it secures.

b. Justice

The aim of justice is to punish only the blameworthy in a manner that is proportional to the circumstances and the severity of the crime committed.

2. Theories

a. Johannes Andenaes

Punishment may serve to generally deter criminal behavior, to stimulate habitual law-abiding behavior, and to strengthen morality if the temptation to commit crimes is outweighed by the risk of punishment.

b. Jeremy Bentham

All laws should be made for the purpose of increasing the total benefit to society, and to exclude anything that detracts from this benefit. Punishment should only be allowed where it excludes some greater evil.

c. Morris Cohen

Criminal behavior may not be curable at a price that society can or should bear.

d. John Dewey

Criminality is a social, not a moral problem. Punishment is necessary because conduct is always shared and ignoring guilt thereby encourages imitation. However, society must accept some of the moral blame for criminals who often come from the underprivileged classes. Therefore society should gear punishment toward rehabilitation rather than retribution.

e. Emile Durkheim

Punishment serves to maintain social cohesion and solidarity by reaffirming social values and expressing the emotional reaction to the loss that the crime has caused.

f. H.L.A. Hart

Punishment must involve an unpleasant consequence, and must address the particular offense committed by the person to be punished. Punishment must be for an offense against legal rules, and imposed by an authority composed by the legal system. To have reform rather than punishment as the dominant objective would be to sacrifice the opportunity to influence the larger class of potential offenders who have not yet broken the law, but may.

g. G.W.F. Hegel

The primary purpose of punishment is to right the wrong committed. A crime must be annulled because it was the rational choice of the criminal to infringe on the rights of another; therefore the measure of punishment must come from the severity of the act, not from desires to reform or deter.

h. Oliver Wendell Holmes

Retribution is only vengeance in disguise in that it does not take repentance into account.

i. Immanuel Kant

Punishment must be based on the ground that the defendant committed a crime, not on the basis that it would benefit either the defendant or society. Retaliation is the only certain way to achieve a just penalty. The standard for retaliation is equality: An individual should suffer himself any undeserved evil that he inflicts on another.

j. J. Mabbot

Retributive punishment treats a criminal as a rational person responsible for his actions; whereas reformative punishment does not respect the fact that he has free choice. Punishment therefore should not be determined by the benefit it will confer on either society or the criminal.

k. Michael Moore

Rehabilitation is utilitarian if the treatment is to make criminals safe to return to the streets and to decrease the expense of incarceration. Rehabilitation should not be imposed in order to give the criminal a better life because there are other disadvantaged non-criminals who are more deserving of such benefits.

l. Herbert Morris
Society consists of rules which confer on each individual the benefits of noninterference with his rights by others. Society also confers on its members the burdens of self restraint over actions that would interfere with another's rights. Punishment grants to those that comply with the rules the assurance that they will not assume another's burden; it induces compliance so that distribution of the benefits and the burdens is fair; and it punishes those who take more than their fair share through noncompliance with the rules.

m. Jeffrie Murphy
Capitalist society encourages and reinforces the motives that lead to criminality.

n. James Fitzjames Stephen
Punishment rightly expresses and justifies the morally right hatred excited by the commission of a crime.

o. James Q. Wilson
Incapacitation cannot be the sole purpose of the prison system. If it were, all minor offenders would be jailed for life. In order for incapacitation to work, offenders must be likely to repeat their crimes; offenders removed from the street must not be immediately replaced by new ones, and prison must not increase post-release criminal activity.

II.   SOURCES OF THE CRIMINAL LAW

A.   Common Law

1. No Federal Common Law Crimes
There are no federal common law crimes. All crimes must be clearly defined by a specific criminal statute. To allow a court to create law would violate the Separation of Powers Clause.

2. State Common Law Crimes
Most states do not allow courts to create common law crimes. This would violate due process because it would not give a potential criminal any forewarning that his conduct will be interpreted as illegal.

B.   Statutes

1. Federal Power to Create Criminal Statutes
Derived from Art. I, § 8 of the Constitution.

2. State Power to Create Criminal Laws
Derived from the police power granted to the state in the Constitution.

3. Interpretation
The courts must look to the intent of the legislature, and cannot enlarge the meaning of the terms of a statute to include actions that were beyond the contemplation of the legislature.

C.   Administrative Agencies

1. Delegation
A legislature may delegate enforcement and regulatory powers to an administrative agency as long as the legislature clearly defines criminal conduct and provides sufficient standards to guide the law's administration.

2. Discretionary Enforcement
An administrative agency can create regulations incidental to enforcement, but may not create additional requirements or punishments.

D.   Federal-State Dichotomy

1. Federal Interest
The courts will construe a statute in its broadest terms in order to allow federal enforcement to encroach on states' enforcement rights if the matter is deemed one of federal interest.

2. Finding Federal Interest
Generally, the courts will find preemptive federal interest if there is a federal statute governing that type of crime. This is so even if:

   a.   The federal court cannot regulate the state interest or statutory scheme involved, and

   b.   The crime took place entirely intrastate.

III.   LEGALITY: LIMITS ON THE CRIMINAL LAW

A.   Due Process
Constitutional protection against arbitrary or discretionary enforcement of the law.

1. Fair Notice Standard
A criminal statute is not unconstitutional on due process grounds if it is sufficiently clear to provide notice prior to prosecution that particular conduct is prohibited.

2. Vagueness

   a.   A criminal statute is unconstitutionally vague if the statute does not:

      i.   Provide clearly defined legal standards by which enforcers may judge which conduct is prohibited;

      ii.   Provide a commonly understood definition of the illegal conduct; and

     iii.   Clearly describe what an individual must do to satisfy the statute.

   b. Subjective fear of prosecution under a vagueness/fair notice standard does not give a potential defendant standing to sue absent actual prosecution under the statute.

3. Overbreadth
A criminal statute is overbroad if:

   a. It is wide enough to restrict constitutionally protected conduct (e.g., free speech); and

   b. In the absence of a substantial federal interest in regulating the conduct, there is a less-broad alternative.

4. Due Process Standard
Generally, a statute is only overturned as violative of Due Process if it aims to deter conduct that is constitutionally protected. A statute is less likely to be overturned if the court finds a public policy interest for prohibiting the particular conduct.

   a. Private Activity
If a right, such as the right to privacy, is not specifically protected by the Constitution, the court will defer to the legislature, and any federal public policy interest will preempt the private right.

   b. Commercial Activity
Commercial enterprises have fewer protected rights than private citizens. Therefore, commercial activity that corresponds to a constitutionally protected private activity is often not protected.

5. Applications of Due Process – Encroachment on Private Rights

   a. Inchoate Crimes
It is permissible to punish contemplated acts, as well as overt acts. This is true as long as the judgement of future criminality is based on a person's intent and not based on:

     i.   Status (such as employment status, or being an alcoholic or a known criminal) or;

     ii.   Acts which would be considered legal but for a judgment about the defendant's character.

Note: The adoption by many states of the Model Penal Code has led to the ratification of vagrancy laws which would be impermissible under a federal standard.

   b. Privacy
It is constitutionally permissible to criminally regulate both public and private morality.

     i.   It is permissible to prohibit private consensual acts which are considered immoral.

     ii.   The Supreme Court is sharply divided on this issue. The prohibition of private consensual immoral conduct is permissible if the acts:

       (1)   Relate to the perpetration of a crime infringing on the rights of others, and

       (2)   Relate to future criminality, and

       (3)   There is no less restrictive alternative to prohibit future criminality.

     iii.   The court will more likely defer to the legislature if the conduct is not specifically protected by the Constitution.

   c. Sentencing
      It is permissible to increase a sentence or parole time based on
      new additional evidence of the severity of the crime. However,
      it is not permissible to impose harsher sentencing procedures
      if they were not in practice at the time of the commission of the
      crime.

B. Equal Protection
   A statute may not arbitrarily classify the type of person to whom it
   applies. For example, a statute is unconstitutional if it prohibits the
   use of contraceptives by men but not by women.

   1. When Due Process is Violated
      A statute violates due process if:

      a. The classification of people to whom it applies does not have
         a fair, substantial and reasonable relation to the conduct
         prohibited by the act.

      b. Individuals who are similarly situated in relation to the statute
         are not all required to conform to the same standard of conduct.

   2. Test for Constitutionality:

      a. Does the classification further the legitimate purpose of the
         act?

      b. Is there a nondiscriminatory alternative classification that will
         accomplish the purpose of the act?

      c. Does the classification make the statute more effective in
         accomplishing its purpose?

      d. If the statute is constitutional on its face, is impermissible
         discrimination an intended result?

C. Proportionality – Cruel And Unusual Punishment Under The Eighth Amendment

  1. Theoretical Standards:

    a. The punishment should be sufficient to outweigh the profit of the offense.

    b. Given a choice between two crimes, the punishment should make the defendant choose the lesser crime.

    c. The more likely it is that the criminal will get away with the crime, the greater the potential punishment should be.

    d. The punishment should not be more severe than that required to deter.

  2. Constitutional Standards
    The sentence must balance the nature of the crime committed with the severity of the punishment.

    a. Test for Constitutionality
    For a sentence to be constitutional, the defendant must deserve the level of punishment to which he is sentenced. This is measured by evolving standards of decency:

      i. Are similar or more serious crimes committed in the same or other jurisdiction punished less severely?

      ii. Is there a less serious punishment which will achieve the purpose for which this punishment was inflicted?

    Note: A statute that is valid on its face may be invalid when applied to a particular set of facts or to a particular defendant.

    b. Deference To Legislative Decisions
    The Supreme Court will defer to the legislature, except in cases of extreme disproportionality or very severe punishment. However, the Court is narrowly divided on this point.

3. Specific Rules

   a. Sentencing
      It is not cruel and unusual punishment to sentence co-criminals disproportionately if due to differing circumstances or pleas.

   b. Imprisonment

      i. Constitutionally Valid
         Imprisonment is *not* cruel and unusual punishment even if the punishment fails to take into account:

         (1) The defendant's past good behavior, or

         (2) The defendant's more useful status in employment other than prison, or

         (3) The fact that the defendant need not be deterred from future crime, or

         (4) The fact that the defendant is not a threat to society.

      ii. Cruel and Unusual
         Imprisonment is cruel and unusual punishment if it punishes addiction.

      iii. Recidivist statutes
         Imprisonment is not cruel and unusual punishment if under a recidivist statute a defendant is punished more severely for his present crime on the basis of his past criminal behavior. These statutes have been upheld as constitutional if:

         (1) The severity of the past crimes is taken into account under the above balancing test, or

         (2) The sentence allows for parole.

c. The Death Penalty

   i.   The death penalty is not cruel and unusual punishment:

   (1) If it is imposed for the crime of murder, and

   (2) The statutory scheme provides for standards to ensure unarbitrary application. Such standards include:

      (a) Separate judgment and sentencing, and

      (b) Specific standards by which to consider the circumstances under which the crime was committed, and

      (c) Automatic appeal, and

   (3) All the mitigating factors that the defendant presents as a basis for a sentence less than death are admitted for consideration by the sentencer.

   ii.   The death penalty is cruel and unusual punishment if:

   (1) It is imposed for rape, or

   (2) It is imposed for a felony during which the defendant neither caused nor intended to cause the victim's death, or

   (3) It is imposed on a defendant who has lost his sanity at any time before execution and after sentencing.

CASE CLIPS

Regina v. Dudley and Stephens (1884) KS
Facts: Ds were stranded on a disabled boat 1000 miles from land. Near starvation, they decided to kill the weakest among them without his consent

and live off his flesh until they were rescued. They would not have survived had they not killed the victim.

Issue: Does dire necessity to conserve one's own life overcome the rule that the taking of another life is justified only in the case of self defense?

Rule: Private necessity does not justify murder, except in the case of self defense.

Note: The court based its judgment on the impossibility of measuring the comparative worth of lives.

United States v. Bergman (1976) KS, L

Facts: D, a noted philanthropist and nursing home operator, defrauded Medicaid. In a plea bargain, government prosecutors agreed to drop the main charges of fraud and larceny, in return for a guilty plea to the much narrower charge of bribery of a state legislator.

Issue: What is the purpose of imprisonment?

Rule: The purpose of imprisonment is punishment, not deterrence. Punishment must be proportional to the crime committed and should not reflect the defendant's past deeds or public desire for retribution.

State v. Chaney (1970) KS

Facts: D, a member of the U.S. Army, picked up a woman in his car, beat her, forcibly raped her, and took her money. The trial judge believed the victim's story, but sentenced D to one year with immediate parole, claiming that the interests of all would be better served with D in the military.

Issue: In sentencing, may a court consider a defendant's prior good behavior and more useful status in service in a place other than prison?

Rule: Prior good behavior and a defendants's employment worth cannot be allowed to mitigate punishment. This would undermine the goals of deterrence, community retribution, reaffirmation of societal norms, reformation, and public protection.

United States v. Jackson (1987) KS

Facts: Jackson robbed a bank thirty minutes after being released from prison, where he had been serving time for two previous bank robbery convictions. Jackson was sentenced to life in prison without possibility of parole under a statue forbidding possession of weapons by career criminals.

Issue: Is a life sentence permissible under a statute calling for a minimum term in prison with no possibility of parole?

Rule: A life sentence is permissible under a statue calling for a minimum term in prison with no possibility of parole. If specific deterrence has failed, a court is entitled to consider general deterrence and incapacitation.

Concurrence: The court is unauthorized to reduce the sentence, but the sentence is too harsh. A long prison term that would keep defendants locked up until they reach an age that makes them harmless would be just as effective as life in prison.

United States v. Johnson (1992) KS

Facts: Johnson was a single mother who cared for five children. Johnson was convicted of stealing money from her employer by inflating paychecks and receiving kickbacks from other employees for whom she inflated checks. The court reduced her sentence because of her family circumstances. The Sentencing Commission had previously issued a policy statement providing that family responsibilities are ordinarily not relevant in fixing a sentence.

Issue: Can a court reduce a sentence based on a factor which the Sentencing Commission has already concluded is not a reason for a "downward departure"?

Rule: Courts may reduce sentences based on extraordinary circumstances. The Sentencing Commission takes into account ordinary circumstances, but extraordinary circumstances may be grounds for a "downward departure."

Bowers v. Hardwick (S.Ct. 1986) KS, L, W, DS, MIB

Facts: D committed an act of sodomy with another consenting male in the privacy of his home. The act was prohibited by state statute and punishable by twenty years imprisonment.

Issue: Does the criminalization of consensual sodomy violate the Due Process Clause of the Fifth Amendment?

Rule: (White, J.) There is no fundamental right to engage in homosexual sodomy. The state has the historic right to regulate moral and sexual activity.

Concurrence: (Burger, J.) The punishment of twenty years for consensual sodomy is excessive and will create serious Eighth Amendment problems.

Dissent: (Blackmun, J.) Prohibition of private consensual sexual activity violates the right to privacy and individual liberty protected by the Fourth, Eight and Ninth Amendments. The court should examine the values underlying the privacy right, not the values underlying the majority's concept of a decent society.

Harmelin v. Michigan (S.Ct. 1991) KS

Facts: Harmelin was convicted of possessing 672 grams of cocaine and sentenced to a mandatory life term without possibility of parole. Harmelin claimed his sentence was unconstitutionally cruel and unusual because it was significantly disproportionate to the crime he had committed.

Issue: Does the Eighth Amendment, which prohibits cruel and unusual punishment, contain a proportionality guarantee?

Rule: (Scalia, J.) There is no proportionality guarantee in the Eighth Amendment. The framers of the Constitution chose not to include a guarantee against disproportionate sentences.

Concurrence: (Kennedy, J.) The Eighth Amendment does not require strict proportionality given the primacy of the legislature, the variety of legitimate penological schemes, the nature of the federal system, and the requirement that proportionality review be guided by objective standards.

Dissent: (White, J.) The Eighth Amendment does contain a proportionality guarantee, and the *Solem* test should be applied.

Note: This case overrules *Solem v. Helm* which held that there was a proportionality guarantee in the Eighth Amendment, but it does not disturb the rule that "death is different" for proportionality review.

Shaw v. Director of Public Prosecutions (1962) KS, MIB

Facts: D published a "Ladies' Directory" of available prostitutes, and was convicted of conspiracy to corrupt public morals.

Issue: May a court interpret the common law to address new crimes that have not been specifically outlawed by the legislature?

Rule: Courts have the power to enforce the supreme and fundamental purpose of the law, which is to conserve the safety, order and moral welfare of the State. This is so even if an act has not yet been specifically addressed by the legislature.

Dissent: Parliament is the only proper place for the extension of the law, especially when the criminality of the conduct is controversial. This is necessary so that the public have fair notice of what is illegal.

Keeler v. Superior Court (1970) KS, L, KW, MIB

Facts: D and his wife had obtained an interlocutory divorce decree. D, upon learning that his wife was pregnant by another man, became very upset and shoved his knee into her abdomen, declaring: "I'm going to stomp it out of you." The fetus, which was viable (could have lived outside the womb), died due to severe skull injuries.

Issue: May a court define an unborn but viable fetus as a "human being" so as to come within the meaning of the state murder statute?

Rule: Courts cannot enlarge the meaning of a statute beyond the plain intent. This would violate the Separation of Powers Clause of the Constitution; only the legislature can make laws. This would also violate due process by denying the defendant fair warning that his acts have become outlawed.

Dissent: At the time this statute was passed, the legislature had given the court permission to construe the terms of the statute as needed to serve the ends of justice.

Nash v. United States (S.Ct. 1912) KS

Facts: D was indicted for conspiracy in restraint of trade and conspiracy to monopolize trade pursuant to the Sherman Antitrust Act.

Issue: Is a statute void for vagueness under the Due Process Clause if it makes contemplated, rather than overt, acts illegal?

Rule: Statutes are not unconstitutionally vague merely because they rely on the jury for their interpretation, rather than delineating a clear cut standard between legal and illegal conduct.

Papachristou v. City of Jacksonville
(S.Ct. 1972) KS, J, MIB

Facts: Four different groups of defendants were arrested on a vagrancy ordinance for stopping in front of a used car lot that had been broken into several times, walking back and forth on a block while waiting for a friend, pulling up to a residence where police were arresting another man, and leaving a hotel, respectively.

Issue: Are vagrancy statutes which, based on an enforcer's judgment of the defendant's character, prohibit a defendant from taking part in activities which are generally considered innocent, void under the Due Process Clause?

Rule: (Douglas, J.) Vagrancy laws that require a defendant to show a lawful purpose or object for his wanderings, thereby allowing punishment by analogy or on suspicion, are contrary to Due Process.

State v. Palendrano (1972) L

Facts: D was indicted as a Common Scold, a common law crime that prohibited a woman from being habitually quarrelsome or noisy.

Issue: Is classification of a criminal offense void on due process and equal protection grounds if it outlaws a type of person rather than a particular type of action?

Rule: A criminal offense classification is void on due process grounds for vagueness if it does not charge a specific, clearly defined violation, and is void on equal protection grounds if it applies only to one sex.

Rose v. Locke (S.Ct. 1975) L, MIB

Facts: D entered the apartment of his neighbor on the pretext of using her phone, and forced her at knife point to submit to two acts of cunnilingus.

Issue: Is a sodomy statute that outlaws "all crimes against nature" void for vagueness under the Due Process Clause when applied to cunnilingus if the statute has never before been construed to include cunnilingus?

Rule: (Per curiam) The terms of a statute are not void for vagueness on due process grounds if the court in its prior decisions has indicated a tendency to construe the statute broadly, and other state courts after which it has modelled its previous interpretations have included the act in question. This is so even if the act has neither been specifically addressed by the statute, nor subjected to plenary review of its soundness.

Dissent: (Brennan, J.) The traditional test of fair warning of illegality has been supplanted by one of whether there is any hint that indicates that a defendant's acts are outside the scope of the statute.

Commonwealth v. Keller (1964) KW

Facts: D, separated but not divorced, twice disposed of the bodies of her newborn children by stuffing them into a cardboard box and hiding them. The first child was allegedly born dead, and the second admittedly born alive. D was convicted of two counts of a common law misdemeanor characterized as "indecent disposition of a dead body."

Issue: Can a defendant be charged with a crime not specifically outlawed by state statute?

Rule: Common law is preserved even after the adoption of statutory criminal law, and in the absence of statutory declaration or specific common law precedent, may be used to cope with novel situations not contemplated by legislators.

Note: Unlike Pennsylvania, the federal system and most states have not retained common law crimes.

Ricks v. District of Columbia (1967) KW

Facts: D, a known and convicted felon, thief, prostitute, vagrant and narcotics user, was observed by police on four separate occasions loitering and soliciting male passersby near a known house of ill repute. On each occasion, police questioned her as to her reason for loitering, her use of drugs, and her employment status. After being warned of the vagrancy law and told to go home, she was arrested for vagrancy.

Issue: Is a vagrancy law based on loitering, leading an immoral life, and wandering without any visible or lawful business, void under the Due Process Clause of the Fifth Amendment due to the vagueness of its terms?

Rule: A vagrancy law is void under the Fifth Amendment if it is so vague by its terms that it fails to provide by means of a commonly understood definition and clearly defined legal standards, a reasonable degree of fair notice as to which conduct is prohibited.

Solem v. Helm (S.Ct. 1983) KW, DS

Facts: During an eleven year period, D was convicted of six nonviolent felonies including fraud, grand larceny and driving while intoxicated. Several years later, D was convicted of uttering a no account check, which normally carried a maximum sentence of five years. D was convicted under South Dakota's recidivist statute which provided that when a defendant was convicted of three crimes in addition to the principal felony, the sentence was life imprisonment without parole.

Issue: Does the Eighth Amendment proscribe as cruel and unusual punishment, a life sentence without the possibility of parole for a seventh nonviolent felony?

Rule: (Powell, J.) Life imprisonment without possibility of parole is prohibited by the Eighth Amendment when the principal felony is of a nonviolent nature, and lesser sentences are imposed for higher degree crimes in the same jurisdiction and for similar crimes in other jurisdictions.

Dissent: The court should defer to legislative decisions because there are no significant differences between this case and *Rummel v. Estelle* (in which there was a possibility of parole) since sentences can be commuted by the governor.

Rummel v. Estelle (S.Ct. 1980) KW, MIB

Facts: On three separate occasions, D was convicted of obtaining small sums of money by fraudulent means. None of the crimes involved injury or threat, and all had a maximum sentence of five to ten years. D was convicted of the third crime under Texas' recidivist statute which mandated a life sentence for all third-time felons.

Issue: May a state recidivist statute mandating a life sentence for all third time felons, regardless of the severity of their crimes, be constitutional under the Eighth Amendment prohibition against cruel and unusual punishment?

Rule: A state has discretion in determining which crimes should result in more severe punishment. Due to the difficulty in formulating standards of punishment, the courts should defer to legislative determinations as to the necessity and utility of a particular punishment.

Dissent: The Eighth Amendment requires that the nature of the offense committed be balanced against the severity of the judgment. The inquiry must include whether the defendant deserves such punishment, measured by evolving standards of decency as reflected in the sentences adopted for the crime in other jurisdictions, and for similar crimes in the same jurisdiction.

United States v. Holmes (1842) W

Facts: Passengers were stranded on a life boat and near starvation. D, a sailor, chose the passenger who he thought was least likely to survive to be sacrificed in order to save the rest. The traditional method was to draw lots.

Issue: Does killing in an emergency in order to save the lives of others constitute murder?

Rule: A man may not kill another in order to save himself, even if by doing so he will save others as well, absent a direct and immediate threat to his or another's life by the person to be killed.

People v. Roberts (1920) W

Facts: At his wife's request, D placed a cup of poison by his wife's bedside so that she could end her life. She was terminally ill with multiple sclerosis.

Issue: Does giving a terminally ill person the means with which to kill themselves constitute murder?

Rule: A person who aids a suicide by intentionally providing a terminally ill victim with the means with which to kill themselves is guilty of murder.

Kolender v. Lawson (S.Ct. 1983) DS

Facts: On fifteen occasions during a two year period, D was detained or arrested for violating a criminal statute that required persons who loiter on the streets to provide "credible and reasonable" identification and to account for their presence at the request of a peace officer.

Issue: Is a statute that requires a person to produce "credible and reliable" identification and to account for his presence at the request of a peace officer void for vagueness under the Due Process Clause?

Rule: A statute that requires a person to produce "credible and reliable" identification and to account for his presence is void under the Due Process Cause because its terms do not describe with sufficient definiteness and clarity what an individual must do in order to satisfy the statute. Such a statute therefore encourages arbitrary enforcement.

Dissent: If an actor is given sufficient notice that his conduct is prohibited, his conviction is not void on vagueness grounds. A statute is not unconstitutionally vague on its face unless it is impermissibly vague in all of its applications. "Credible and reliable" has been defined as "reasonably authentic."

Coker v. Georgia (S.Ct. 1977) DS

Facts: D escaped from jail, broke into a couple's house, stole money and car keys, locked the husband in a closet, and raped the wife at knife point. He then drove away in the victim's car.

Issue: Is the death penalty excessive punishment under the Eighth Amendment for a rape that was committed by an escaped convict during the course of another violent felony?

Rule: The death sentence is grossly disproportionate and excessive punishment for the crime of rape, regardless of the degree of brutality of the rape, the rapist's prior criminal record, or the fact that rape occurred during the commission of another capital crime.

Concurrence: The death penalty may not be disproportionate when the degree of brutality or the amount of physical and psychological damage done is very high.

Dissent: The state legislature has the right to impose the death penalty for rape. The Eighth Amendment does not preclude the imposition of a punishment that is more severe that the crime committed or for a crime that does not involve the death of the victim.

People v. Pointer (1984) J

Facts: D fed her young children a macrobiotic diet despite repeated warnings from social workers and doctors. As a result the children suffered growth retardation and neurological damage. D was sentenced to probation on the condition that she not have custody of any children and not conceive during the probationary period.

Issue: Can a woman, convicted of the felony of child endangerment and found in violation of a custody decree, be prohibited from conceiving a child as a condition of probation?

Rule: Due to the right to privacy, a court may not prohibit a D from conceiving a child as a condition of probation, unless such conduct relates to the crime and to future criminality, and there is no less restrictive alternative.

People v. Gauntlett (1984) J

Facts: D sexually molested his stepson and stepdaughter. The judge described D as a man who had warm personal feelings for his stepchildren, but let them get out of hand. As part of his sentence D was to submit to use of an experimental chemical to reduce his sex drive for a five year probationary period.

Issue: If a court imposes a sentence that is in part unconstitutional, may the unlawful condition be set aside and the balance sustained, or must the defendant submit to resentencing?

Rule: Resentencing, including imposition of a greater sentence, does not violate the defendant's right to protection against double jeopardy, and is available at the court's discretion.

United States v. Ely (1983) J

Facts: As the result of a plea bargain, D received a much stiffer sentence than his two co-conspirators.

Issue: Does a judge abuse his discretion by imposing a stiffer sentence on a defendant who has pleaded guilty as a result of a plea bargain, than that imposed on his co-defendants?

Rule: If co-conspirators have not committed the same crimes under the same circumstances, imposing unequal sentences is not an abuse of judicial discretion.

Marshall v. Garrison (1981) J

Facts: D was convicted of armed robbery and attempting to kill a member of Congress. His parole date was extended due to new evidence of an additional robbery and an evaluation of the severity of the crimes committed.

Issue: Does parole evaluation based on the severity of a defendant's offenses violate the Constitutional proscription of ex post facto laws where the defendant was sentenced prior to the adoption of the severity standard?

Rule: An evaluation of eligibility for parole cannot be based on standards that were adopted subsequent to the commission of the crime.

State v. Anonymous (1978) J

Facts: D followed P to the restaurant where P worked, shouted insults at her, accused her of sleeping with D's husband, and threatening to "get [her] this time." D later telephoned P at the restaurant and repeated the accusations. D was convicted of disorderly conduct and harassment.

Issue: Is a statute that makes it illegal to annoy or interfere with another person, recklessly or with intent or to cause inconvenience, annoyance or alarm, void because it abridges the First Amendment free speech guarantee?

Rule: Under the First Amendment, a statute may restrict speech in a public place only if the speech has a substantial tendency to provoke violent reaction. However, where the means of communication involves an invasion of privacy, any purposeful harassment may be outlawed.

Screws v. United States (S.Ct. 1945) J

Facts: In the early morning hours, D, a Georgia sheriff, went to the home of a young black man and arrested him for tire theft. After handcuffing, the man was taken to the courthouse where he was beaten to death by police using fists and a blackjack. There was evidence that D had a grudge against the victim. D was convicted under a statute that criminalized willful deprivation of rights, privileges, or immunities secured or protected by the Fourteenth Amendment.

Issue: Is a statute void for indefiniteness under the Due Process Clause if it outlaws acts by state officers that wilfully deprive a person of *any* constitutional rights, privileges or immunities?

Rule: (Douglas, J.) A statute which outlaws the deprivation of constitutional rights that have not been specifically and clearly defined is void under the Due Process Clause unless it requires that the defendant have a specific intent to deprive a person of a protected right.

Dissent: (Roberts, J.) This specific intent exception violates the plain constitutional principle of definiteness in criminal statutes and deprives the public and officials of fair warning of which acts are illegal.

Gregg v. Georgia (S.Ct. 1976) J, MIB

Facts: D, a hitchhiker, robbed and murdered two men who gave him a ride. D was found guilty of two counts of armed robbery and two counts of murder.

Issue: Does the imposition of the death penalty for murder constitute cruel and unusual punishment in violation of the Eighth Amendment?

Rule: (Stewart, J.) The imposition of the death penalty is constitutional where the statutory scheme provides for separate judgment and sentencing, specific standards for the trier of fact to consider the surrounding circumstances, and automatic appeal.

Pulley v. Harris (S.Ct. 1984) J

Facts: D was convicted of a capital crime in California, and sentenced to death.

Issue: Does the Constitution mandate review of the proportionality of sentences imposed on similar defendants in capital cases before a death sentence may be imposed?

Rule: (White, J.) Review of the proportionality of a death sentence in light of sentences imposed on others for similar crimes is not mandated by the Constitution as long as there are other standards of review to insure guided and unarbitrary application of the death penalty.

United States v. Grimaud (S.Ct. 1911) MIB

Facts: D was indicted for grazing his sheep on a government reserve without permission.

Issue: Does the Separation of Powers Clause prohibit an administrative agency from enforcing a criminal act of the legislature?

Rule: Congress can delegate any powers that are not strictly and exclusively legislative. An administrative agency can enforce rules made by Congress with punishments specified by Congress, and can "fill up the details" by making regulations incidental to the Act, but cannot create additional requirements or punishments.

United States v. Hudson and Goodwin (S.Ct. 1812) MIB

Facts: D, a newspaper, was indicted in a libel suit for claiming that the President and Congress secretly voted two million dollars as a present to Napoleon in exchange for leave to make a treaty with Spain.

Issue: Does a federal court have jurisdiction to exercise common law in the absence of a specific criminal statute?

Rule: A federal court in a criminal action cannot make common law in the absence of a statute on point. Courts do not make laws; this would be a violation of the Separation of Powers Clause.

Sonzinsky v. United States (S.Ct. 1937) MIB

Facts: Congress imposed a $200 yearly tax on dealers of certain size firearms.

Issue: Does the Constitution prohibit Congress from imposing taxes which have a regulatory effect that is local in character, and therefore should be reserved to the states?

Rule: Congress may levy any tax which is not regulatory on its face. The courts will not attempt to measure the regulatory effect of a tax, or guess the hidden motives of Congress.

United States v. Sharpnack (S.Ct. 1958) MIB

Facts: The Assimilative Crimes Act of 1948 made state law applicable to federal territories that are within that state.

Issue: May a federal statute that adopts state laws for areas within federal jurisdiction be applied to state laws created after the enactment of the statute?

Rule: The Necessary and Proper Clause of the Constitution grants Congress the power to create, define, and punish offenses committed in any state, territory or possession whenever it is necessary to do so in order to effectuate the objects of government.

United States v. States (1973) MIB

Facts: Ds devised a scheme to use fraudulent voter applications and absentee ballots in order to control certain political offices for personal gain.

Issue 1: Must an indictment for mail fraud allege that someone has been defrauded of money or property in order to be valid?

Rule 1: An indictment for fraud is valid whether it refers to the taking by fraudulent means of tangible rights such as property or money, or intangible rights such as the loyal and faithful services of a government employee.

Issue 2: Does application of a federal mail fraud statute to acts done in furtherance of a state scheme constitute an infringement on state regulatory rights?

Rule 2: Congress can forbid any acts done pursuant to a state scheme which it regards as contrary to public policy, whether or not it can forbid the scheme itself.

Concurrence: The federal government may not take over the prosecution of every state fraud merely because the mails are involved.

Perez v. United States (S.Ct. 1971) MIB

Facts: D, loan shark, lent money to the owner of a new butcher shop, and increased his repayment demands from $100 to $1000 weekly, threatening to castrate the owner or break his back if he did not comply.

Issue: Is a federal statute regulating intrastate "loan sharking" unconstitutional under the Commerce Clause?

Rule: The Commerce Clause allows Congress to regulate any class of activities deemed to affect commerce, regardless of whether they occur wholly intrastate.

Dissent: Congress may not regulate intrastate activities unless they have a substantial affect on interstate commerce.

United States v. DeMet (1973) MIB

Facts: D, a Chicago police officer extorted monthly payments from the owner of a bar, threatening to harass the owner about closing time and revoke his liquor license.

Issue 1: Are threats of physical harm necessary to prove the element of fear needed for an indictment of extortion?

Rule 1: Fear of physical harm is not a necessary element of extortion. Fear of economic harm suffices.

Issue 2: Must extorted goods be the subject of interstate commerce at the time the extortion takes place in order to be federally regulated under the Commerce Clause of the Constitution?

Rule 2: Extorted goods may be the subject of interstate commerce at any time before or during the extortion, in order to be federally regulated under the Commerce Clause.

Wayte v. United States (S.Ct. 1985) MIB

Facts: D did not register for the Selective Service System as required by law, but wrote to several government officials, including the President, stating his intent not to register.

Issue: Does a passive enforcement policy under which the government prosecutes only those who report themselves or are reported by others violate the First and Fifth Amendments on the ground of selective prosecution?

Rule: The Government's prosecutorial discretion is broad, and discrimination is valid as long as it is not based on unjustifiable standards or arbitrary classification, and impermissible discrimination was not an intended result.

Commonwealth v. Bonadio (1980) MIB

Facts: Ds had sex on stage at a pornographic theater.

Issue 1: Does a statute that prohibits consensual deviate sexual intercourse (oral or anal sex) exceed the valid police power of the state in regulating public, health, safety, welfare and morals?

Rule 1: A statute enacted pursuant to the police power to regulate morality cannot enforce a majority morality on persons whose conduct does not harm others, but must protect an individual's right to be free from interference in pursuing his/her own morality.

Issue 2: Does a statute that proscribes deviate sexual acts, but excludes married persons, violate the Equal Protection Clause?

Rule 2: The Equal Protection Clause prohibits classifications of persons to be affected by a statute if those classifications do not have a fair and substantial relation to the object of the regulation.

Doe v. Duling (1986) MIB

Facts: The Does challenged Virginia laws against consensual intercourse and cohabitation by unmarried members of the opposite sex. Although neither was threatened with prosecution, they claimed that fear of prosecution had curtailed their individual liberty.

Issue: Do individuals to whom an unenforced statute applies have standing to challenge the constitutionality of the statute if they have a subjective fear of prosecution?

Rule: Absent objective threatened injury, judicial review of criminal laws is an appropriation of power by the judiciary and violates the Separation of

Powers Clause. A subjective chilling effect on personal behavior is not a valid threat for purposes of authorizing judicial review of a statute.

State v. Rocker (1970) MIB

Facts: Ds were arrested for nude sunbathing on a public beach.
Issue: What level of intent is necessary for nude sunbathing to become the common nuisance of indecent exposure?
Rule: To be guilty of common nuisance, one need only have the intent to commit acts that one knows are likely to be seen by others.

Caminetti v. United States
Diggs v. United States
Hays v. United States (S.Ct. 1916) MIB

Facts: All three Ds were charged under the White Slavery Act for transporting a woman across state lines for the purpose of debauchery to enable her to become a mistress and concubine.
Issue: Is a statute prohibiting the interstate transportation of women for the purpose of debauchery or any other immoral practice limited to "commercialized vice" (i.e., the trafficking of women for economic gain)?
Rule: By its terms, a statute prohibiting the interstate transportation of women for the purposes of debauchery and any other immoral practice applies to both commercial and noncommercial vice.
Dissent: "Immoral" is too comprehensive a word; the court's interpretation provides no limits. The act, according to its legislative history, was meant to apply only to prostitution.

Griswold v. Connecticut (S.Ct. 1965) MIB

Facts: Ds, a doctor and a Planned Parenthood executive, were found guilty as accessories to the crime of preventing conception because they gave instruction and medical advice on contraceptives to a married couple.
Issue: Does a statute that prohibits both married and unmarried couples from preventing conception violate the Due Process Clause of the Fourteenth Amendment?
Rule: (Douglas, J.) A law forbidding the use of contraceptives, rather than their manufacture or sale, is void because it is unnecessarily broad and violates the constitutional right to privacy.
Dissent: (Black, J.) This law is not unconstitutionally vague, and therefore the Due Process Clause does not apply.

Roe v. Wade (S.Ct. 1973) MIB

Facts: A single pregnant woman wished to have an abortion "by a licensed physician under safe, clinical conditions." Abortion was criminally prohibited except to protect the life of the mother.

Issue: May a state impose regulations restricting a woman's right to terminate a pregnancy?

Rule: (Blackmun, J.) In the absence of a precise definition of when life begins, a statute is unconstitutional if it adopts a particular theory of life that infringes on the personal integrity of individuals without showing a compelling state interest. The measure of a compelling state interest must take into account the stage of the pregnancy, and balance the private rights and interests of the individual against those of the state.

Dissent: Abortion does not involve the right to privacy because an operation is not private. The fact that a majority of states have abortion laws shows that the right to abortion is not widely accepted.

Dissent: There is no constitutional warrant to permit the court to value the rights of pregnant mothers over the continued existence of the potential life that they carry.

Eddings v. Oklahoma (S.Ct. 1982) MIB

Facts: D, a juvenile runaway, shot and killed a highway patrol officer who had stopped D's car. At sentencing, the court allowed testimony of aggravating circumstances, but denied evidence of mitigating circumstances. D was sentenced to death.

Issue: Do the Eighth and Fourteenth Amendments prohibit the imposition of the death penalty where it was imposed without consideration of all of the mitigating factors that the defendant presented?

Rule: The Eighth and Fourteenth Amendments require that a sentencer must consider as a mitigating factor all circumstances and aspects of a defendant's character that the defendant offers as a basis for a sentence less than death.

Dissent: In considering the imposition of the death penalty, a sentencer must consider all mitigating factors offered by a defendant; however, he need not accept all proffered factors as true on their face.

Enmund v. Florida (S.Ct. 1982) MIB

Facts: A man and woman drove to a house and asked for water for an overheated car. They fatally shot and robbed the elderly couple who owned the house. D, an accomplice, drove the car in which the murderers escaped. D was sentenced to death for conspiracy to murder for monetary gain.

Issue: Is the death penalty valid under the Eighth and Fourteenth Amendments for a defendant who neither took, attempted to take, nor intended to take a life?

Rule: Under the Eighth and Fourteenth Amendments, a defendant cannot be sentenced to death solely for participating in a felony in which a person was killed if the defendant did not actually cause or intend to cause the victim's death.

Dissent: The Constitution does not require intent as a requisite for imposition of the death penalty, only that the punishment be proportional to the harm caused and to the defendant's blameworthiness. There was evidence that the defendant here masterminded the crime.

Ford v. Wainwright (S.Ct. 1986) MIB

Facts: D was convicted of murder and sentenced to death. Eight years later, D succumbed to paranoid schizophrenia which made him believe that he was Pope John III, and that he could not be executed because he owned all the prisons and could control the Governor through mind waves. His ability to comprehend his death sentence was determined by three psychiatrists. A rehearing of his competency to suffer execution was denied.

Issue: Is the execution of a defendant who has lost his sanity subsequent to trial and sentencing prohibited by the Eighth Amendment as cruel and unusual punishment?

Rule: The Eighth Amendment prohibits the execution of a defendant who has lost his sanity subsequent to sentencing if the defendant is barred from presenting evidence relevant to his sanity, denied an opportunity to impeach the state psychiatrists' opinions, and if the executive branch controls the ultimate decision of whether to execute.

Dissent: Creating a constitutional right to a judicial determination of sanity serves as an invitation to those who have nothing to lose to advance spurious claims of insanity.

Coates v. City of Cincinnati (S.Ct. 1971) MIB

Facts: D, a student involved in a demonstration, was convicted under an ordinance that made it illegal for three or more persons to assemble on a city sidewalk and act in a manner that would annoy passersby.

Issue: Is a statute which forbids conduct annoying to passersby unconstitutionally vague under the First and Fourteenth Amendments?

Rule: A statute that forbids three or more persons from engaging in conduct annoying to passersby is unconstitutionally vague because it subjects the right of assembly to an unascertainable standard, and unconstitutionally broad because it authorizes the punishment of constitutionally protected conduct.

Dissent: A statute that prohibits annoying passersby is not vague on its face since a reasonable man should know that some types of conduct, such as blocking passage, are clearly covered. It may, however, be vague as applied to certain circumstances.

Gooding, Warden v. Wilson (S.Ct. 1972) MIB

Facts: D threatened to kill and "cut to pieces" two police officers who were trying to restore access to a building. D was convicted of using "opprobrious words or abusive language tending to cause a breach of the peace."

Issue: Is a statute that prohibits speech "tending to cause a breach of the peace" overbroad on its face because it may be applied to conduct protected under the First and Fourteenth Amendments?

Rule: The First and Fourteenth Amendments proscribe a statute that prohibits speech *"tending* to cause a breach of the peace" because such a statute can and has been construed to apply to speech beyond the constitutionally unprotected class of words known as "fighting words."

Dissent: A statute cannot be determined to be vague on its face because of previous interpretations; this must be determined by construction of its terms. The term "tending to cause a breach of the peace" restricts the application of the statute to fighting words.

Village of Hoffman Estates v.
Flipside Hoffman Estates, Inc. (S.Ct. 1982) MIB

Facts: The Flipside (D), a store that sold novelties and smoking accessories, was warned that it was in violation of a law that required the licensing of stores selling items which could be used in conjunction with marijuana.

Issue: Is an ordinance that requires a business to obtain a license if it sells any items "designed or marketed for use with illegal ... drugs" unconstitutionally vague and overbroad on its face?

Rule: An ordinance that requires a business that sells items designed or marketed for use with illegal drugs to obtain a license is neither unconstitutionally broad nor vague on its face, since commercial activity promoting or encouraging drug use is not constitutionally protected speech, and the statute does not threaten to inhibit protected rights.

Eisenstadt v. Baird (S.Ct. 1972) MIB

Facts: D delivered a lecture on contraception to a group of students from Boston University and gave a contraceptive to one female student.

Issue: Does a statute that prohibits the dispensation of contraceptives to unmarried couples for the purpose of contraception, but not for the purpose of disease prevention, violate the Equal Protection Clause of the Fourteenth Amendment?

Rule: A statute that prohibits the dispensation of contraceptives to unmarried couples for the purposes of contraception, but allows it for the purpose of preventing disease, violates the Equal Protection Clause of the Fourteenth Amendment by providing dissimilar treatment for married and unmarried persons who are similarly situated.

Concurrence: The purpose of the statute is not furthered by the restriction of those who may dispense nondangerous contraceptives since it applied only to those that are not distributed in order to prevent the spread of disease.

Dissent: The court ignores the state's legitimate interest in protecting the health of its citizens by requiring that contraceptives be dispensed only through medical channels.

Michael M. v. Superior Court of Sonoma County
(S.Ct. 1981) MIB

Facts: D, a seventeen-year-old male, had sex with a sixteen-year-old girl that he met at a bus stop. Both had been drinking.

Issue: Does a statute that prohibits sexual intercourse with a girl under the age of eighteen violate the Equal Protection Clause of the Fourteenth Amendment because it penalizes only males for adulterous relations?

Rule: A statute that prohibits sexual intercourse with a female under the age of eighteen is constitutional under the Equal Protection Clause because the gender-based classification has a substantial relationship to the legitimate objectives of preventing teenage pregnancies and is based on the real distinction that young men and women are not similarly situated with respect to the risks and consequences of intercourse and pregnancy.

Dissent: The State has not shown that a gender-based statute is more effective than a gender-neutral one in deterring minor females from engaging in intercourse. Gender-based statutes rely on the outmoded stereotype that young women are incapable of consenting to sex.

Dissent: The fact that a female confronts a greater risk of harm has not deterred young females from engaging in sex in the past, and does not justify granting females a license to use their own judgement on whether or not to engage in intercourse.

Chapter 3

ACTUS REUS AND MENS REA

I. INTRODUCTION

For behavior to be punishable, an actor must (1) commit an overt criminal act, called an actus reus, and (2) have a culpable intent, known as a mens rea.

II. ACTUS REUS

An actus reus is an overt criminal act.

A. Actions

1. Voluntary Acts
   A criminal act, or failure to act, must be voluntary. See, MPC § 2.01.

2. Involuntary Acts
   Generally, one is not punished for acts that were outside of one's control. See, MPC § 2.01(2).

   a. Deterrent Effect
      There is little reason to punish involuntary acts because they cannot be deterred.

   b. Blameworthy
      Individuals should not be blamed for acts they did not consciously or willfully commit.

   c. Not Required of Every Element
      It is not necessary, however, that every part of the act leading up to the harm be voluntary for the actor to be blameworthy.

      Example: An individual who knows he is using medication that causes fainting, voluntarily decides to go for a drive. While driving, he faints and runs over a pedestrian. Although unconscious at the time of the accident, the driver consciously chose to go driving knowing that he might faint and, therefore, is liable for the harm.

3. Punishing Status

Statutes that prohibit a particular status (e.g., a statute declaring that drug addiction is a crime), are generally unconstitutional and thus should be viewed cautiously. However, one may be punished for actually being intoxicated due to the threat posed to the public by intoxicated persons.

4. Possession

Possession of an illegal object is a crime only if the possessor is aware of the object's presence. See, MPC § 2.01(4).

a. Possession is punishable if it is:

   i.   Actual, such as on one's person, or

   ii. Constructive; being under one's dominion or control.

b. Knowledge that the substance or object is illegal is not necessary for punishment.

B. Omissions

(See, MPC § 2.01(3))

Failure to act can constitute a crime where there is a legal duty to act. In general, an individual is under no legal obligation to help another. However, some circumstances do create a duty.

1. Special Relationship

Parent-child, husband-wife, or a similar special relationship gives rise to legal responsibility.

2. Statute

Statutes may impose a legal duty to act. Example: legislation requiring a night club owner to provide safety exits.

3. Contract
A contract can create a legal duty to act. Example: the employment contract of a lifeguard or nurse.

4. Assumption of Care
Once a person begins to render aid, he is under a duty to continue to aid. Abandonment may be criminal.

5. Creation of Danger
One who creates a danger may have a duty to aid those who he imperiled.

C. Multiple Charges
(See, MPC § 1.07(1))
A single act may violate several statutes, and the perpetrator may thus be charged with several offenses.

1. Lesser Included Offenses
If all the elements of a lesser crime are part of a larger crime, one may not be charged with both crimes.

2. Fairness Factors
In deciding the fairness of bringing multiple charges for a single offense, the court will consider:

a. Whether the offenses require proof of different facts,

b. Whether the statutes are intended to prevent the same result, and

c. Whether the offenses require different criminal intent.

III. MENS REA

It is widely believed that to justify punishing an individual for a particular act, the act must be accompanied by a blameworthy state of mind.

A.   General and Specific Intent Crimes
Under common law, crimes were often classified as either "general intent" or "specific intent."

1. Specific Intent

   a. Defined
   Specific intent crimes require that the accused intend both the criminal conduct and its particular result. For example, to be convicted of assault with intent to kill, the state must prove a defendant both intended his actions and intended for the act to result in the victim's death.

   b. Defenses
   A person charged with a specific intent crime may offer evidence to show that she was unable to form the requisite intent and thus cannot be convicted.

      i.   Intoxication
      Intoxication may render a person incapable of forming a particular intent.

      ii. Diminished Capacity
      Some jurisdictions allow a defendant to introduce evidence of diminished mental capacity that rendered him incapable of forming a requisite specific intent. See also, Ch. 8.

      iii. Mistake of Fact
      An honest mistake of fact is a valid defense when one is charged with a specific intent crime.

2. General Intent

   a. Defined
   General intent crimes require only proof that a defendant intended the particular criminal act, and not the result.

    b. Intoxication

        Intoxication is not a valid defense to a general intent crime because drunken individuals intend their acts, although they may not realize certain consequences. See also, Ch. 8.

B.   Categories of Mens Rea
      (See, MPC § 2.02)

      Many jurisdictions have discarded the distinction between general intent and specific intent crimes. Instead, many states follow the Model Penal Code, which divides mens rea into four categories. In addition, some crimes, called strict liability offenses, do not require any culpable mental state.

      Different elements of a crime may have different mens rea requirements. For example, if a person is charged with statutory rape (sex with a person below a certain age), conviction will require that the person *intended* to have sex, but will only require that the person have been *negligent* as to ascertaining the other person's age.

    1. Purpose or Intent

        In some jurisdictions, the term "intent" is used instead of purpose. See, MPC § 2.02(2)(a).

        a. Model Penal Code Definition

            According to the Code, one acts purposely if one's conscious object is to engage in certain conduct or bring about a certain result.

        b. Malice Requirement

            Some jurisdictions once required proof of a malicious intent in order to convict a defendant of certain crimes.

        c. Inference of Intent

            Recent Supreme Court decisions suggest that intent may be inferred if circumstantial evidence sustains such an inference beyond a reasonable doubt.

2. Knowledge
   (See, MPC § 2.02(2)(b))

   a. Definition
      A person acts knowingly if he is aware of the nature or circumstances of his conduct.

   b. Aware of Probability
      If the crime involves a particular result, a person acts knowingly if he is aware that his conduct is practically certain or highly probable to cause the particular result. See MPC, § 2.02(7).

   c. Willfulness
      According to the Code, proof that a defendant acted knowingly also satisfies statutes requiring "a willful act." See, MPC § 2.02(8).

   d. Knowledge Inferred
      Knowledge may be inferred when one makes a conscious effort to disregard the obvious.

   e. Burden on Prosecution
      According to the Code, when the requisite mens rea for a crime is "knowingly," the prosecution has the burden of showing that the particular defendant had such knowledge.

3. Recklessness
   (See, MPC § 2.02 (2)(c))

   a. Defined
      A person acts recklessly, or wantonly, when he ignores the substantial risk of a particular result or situation, and the disregard is a gross deviation from the amount of care that would be shown by an ordinary person.

      MPC § 2.02(3) states that if a culpability level is not specifically proscribed, the requisite level is at least that of recklessness. Furthermore, if only one level is mentioned, it applies to all elements of the crime. See MPC, § 2.02(4).

   b. Awareness Requirement
      In order to be convicted of a recklessness crime, the Code and some jurisdictions require that a particular defendant be aware of the risk. Other jurisdictions require only that a defendant overlook a risk that would have been recognized by a reasonable person.

4. Negligence
   A person acts negligently when he acts without being aware of a substantial risk, and a reasonable person would have exercised greater care. See, MPC § 2.02(2)(d).

C.   Strict Liability
    (See, MPC § 2.05)
    A strict liability crime requires no culpable state of mind. The defendant is absolutely liable for the result, even if there is no intent, knowledge, recklessness, or negligence on his part.

    1. Public Interest Requires Accountability
       Strict liability is imposed when there is a strong public interest in preventing a certain harm. In order to force individuals to avoid such harm, they are held absolutely liable, regardless of state of mind.

    2. Difficulty in Finding Culprit
       Strict liability is often imposed for safety regulations because it is difficult to find an actual intention to violate such standards.

    3. Statutory Rape
       Strict liability generally applies to the crime of statutory rape, so individuals will make certain that their sexual partners are of legal age. See further, Ch. 4, I, E.

    4. Public Welfare Offenses
       Some courts have held that strict liability should only be imposed on public welfare offenses.

5. Common Law Offenses
Strict liability may not be imposed by statute on a crime that was traditionally a common law offense, unless it was always a strict liability offense.

D. Mistake of Fact
(See, MPC § 2.04(1))

1. Generally
In many jurisdictions a reasonable mistake of fact serves as a valid defense to negate a culpable state of mind.

2. Model Penal Code Approach
Under the Code, a good faith mistake of fact, even if it is unreasonable, will serve as a valid defense if the mistake negates the requisite intent.

3. Strict Liability Offenses
Mistake of fact is not a defense to a strict liability crime, because such offenses require no culpable mens rea. However, some courts have argued that in statutory rape cases, a reasonable mistake should relieve a person of liability.

E. Mistake of Law
(See, MPC § 2.04(3))

1. Generally
A mistake of law is no excuse for criminal behavior because members of a society are expected to know right from wrong and act accordingly.

2. Knowledge of Action, Not Illegality
Legislation may deem one culpable for "knowingly violating a regulation." Even with this kind of offense, ignorance of the law is no excuse. The Supreme Court has held that "knowing" requires that one know what one is doing, but one need not know of the illegality of the act to be convicted.

3. Exceptions
Ignorance of the law can be a valid defense in certain limited cases:

a. If a statute is not readily available;

b. If one acted upon an earlier judicial decision that was subsequently overruled;

c. If one acted upon an interpretation of a law by a public official responsible for enforcement or other administration.

4. Model Penal Code
The Code allows any good faith or honest mistake, even one of law, to negate culpability.

CASE CLIPS

Martin v. State (1944) KS, KW

Facts: D was charged with being drunk on a public highway after police officers forcibly removed him from his home and placed him on the road.
Issue: Must an act be voluntary to constitute a crime?
Rule: To be convicted of a crime, the violation must be voluntary. One cannot be blamed for an act he was forced to perform.

People v. Newton (1970) KS, J

Facts: D struggled with police officers who had pulled him over. After being shot in the abdomen, D shot and killed a police officer. D claimed he was unconscious when he killed the officer.
Issue: Is unconsciousness a valid defense to a criminal charge?
Rule: Unconsciousness is a complete defense to a charge of criminal homicide, so long as it is not self-induced.

Pope v. State (1979) KS

Facts: D invited a young mother and infant to stay at her home. D did nothing while the mother savagely beat the infant. D was charged with child abuse.

Issue: Can one be held liable for failing to help another?

Rule: One has no legal obligation to help a child unless one is a parent or guardian or if the obligation is imposed by a statute. One cannot be punished for failing to fulfill a moral obligation to aid another.

Jones v. United States (1962) KS, J, KW

Facts: A baby was placed under the care of D, a friend of the baby's family. The baby died of malnutrition and neglect. D was convicted of involuntary manslaughter.

Issue: When does the failure to preserve the life of another constitute a crime?

Rule: Failure to protect the life of another when under a duty to do so is criminal only if there is a special relationship between the parties (e.g., parent-child), if one has voluntarily assumed care for another, or the duty is imposed by statute or contract.

Barber v. Superior Court (1983) KS

Facts: The family of a severely ill and comatose hospital patient asked that Ds, two physicians, remove all life-sustaining equipment. Ds complied and a short while later the patient died. Ds were charged with murder and conspiracy.

Issue: Does a physician have a duty to preserve life when there is no chance of meaningful recovery?

Rule: There is no duty to continue medical treatment when qualified authorities feel such treatment is ineffective and futile.

Regina v. Cunningham (1957) KS, L

Facts: D, hoping to steal some money, ripped a gas meter out of the wall. Gas escaped, causing D's elderly neighbor to become ill. D was charged with a "malicious" crime?

Issue: In order to be convicted of a malicious act, must one foresee the harm?

Rule: Malicious does not merely mean wicked. To be malicious, one must actually foresee the harm that occurs.

Santillanes v. New Mexico (1993) KS

Facts: Santillanes cut his seven-year-old nephew's neck with a knife during an altercation. He was convicted of child abuse under a statute that defined the mens rea of the crime as negligence. The court instructed the jury on a civil negligence standard, but Santillanes argued that the correct standard was that of criminal negligence.

Issue: When the legislature has included, but not defined, the mens rea element in a criminal statute, how should the courts determine what specific degree of mens rea is required?

Rule: In the absence of clear legislative intent, courts should construe statutory language to require criminal intent as an essential element of the crime. When moral condemnation attaches to a crime, the crime should typically reflect a mental state warranting such condemnation.

United States v. Jewell (1976) L, J, KS

Facts: D's car was stopped at the Mexican border, and 110 pounds of marijuana were discovered in a hidden compartment. D claimed he did not know it was there.

Issue: Is purposeful ignorance equivalent to positive knowledge?

Rule: Knowledge can be inferred when one makes a conscious effort to disregard the obvious.

Dissent: Knowledge of a condition should only be inferred if a defendant realizes there is a high probability of the condition.

Regina v. Prince (1875) KS, KW, J

Facts: D ran off with a fourteen-year-old girl who claimed to be eighteen. D was charged with abducting a girl under eighteen.

Issue: May one be held liable for a crime when due to a mistake of fact one reasonably believed the action was legal?

Rule: In certain cases where there is a strong public interest, a state can make an offense a strict liability crime so that people will be warned that they act at their own peril.

Dissent: One should not be punished absent a criminal intent.

People v. Olsen (1984) KS, DS

Facts: D had sex with a girl he believed was over sixteen, but was actually under fourteen, the statutory age of consent.

Issue: Is a good faith reasonable mistake of fact as to the age of a sexual partner a defense to a statutory rape charge?

Rule: There is a strong public policy interest in protecting children below the age of consent, and in order to deter lewd acts, mistake of fact is not a valid defense.

Dissent: Conviction without fault often smacks of cruel and unusual punishment. A reasonable inquiry as to the person's age should be sufficient to avoid liability.

Morissette v. United States (S.Ct. 1952) KS, DS, J, MIB

Facts: D, a junk dealer, found some old bomb casings on a bombing range and erroneously assumed they were abandoned. D sold the parts as scrap.

Issue: Must one have a criminal intent in order to be punished?

Rule: (Jackson, J.) Generally, in order to protect those who are not blameworthy in mind, a criminal intent is required for punishment. Strict liability may be imposed by legislation, but it is usually not applied to statutes that simply codify common law offenses.

United States v. Staples (S.Ct. 1994) KS, L

Facts: Staples was convicted of possession of an unregistered firearm pursuant to the National Firearms Act, which defines a firearm as "a weapon capable of automatically firing more than one shot with a single pull of the trigger." Staples testified that he never fired the weapon automatically, and that he did not know it was capable of firing automatically. Staples was denied a jury instruction that would have required the government to prove that he knew the gun would fire automatically.

Issue: When a statute is silent as to the mens rea required for a violation, what mens rea standard should be applied?

Rule: (Thomas, J.) When a statute is silent as to mens rea, some form of mens rea will be implied as an element of the crime. Offenses that require no mens rea are disfavored, and some indication of congressional intent, express or implied, is required to dispense with mens rea as an element of a crime.

Concurrence: (Ginsburg, J.) The question is not whether knowledge of possession is required, but what level of knowledge suffices: (1) knowledge simply of possession of the object; (2) knowledge that the object is a dangerous weapon, (3) knowledge, beyond dangerousness, of the characteristics that render the object subject to regulation. Since only a limited class of firearms were regulated, and all firearms are dangerous, the third reading is the proper mens rea requirement in this case.

State v. Guminga (1986) KS

Facts: D's employee served alcohol to a seventeen-year-old girl who was accompanied by two state investigators. D was charged with violation of a statute that made an employer liable for the sale of alcoholic beverages to a minor by an employee.

Issue: Is vicarious criminal liability for an employee's criminal conduct violative of due process?

Rule: Vicarious liability is violative of due process when the defendant neither has knowledge of the conduct nor gives express or implied consent to the conduct.

State v. Baker (1977) KS

Facts: D was convicted for driving his car at 77 mph in a 55 mph zone. D's cruise control mechanism had malfunctioned, causing him to speed.

Issue: Does malfunction of one's cruise control mechanism negate an intent to drive over the speed limit?

Rule: By activating cruise control, one voluntarily delegates partial control of the car, so malfunction is no excuse. Break failure, however, is an excuse because in that situation a driver does not voluntarily relinquish control.

Regina v. City of Sault Ste. Marie (1978) KS

Facts: Not provided.

Issue: Is absolute liability justified in public welfare offenses?

Rule: There is a middle ground between absolute liability and the requirement of full mens rea. A defendant charged with an absolute liability offense should be allowed to prove he did not act negligently.

People v. Marrero (1987) KS

Facts: D, a federal corrections officer, mistakenly thought a state law exempted both state and federal corrections officers from the requirement of licensing their guns. In fact, the law only exempted state corrections officers.

Issue: Does one's personal misreading of a statute excuse criminal conduct?

Rule: Mistake of law does not excuse criminal conduct.

Dissent: One should not be punished for conduct that, in good faith reliance on a statute, one believes is lawful.

Cheek v. United States (S.Ct. 1991) KS, MIB

Facts: Cheek was convicted for willfully failing to file a federal income tax return. Cheek asserted that he sincerely believed that he owed no taxes, and the tax laws were unconstitutional. The court instructed the jury that only a good-faith, reasonable mistake of law negates willfulness. Cheek argued that even an unreasonable mistake of tax laws can negate willfulness.

Issue: Does an unreasonable mistake of law negate willfulness to violate a federal income tax statute?

Rule: (White, J.) In criminal tax cases, an unreasonable mistake of law negates willfulness. Willfulness requires the government to prove that the law imposed a duty on the defendant, that the defendant knew of this duty, and that he voluntarily and intentionally violated that duty. If the defendant is not aware of the duty, no matter how unreasonable the belief, the government cannot maintain its burden.

United States v. Albertini (1987) KS

Facts: D engaged in a peace protest on a naval base, despite receiving a letter prohibiting such action. He was convicted, but the Circuit Court reversed the conviction. D then held another protest. However, the Supreme Court reversed the Circuit Court's decision. After the Supreme Court's decision, D was charged for the second protest.

Issue: Can one be convicted for criminal conduct when that conduct had been held legal, but afterwards illegal?

Rule: Just as a state cannot pass ex post facto laws, one cannot be convicted for reliance on a court opinion that is later reversed.

Lambert v. California (S.Ct. 1957) KS, KW, DS, J

Facts: A local statute required all persons who had been convicted of a felony to register with the police if they were in town for more than five days. D was unaware of the statute and did not register.

Issue: May a person be convicted for failing to do a required act when one is unaware of that duty?

Rule: (Douglas, J.) It is a violation of due process to punish someone for failing to do a certain act when the person had no notice of the responsibility.

Dissent: (Frankfurter, J.) Many laws require specific action and do not require an element of knowledge for conviction.

State v. Rocker (1970) L, MIB

Facts: Ds openly sunbathed in the nude at a public beach and were charged with creating a common nuisance.

Issue: To be charged with creating a common nuisance, must one have intended the act to be criminal?

Rule: One need only have a general intent, or intent to commit acts one knows are likely to be seen by others to be guilty of creating a common nuisance.

United States v. Melton (1973) L, MIB

Facts: D entered another person's home at night and was found there, lying on the floor. D did not have any weapons and nothing had been stolen.

Issue: May one be convicted of burglary if there is no evidence of an intention to steal?

Rule: Evidence of intent to commit larceny or attack the dweller is required for a burglary conviction.

Dissent: An intent to steal can be inferred from the act of breaking into another's home.

State v. Odom (1974) L

Facts: D shot a man in an unemployment office, then shot at responding police officers. Shortly before he was apprehended, D pointed his unlicensed gun at a policeman, but did not shoot.

Issue: Is mere possession of an unlicensed gun prima facie evidence of an intent to commit a violent crime?

Rule: Mere possession of an unlicensed weapon is not prima facie evidence of intent to commit a violent crime. Intent must be proven beyond a reasonable doubt.

Dissent: Intent to commit a violent crime should be inferrible from possession of an unlicensed weapon, with a defendant given an opportunity to rebut the presumption.

Sandstrom v. Montana (S.Ct. 1979) L

Facts: D was on trial for murder. The jury was instructed that the consequences of one's voluntary acts are presumed to be intended.

Issue: May the burden of disproving intent be placed on the defense?

Rule: It is unconstitutional to presume an intent. The burden of proof is on the prosecution.

State v. Beale (1973) L

Facts: Police told D's wife that certain goods in D's store were actually stolen property and could not be sold. D nonetheless sold the goods, and claimed he believed they were not stolen material.

Issue: To be convicted of "knowingly" committing a crime, must the defendant actually know of the illegality, or is it enough that a reasonable person would have known under the circumstances?

Rule: When a crime requires knowledge, the actual defendant must have the requisite knowledge. It is not enough to show a reasonable person would have had such knowledge.

Barnes v. United States (S.Ct. 1973) L

Facts: D forged endorsements and deposited four government checks that were mailed to others. D claimed that he received the checks from an unidentified door-to-door furniture salesman.

Issue: Can knowledge be inferred from circumstances?

Rule: (Powell, J.) If a jury can infer beyond a reasonable doubt from the circumstances that a defendant had certain knowledge, the inference does not violate due process.

Dissent: (Douglas, J.) For knowledge to be inferred from the circumstances, there must be strong evidence proving the elements of the specific offense.

Dissent: (Brennan, J.) Knowledge must be proven beyond a reasonable doubt.

State v. Jones (1956) L

Facts: D accidentally shot someone on a hunting trip, and was charged with negligently shooting and wounding another.

Issue: Is the criminal law negligence standard higher than civil law?

Rule: The criminal law punishes negligence that is gross and culpable, while the civil law requires mere carelessness.

Dissent: In order to be an effective deterrent, the standard for criminal negligence should be no different than the standard for civil negligence.

State v. Cushman (1974) L

Facts: D threatened a police officer with a gun that D knew was not loaded. Nonetheless, D was charged with recklessly endangering a person with death or serious injury.

Issue: In order for a defendant to be punished for recklessly endangering another, must the victim be in real danger?

Rule: One may be guilty of reckless endangerment even if there is no actual risk of harm.

Dissent: There can be no reckless endangerment when there is no real danger.

State v. Stepniewski (1982) L

Facts: Ds, contractors, failed to file certain project completion forms as required by state law. D's were charged with intentional violation of trade practices.

Issue: Must one have intended to violate the law in order to be guilty of intentional violation of trade practices?

Rule: If one is neglectful where the law imposes a duty, it may be inferred that one intentionally neglected that duty.

Dissent: Criminal liability should not be imposed on inadvertent failure to comply with regulations.

State v. Campbell (1975) L

Facts: D found and kept some ammunition and binoculars. A statute required anyone who found property to either advertise the discovery in the newspaper or notify police before appropriating it.

Issue: Must statutorily created offenses require criminal intent?

Rule: A criminal statute is unconstitutional if there is no intent requirement, unless the offense is a common law crime or a strict liability crime.

Director of Public Prosecutions v. Morgan (1975) L, DS

Facts: Ds, one of whom was the victim's husband, had intercourse with a woman who resisted. Ds claimed that they believed the resistance was merely an act.

Issue: Is an honest but unreasonable belief that there is consent a valid defense to a rape charge?

Rule: One who is charged with rape need only prove that he actually believed there was consent. The belief need not be reasonable.

Concurrence: A belief that there is consent bars a rape conviction.

Dissent: All defendants can assert they believed a rape victim consented. There should be a reasonableness standard.

Dissent: In order to excuse otherwise criminal behavior, any mistake of fact must be reasonable.

Note: After this decision, Parliament passed a statute allowing for rape convictions if one is reckless as to a victim's consent.

State v. Caddell (1975) L
Facts: D kidnapped and tried to rape a fourteen-year-old girl. D claimed that he was not conscious of the events at the time of the kidnapping.
Issue: Which side has the burden of proving a defendant was conscious or unconscious of a criminal act?
Rule: Unconsciousness is an affirmative defense, and thus a criminal defendant has the burden of proving to the jury that he was not conscious during commission of a crime.

People v. Gory (1946) L
Facts: A quantity of marijuana was found in an open locker belonging to D, an inmate. D claimed he was unaware the marijuana was there, but was nonetheless convicted of possession.
Issue: In order to be convicted of possession, must one be aware of the object's presence?
Rule: Knowledge of an object's presence is the essence of possession, and thus to be convicted one must knowingly have the objects in one's possession.

Wheeler v. United States (1985) L
Facts: Police found a quantity of heroine underneath a pillow in a motel room. D was present and admitted she lived there with a roommate. Two other individuals were also in the room at the time of the search.
Issue: Must actual in-hand possession of an illegal substance be demonstrated to attain a conviction for possession?
Rule: The inference that a defendant knows of an object's presence, if combined with other circumstances implying illegal action, is enough to prove constructive possession.

County Court of Ulster County v. Allen (S.Ct. 1979) L
Facts: The three Ds were sitting in an automobile in which two handguns were found. The guns were visible and lay in an open handbag that belonged to a fourth passenger, a minor who was not charged in this case. A statute allowed the presumption of possession by all persons occupying a vehicle.
Issue: May shared possession be inferred from one's presence in a vehicle?

Rule: (Stevens, J.) The facts of a particular case can permit a presumption of possession when it appears to be a completely rational presumption.

Dissent: (Powell, J.) The inference of possession is not rational because mere presence in certain places such as an automobile does not indicate dominion or control over all objects within it.

State v. Williquette (1986) L

Facts: D, a mother, knew that her husband regularly abused her children, but she did nothing to stop the abuse and often left the children alone with their father. She was charged with child abuse even though she did not personally abuse the children.

Issue: Can an omission or a failure to take action be a crime?

Rule: The failure to act is a crime when there is a legal duty to act. A special relationship, such as parent-child, imposes such a duty.

Gore v. United States (S.Ct. 1958) L

Facts: Defendant allegedly sold drugs on two occasions. For each single act the defendant was charged with three different offenses.

Issue: Can a single act constitute several different offenses?

Rule: (Frankfurter, J.) A single act may constitute several offenses if each offense requires proof of an additional fact which the other does not.

Dissent: (Warren, C.J.) Similar statutes are often intended to give prosecutors different ways to attain convictions, and are not intended to attach numerous punishments to one act.

Irby v. United States (1967) L

Facts: D pled guilty to one count of housebreaking and one count of robbery, and received consecutive sentences. After serving several years, D moved to be released from prison, alleging that the sentences could not run consecutively.

Issue: Can two separate consecutive sentences be imposed for two violations that were part of a single criminal act?

Rule: If different statutes are intended to prevent different dangers to society, a single act violating both statutes may be punished by consecutive sentences.

Concurrence: Consecutive sentences should be imposed for different offenses when each violation involves a larger or different degree of intent.

Dissent: A defendant with only one criminal purpose should only be punished for one crime.

Proctor v. State (1918) KW
Facts: Defendant was convicted of "keeping a place with intent to unlawfully sell liquor."
Issue: Is the intent to commit a crime punishable if not accompanied by an overt criminal act?
Rule: The law is not concerned with guilty intent unless the intent is accompanied by an overt unlawful act.

People v. Newton (1973) KW
Facts: D became unruly during an airline flight. The pilot made an unplanned stop in New York, where D was arrested for having an unregistered weapon in violation of New York law.
Issue: Is one liable for violating a jurisdiction's law if one's presence in that jurisdiction was not voluntary?
Rule: One is not liable for violating a jurisdiction's law if one's presence is not attributable to a voluntary act.

People v. Grant (1977) KW
Facts: D, an epileptic, struck a police officer and was convicted of battery. D claimed that at the time of the attack he was having a seizure and could not control his actions.
Issue: Is one criminally liable for involuntary actions?
Rule: Automatism, or the inability to consciously control one's acts is a defense, unless the defendant recklessly brings about the automatism, for example by drinking.

People v. Beardsley (1907) KW, W
Facts: D, a married man, invited another woman to visit his house while his wife was away. At the house, the woman took a large dose of morphine, became ill, and died. D did not call for help and was convicted of manslaughter.
Issue: Does one owe a legal duty of care to a visitor in one's home?
Rule: Failure to care will result in a charge of criminal manslaughter only when there is a legal duty to care. No such duty is owed to one who voluntarily visits another's home.

Commonwealth v. Cali (1923) KW, J

Facts: In order to collect insurance proceeds, D purposely refrained from trying to put out a fire.

Issue: If harm is begun accidentally, may one be criminally culpable for failing to prevent further harm?

Rule: One has a duty prevent further harm when one accidentally causes the initial harm.

United States v. Balint (S.Ct. 1922) KW

Facts: Ds were indicted for selling opium derivatives. Ds contended they did not know the items were illegal drugs. The relevant statute did not require knowledge.

Issue: Is knowledge of illegality a prerequisite for conviction?

Rule: (Taft, J.) Knowledge is not required for conviction so long as it is not specified in the statute, and there is legitimate public policy for making the offense a strict liability crime.

Liparota v. United States (1985) L, DS

Facts: D owned a sandwich shop and accepted food stamps for less than face value in violation of federal food stamp statutes.

Issue: When charged with violating federal regulations, must an element of knowledge be proven by the prosecution?

Rule: Ambiguous criminal statutes should be interpreted in favor of the accused, and in such instances it must be proven that the actor knew the conduct was illegal.

Dissent: Conviction should only require that defendants know the nature of their acts, and not that they know those acts are illegal.

United States v. Dotterweich (S.Ct. 1943) KW

Facts: D, president of a drug company, was convicted of an offense when the company mislabelled drugs, even though D himself did not know of the mislabelling.

Issue: May a corporate officer be culpable for an act without knowledge of the act's occurrence?

Rule: (Frankfurter, J.) In order for the law to have a truly deterrent effect, the legislature may impose strict liability on certain offenses, and thus actual knowledge of a violation is not necessary for conviction.

Dissent: (Murphy, J.) Liability should not be imposed on one lacking knowledge or intent.

People v. Hutchison (1977) KW

Facts: D was not aware that a passenger had left an open bottle of whiskey in his cab. D was convicted of illegal transportation of alcohol.

Issue: May one be convicted of a crime when one is unaware the violation is occurring?

Rule: One generally may not be convicted of an offense if one does not intend the act or is unaware of it.

Dissent: The legislature has the right to create strict liability offenses.

Regina v. Faulkner (1877) KW, J

Facts: D, a sailor, was trying to steal some rum when he lit a match and accidentally set the boat on fire.

Issue: May one be charged for a crime that is the accidental result of a lesser crime?

Rule: One cannot be convicted for an act that is the unintended and unforeseeable consequence of a lesser offense.

State v. Guest (1978) KW

Facts: D had sex with a fifteen-year-old girl whom he believed was at least sixteen. State law made it illegal to have sex with a girl under sixteen.

Issue: Is a reasonable mistake of fact as to a person's age a valid defense to a statutory rape charge?

Rule: A reasonable mistake as to a person's age is a valid defense to a statutory rape charge.

Note: In many states, statutory rape is a strict liability offense.

People v. Bray (1975) KW

Facts: D mistakenly wrote on his application for a gun license that he had never been convicted of a felony. D did not realize that his earlier conviction was for a felony.

Issue: Can mistake of fact be a valid defense?

Rule: Mistake of fact can be a valid defense except when one is charged with a strict liability crime.

People v. Wetmore (1978) KW

Facts: D was found in another man's apartment, wearing the other man's clothes and cooking the other man's food. D had just left the hospital and believed he was in his own apartment.

Issue: Can mental illness preclude a finding of the specific intent required for conviction of a crime?
Rule: If one lacks the mental capacity to form the requisite specific intent, one is entitled to a diminished capacity defense.

State v. Cameron (1986) KW
Facts: Intoxicated, Cameron attacked a man with a broken bottle. She was convicted under a statute that punished the purposeful use of a weapon.
Issue 1: Is voluntary intoxication a viable defense?
Rule 1: Voluntary intoxication is a defense to a criminal charge that contains as an essential element of proof that a defendant acted purposely or knowingly.
Issue 2: What level of intoxication must be demonstrated before a trial court is required to submit the issue to a jury?
Rule 2: Evidence of voluntary intoxication must be sufficient to show that the consumption of alcohol has rendered the defendant incapable of forming an intent to commit an offense.

State v. Hatch (1973) KW
Facts: D, a resident of Massachusetts, was driving through New Jersey and had two guns in his car. D had a Massachusetts permit to carry guns, but he did not have the guns in a case or trunk as required by New Jersey law.
Issue: Is ignorance of the law a valid defense?
Rule: Ignorance of the law is no excuse. People have a responsibility to know and abide by the law, especially when engaged in a highly regulated area of conduct.

Hopkins v. State (1950) KW
Facts: D advertised on a billboard that he was a notary public, after a State Attorney advised him the ad was legal. D was charged with violating a statute that forbid the solicitation of marriages.
Issue: May one be convicted of a crime after acting on the advice of a State Attorney?
Rule: Ignorance of the law, even in good faith reliance on a State Attorney, is no excuse.

State v. Mercer (1969) DS

Facts: D, a soldier whose marriage was failing, shot and killed his wife, sister-in-law, and nephew. He claimed that at the time of the shooting he was completely unconscious of what was taking place.

Issue: May one be held criminally liable for acts committed while unconscious?

Rule: A person may not be held liable for acts committed while unconscious. Criminal liability requires that acts be voluntary.

Note: Unconsciousness is not a complete defense and will not work when the unconsciousness is the result of voluntary acts such as intoxication.

Robinson v. California (S.Ct. 1962) DS

Facts: A police officer saw D's scarred arms and suspected that D was a heroine addict. D was not on drugs at the time, but California law made it criminal to "be addicted to the use of narcotics."

Issue: Can one be punished for a condition or status, absent the commission of a criminal act?

Rule: Punishing an individual simply for an ongoing affliction is cruel and unusual punishment and is therefore unconstitutional.

Dissent: A statute making addiction an offense punishes habitual use and is not cruel and unusual.

State v. Bugger (1971) DS

Facts: Defendant's automobile was parked on the shoulder of a road. Defendant was found asleep and intoxicated in the car. He was convicted of being in physical control of a vehicle while intoxicated.

Issue: Is a person sleeping in a car in actual physical control of it?

Rule: Lying asleep in an automobile does not constitute actual physical control of the vehicle.

Dissent: Being intoxicated in an automobile presents a significant threat to society that amounts to criminal control of a vehicle.

Davis v. Commonwealth (1985) DS

Facts: D claimed to be her mother's caretaker. Defendant's mother died of freezing and starvation after defendant failed to provide heat, food, liquid or other necessities. Defendant was convicted of involuntary manslaughter.

Issue: May one be held criminally negligent due to a breach of duty to care?

Rule: When a legal duty to care exists, an individual may be criminally negligent for omitting to perform a duty, provided the negligence is flagrant, reckless, or wanton.

Commonwealth v. Williams (1985) DS

Facts: D fired one shot from a gun after a police officer started to question him. D was charged with four different offenses for the one act, including a weapons charge, a firearms charge, resisting arrest and assault.

Issue: May a person be charged with numerous offenses when they are all based on one single act?

Rule: An individual may be punished for numerous offenses arising from the same act if each statute is aimed at protecting a different harm or evil.

Alvarado v. State (1986) DS

Facts: D wanted to give a child a bath, but the child resisted. D got angry, and placed the fully clothed child in the tub, not realizing that the water was scalding hot.

Issue: To be punished for intentionally and knowingly injuring a child, must one know that one's conduct will cause injury?

Rule: To punish one for intentionally and knowingly injuring a child, the state must prove one actually knew the likelihood of or intended serious bodily injury.

State v. Gordon (1974) DS

Facts: D was escaping from prison and took another man's car, but promised to return it as soon as possible. On trial for robbery, D contended he did not have the requisite intent to permanently deprive the owner of the property.

Issue: Does robbery require a specific intent to deprive the owner of the property?

Rule: Robbery is a specific intent crime. However, indifference to the owner's ability to get the goods back is sufficient proof of intent to permanently deprive.

United States v. Adamson (1983) DS

Facts: D, the president of a bank, made illegal loans and was charged with willful misapplication of bank funds. At trial, the judge stated that reckless disregard was the equivalent of intent to injure.

Issue: May recklessness be equated with intent to injure?

Rule: "Willful" implies knowledge or intention, not mere recklessness. Recklessness should not be equated with the higher mens rea of intent or knowledge.

Dissent: A reckless disregard of rules can amount to acting with knowledge.

Wilson v. Tard (1984) DS

Facts: D and three others were discussing who should be the first to use some heroin that was in their possession. D shot one of the others, but claimed he had believed the weapon was not loaded and had only pointed it at the victim as a prank.

Issue 1: Can recklessness be presumed from one's acts?

Rule 1: Recklessness cannot be inferred. It must be proven beyond a reasonable doubt.

Issue 2: Who has the burden of proving whether or not a mistake of fact was reasonable?

Rule 2: The prosecution must prove by a preponderance of the evidence that a mistake of fact was not reasonable.

United States v. Burton (1984) DS

Facts: D did not file income tax returns, claiming he did not realize that wages qualified as income.

Issue: May a person be punished for a good faith mistake as to one's legal duty?

Rule: A good faith misunderstanding of one's duty under the law constitutes a valid defense. No standard of objective reasonableness is applied. One may only be punished for intentional violations of a known legal duty.

Ostrosky v. State (1985) DS

Facts: Ds were charged with fishing without a permit, but a lower court found the law unconstitutional. The state appealed, and was granted a stay to enforce the law, pending the state supreme court's decision. Ds, relying on the first decision, then went fishing again, and were again arrested. The state supreme court subsequently held the law constitutionally valid.

Issue: Is reasonable reliance on a judicial decision a valid defense?

Rule: The defense of a mistake of law in reliance on a judicial decision is an affirmative defense which the defendant must prove by a preponderance of the evidence.

Dissent: A legislature is free to reject the mistake of law defense.

Kizer v. Commonwealth (1984) DS

Facts: D, a sailor, had been separated from his wife for three weeks and had not had sexual relations with her for six months. D forcibly raped his estranged wife because he "was hard up for sex."

Issue: In marital rape cases, must a wife's intent to end the marriage be objectively or subjectively manifested?

Rule: In addition to satisfying the general elements of rape, a victim of marital rape must prove that she lived apart from her husband, has refrained from having sex with him, and has manifested her intent to end the marriage in a manner that has convinced her husband of her intent.

Dissent: In a marital rape case, a court should view the situation in an objective manner, not from the husband's perspective.

United States v. Yermian (S.Ct. 1984) J

Facts: D knowingly made false statements about his criminal record on an employment application, although he did not know the form would be sent to a federal agency. Federal law forbid making false statements in an area within the jurisdiction of a federal agency.

Issue: Must a defendant know that his conduct violates the law to be punished?

Rule: (Powell, J.) To be culpable, a defendant must intend his actions, but the defendant need not intend to break the law or have knowledge that his conduct violates a statute.

Dissent: (Rehnquist, J.) When a statute is ambiguous, knowledge should be required for a conviction.

United States v. Park (S.Ct. 1975) J, MIB

Facts: D was president of a food corporation that had been cited for numerous health code violations. D was charged with adulterating food even though he claimed he had no knowledge or control over the food in question.

Issue: Must one know of or participate in certain delegated acts to be convicted of a crime?

Rule: (Burger, J.) When enforcement of a statute is necessary to protect the public welfare and there is no alternative means of enforcement, liability may be imposed on an employer for acts delegated to employees, even if the employer did not participate in or know of the illegal acts.

Dissent: (Jackson, J.) An individual should not be convicted of a crime unless there has been behavior amounting to at least common-law negligence. In order to punish someone, there must be constructive and not mere formal responsibility for delegated duties.

People v. Hood (1969) J

Facts: D was drunk and tried to force his way into his ex-girlfriend's house. The police attempted to arrest D, and a scuffle ensued, during which D shot a police officer once in each leg. D was charged with assault with a deadly weapon.

Issue: Can voluntary intoxication negate intent when one is charged with a general intent crime?

Rule: General intent crimes such as assault are frequently committed by drunks, and the criminal law should deter such behavior. Intoxication is no defense to general intent crimes.

United States v. International Minerals & Chemical Corp. (S.Ct. 1971) J

Facts: D shipped chemicals that were improperly labelled. Federal law forbid "knowing" violation of regulations. Ds claimed they did not know of the regulations.

Issue: Is ignorance of an applicable law a valid defense?

Rule: (Douglas, J.) Ignorance of the law is no excuse. One is guilty of a violation if one is are aware of the facts that constitute the illegal action.

Dissent: (Stewart, J.) If a statute punishes someone for "knowingly" violating a statute, one should only be punished if one is actually aware of the violation.

People v. Decina (1956) J

Facts: D had an epileptic seizure while driving and killed four children. He was convicted of negligent homicide.

Issue: Is one culpable for involuntary acts resulting from a known condition?

Rule: One may be criminally culpable for involuntary acts caused by a condition if the individual knows of the condition, and disregards the possible consequences.

Dissent: One should not be culpable for acts committed while unconscious.

Commonwealth v. Olshefski (1948) MIB

Facts: D's coal truck was weighed by one authority, who said it was within legal limits. The next day, a different officer using a different scale found that D's truck weighed too much, and charged D with a violation.

Issue: Is a mistake of fact a legitimate defense to a criminal charge?

Rule: When a crime is established by statute, there is no intent requirement, and one may be convicted irrespective of one's intent or belief.

Ex Parte Marley (1946) MIB

Facts: D owned a meat market. One of his employees, unbeknownst to D, sold meat based on a weight that was greater than the actual weight.

Issue: May an employer be liable for statutory violations by an employee, absent proof of any personal wrongdoing?

Rule: Where a statute lacks qualifying words such as knowingly or intentionally, guilty knowledge and intent are not elements of the case. When there is a strong public interest at stake, one has a duty to know the law regulating one's conduct.

Dissent: It is unfair to convict individuals who are free of any moral culpability.

Braun v. State (1962) MIB

Facts: D married a second wife, mistakenly believing his first wife had divorced him. D was charged with bigamy.

Issue: Is mistake of fact a valid defense to a bigamy charge?

Rule: Neither mistake of fact nor mistake of law is a valid defense to a bigamy charge.

People v. Hernandez (1964) MIB

Facts: D had consensual sex with a girl whom he believed was eighteen but was actually seventeen years and nine months old.

Issue: Is mistake of fact a valid defense to a statutory rape charge?

Rule: An honest and mistaken belief is a valid defense to a statutory rape charge, as well as any statutory crime, unless it is barred by legislation.

People v. Young (1962) MIB

Facts: D interfered in a struggle on behalf of another person. D did not realize the opponent was an undercover police officer.

Issue: Is a mistake of fact a valid defense when one interferes in a struggle to aid another?

Rule: One who interferes to aid another in a struggle does so at one's own peril. Mistake of fact is no defense.

Dissent: Criminal intent requires awareness of wrongdoing. An honest and reasonable belief in facts that, if true, would make an act legal, is a valid defense.

Chapter 4

CRIMES AGAINST THE PERSON

I.   RAPE

A.   Definitions

1. Common Law
    At common law the crime of rape was a felony, defined as unlawful sexual intercourse (requiring penetration) of a woman not the rapist's wife, by force and against her will.

2. Statutes

    a. Most state statutes have adopted a definition of rape that is substantially the same as the common law definition.

    b. There is now a trend among some states, led by Michigan, to adopt statutes that propound that:

        i.   Rape is any violation of bodily integrity by a forced sexual act (penetration is not necessary), and

        ii. Rape is an act of violence motivated by the need to express anger and hatred through domination, and

        iii. Rape should be a degree crime to adjust to the varying degrees of violence rape encompasses.

3. Model Penal Code
    The Code defines rape as sexual intercourse imposed by a male on a female by the use of force or threat of imminent use of force, or by rendering her unable to consent. The Code divides rape into degrees and includes non-consensual sexual acts in addition to intercourse under the definitions of second and third degree rape.

B.   Elements of Rape

Mnemonic: <u>**FAN**</u>

1. <u>F</u>orce

    a. Common Law
        Common law required that actual force or verbal threat of force
        be present in order for a woman to prove that the rape occurred
        against her will.

    b. Statutes
        Most statutes require that rape be committed by force or threat
        of force unless the victim is incapable of consent. Some states
        recognize that a threat of force may be a nonverbal threat of
        harm to someone other than the victim, or a combination of the
        totality of circumstances. Most states recognize the impetus of
        implied force or threats of nonviolent acts only when a rape
        involves children.

    c. Model Penal Code
        Section 213 focuses on the rapist's behavior, and differentiates
        between degrees of force. Generally, in the absence of a
        mentally impaired victim, the Code requires use of force or
        threat of imminent death, serious bodily injury, extreme pain,
        or kidnapping. The threats may be of harm to be inflicted on
        someone other than the victim.

2. "<u>A</u> Woman Not His Wife"

    a. Marital Exception

        i.   Common Law
              Common Law exempted husbands from the crime of rape
              because a wife was considered to have consented to inter-
              course through marriage.

    ii.   Statutes
Most states have retained the marital exemption. However, most states recognize that a married woman has the same legal rights as a man or non-married woman, and that nonconsent is no harder to prove in cases of marital rape than in other instances of rape.

    iii.   Model Penal Code
Section 213.1 recognizes a marital exemption. However, a wife may bring assault charges if there is a physical threat. Section 213.6(2) applies this exemption to any couple living together as man and wife, regardless of legal status.

  b. Gender Distinctions

    i.   Common Law
At common law, only a woman could be raped, and only a man could rape.

    ii.   Statutes
Today, most states agree that young boys and men may also be raped, and that a woman may be a rapist. Therefore many courts have held gender distinctions in rape statutes serve no valid purpose and violate Equal Protection.

    iii.   Model Penal Code
Section 213.1 defines rape as forced sexual intercourse on a female by a male and as a first degree felony. However, § 213.2 recognizes sexual violation in any other combination of the sexes as the second degree felony of deviate sexual intercourse.

3. Nonconsent

   a. Common Law

      i. Active Proof of Nonconsent
          Common law equated nonconsent with "against her will."
          Therefore, a woman would have to prove that she actively
          resisted in order to convey her nonconsent.

          (1) Resistance to the Utmost
              Originally the level of resistance that was required of the
              woman was "resistance to the utmost." This failed to
              take into account strength disparity, or the increased
              danger of harm that resistance might cause.

          (2) Reasonable Fear Exception
              Eventually, states began to recognize an exception to the
              resistance rule. In cases of reasonable fear of imminent
              and serious bodily harm, a woman's lack of consent was
              implied.

      ii. Incapability
          The common law has always recognized cases where a
          woman is incapable of consent. These include: mental
          illness, youth, unconsciousness, or mental impairment
          caused by the deliberate administration of drugs or alcohol
          by the rapist.

   b. Statutes

      i. Reasonable Fear
          Today, many states recognize that any genuine fear that is
          reasonably grounded adequately demonstrates nonconsent,
          even in the absence of serious or immediate harm or threat
          of harm.

      ii. Active Resistance Requirement
          While most courts require that nonconsent be expressed,
          some recognize that resistance need not be active and may

involve submission, because they recognize that non-resistance may not be due to acquiescence, but rather to caution, fear, or a desire to end the episode quickly.

c. Model Penal Code
Section 213 does not specifically require that a woman express her nonconsent or actively resist a rapist.

C. Intent

1. Common Law
Common law did not focus on the intent of the rapist, but on the state of mind of the victim.

2. Statutes
Most statutes do not specify a mens rea requirement regarding a rapist's perception of consent or do not require specific intent to "commit rape against the will of another." Instead, they focus on the victim's expression of nonconsent. However, the current trend is toward focusing on the defendant's intent.

3. Model Penal Code
Section 213 implies that a rapist must have the intent to commit rape since it requires compulsion or incapacitation of the victim by the rapist. Section 2.02(3) states that if the Code does not specify the culpability required, the elements of the crime are satisfied if one acts purposely, knowingly or recklessly with regard to an element of the crime.

4. Mistake

a. Common Law
At common law, a defendant was not guilty of rape if the accuser did not clearly express her nonconsent.

b. Statutes

    i.   Reasonable Mistake
Some states, such as California, allow reasonable mistake as to the consent of the victim as a defense. The rationale is that one should not be subject to the severe punishment of a felony for a crime that one had no criminal intent to commit.

    ii.   Reckless or Negligent Mistake
Generally if a mistake is reckless or negligent there is no excuse.

c. Model Penal Code
Section 2.04 allows mistake of fact to be used as a defense if it negates the purpose, knowledge, or recklessness required to commit rape.

D.   Proof
At common law, the belief of Sir Matthew Hale that "rape is an accusation easily made and hard to be proved" was adopted by most courts.

1. Victim's Background

a. Common Law
At Common Law, the fact that a victim was unchaste, was a prostitute, or had a prior consensual sexual relationship with the defendant was a defense to the crime of rape.

b. Statutes

    i.   The Federal Rules of Evidence
Reputation or opinion about a victim is never admissible as evidence in federal court. However, a victim's past sexual conduct may be admitted if, at a separate hearing, its probative value is determined to outweigh its prejudicial effect.

ii. Shield Laws
Many states have enacted shield laws which exclude a victim's prior sexual conduct from admission at trial. These states have determined that prior sexual conduct is not probative of consent to rape. Critics of shield laws claim that the laws violate one's Sixth Amendment right to defend oneself by impeaching the credibility of the prosecution's witness.

c. Model Penal Code
Section 213.1 classifies rape as a more serious crime if the victim is not a voluntary companion of the rapist and had not allowed the rapist to have sex with her in the past. Also, § 213.6(3) allows prior sexually promiscuous conduct by the victim to be used as a defense.

2. Corroboration

a. Common Law
Common law did not allow rape to be proven on the uncorroborated testimony of the accuser. However, corroboration could be shown by circumstantial evidence such as the immediate reporting of the crime.

b. Statutes
Most states do not require corroboration of a victim's testimony, but require testimony to be clear and convincing, or at least not unbelievable. Those states that require corroboration often use the fresh-complaint standard, which determines the validity of a victim's accusations based on the promptness of her reporting the crime.

c. Model Penal Code
Section 213.6(5) requires that a victim's testimony be corroborated, although it allows corroboration by circumstantial evidence. Section 213.6(4) also requires that rape be reported within three months of an incident, except under certain circumstances.

3. Expert Testimony
Expert testimony is now admitted by many courts to help explain the testimony of rape victims so that they will not be prejudiced by their reactions to the rape. This testimony is especially useful in cases that involve young children who are unable to fully articulate the circumstances of the rape.

4. Polygraph Tests
Polygraph tests are also being employed to help the jury determine the veracity of the parties; however, many jurisdictions will not admit polygraphs into evidence due to their unreliability.

E.   Statutory Rape
Statutory rape is defined as sexual intercourse with a girl under a predetermined "age of consent." It does not require threat, force, consent, or intent. The only element is that a girl be under a certain age. The "age of consent" is the age below which a child is believed to be incapable of freely choosing to consent in light of a reasonable assessment of her circumstances.

1. Common Law
The common law did not allow reasonable mistake as to a victim's age as a defense to statutory rape.

2. Statutes

a. Strict liability
In the majority of jurisdictions, statutory rape is a strict liability crime, especially if the victim is under age of fourteen.

b. Mistake
The majority of courts do not allow a defense of honest and reasonable mistake as to age because this is an attendant circumstance. However, the modern trend is to follow the Model Penal Code.

3. Model Penal Code

   a. Liability

      i.   The Code makes rape and related offenses more serious violations if the victim is less than ten years of age.

      ii.   Under § 213.3, a male is guilty of "corruption of minors" if he has intercourse with a person under sixteen, or if he has intercourse with a person under 21 years of age to whom he is guardian.

   b. Mistake
   Section 213.6(1) allows no mistake when the child is under ten years, but a reasonable mistake is a defense when the victim is over ten.

II.   KIDNAPPING

A.   Common Law

1. Defined
Historically, kidnapping was the forcible transportation of a person from his own country to another. Later, the element of removal from a country was no longer required.

2. Grading
At common law kidnapping was a misdemeanor, viewed merely as aggravated false imprisonment.

B.   Statutes

1. Defined
Kidnapping is the forcible abduction or confinement of another with the intent to hold for benefit or for the facilitation of the commission of another crime. Many courts have developed limitations on this definition, due to its broadness.

2. Grading
Most states now punish kidnapping as a serious felony and do not distinguish between kidnapping and the lesser crime of false imprisonment.

C. Model Penal Code

1. Defined
Section 212 defines kidnapping as the unlawful (rather than forcible) removal of another. This emphasizes a victim's consent to being moved, rather than the amount of force used.

2. Grading
Under the Code, kidnapping is a felony.

D. Elements

1. Abduction or Confinement
Kidnapping can occur either through seizure and *removal* of a person, or through *confinement* of a person in that place where he was found. The former requires the element of asportation, and the latter requires secrecy.

   a. Asportation
   Asportation is the significant movement of a victim. The requirement of asportation developed to keep lesser crimes from being turned into the felony of kidnapping solely on the basis of some incidental movement of a victim from one place to another.

      i. Any Movement
      At first, most courts accepted any movement, however slight, of a victim from the place of abduction.

      ii. Meaningful Asportation
      Now, most courts require meaningful asportation:

(1) The movement must be greater than that which is merely incidental to another offense being committed simultaneously, and

(2) The movement must cause a substantial increase in risk of harm over and above that of another simultaneous offense.

  b. Duration
  The duration of asportation or confinement generally must be that which increases the risk of harm to the victim.

  c. Secrecy
  Some statutes require secrecy rather than asportation because this addresses unlawful confinement as well. They define kidnapping as unlawful seizure with intent to detain secretly and against a victim's will.

2. Intent
To constitute kidnapping, confinement or abduction must be committed either without lawful justification or with malice.

  a. Malice
  Malice means ill will and signifies any intentional act that is neither justified nor excused.

  b. Consent
  There is no lawful justification for asportation or confinement without a victim's consent;

    i. If a victim is not a criminal in the custody of law enforcement officials, or

    ii. If consent is obtained by deceit, force or threat.

E. Child Custody
Absent a custody award, a parent does not commit kidnapping by taking exclusive possession of his/her child, because each parent has an equal right to custody of the children.

F.   Kidnapping Resulting In Murder
Until kidnapping became a felony in most states, prosecutors would stretch a kidnapping that resulted in death into the felony-murder category. For example, by claiming that the kidnapping took place during the felony of stealing the victim's clothes. There is no death penalty for kidnapping unless the crime results in death.

III.   ASSAULT AND BATTERY

Under the common law, assault and battery were two distinct crimes. The presence of an actual touching distinguished the two.

A.   Battery

1.   Defined
At common law a battery was the unlawful application of force to the person of another. Touching of the victim was an essential element of common law battery; physical injury was not required.

2.   Intent
Battery required intent to injure; however, today some statutes allow battery to be committed recklessly or negligently because battery is a general intent crime.

B.   Assault
At common law, assault was defined as an attempt at battery with present ability to commit the battery. Common law allowed assault to be committed recklessly.

C.   Mayhem

1.   Common Law
Called "maim," this was defined as the infliction of violent injury which makes a victim unable to fight or to harry an opponent. It was classified as a misdemeanor unless it resulted in castration, in which case it was a felony.

2. Statutes
Many statutes continue to prohibit "mayhem," which is now defined as intentional permanent maiming, and is not restricted to curtailing an opponent's ability to fight.

IV.   STATUTORY ASSAULT
(See also, MPC § 2.11)

Modern statutes usually group battery and assault together into the single offense of "assault." Assault crimes are now divided into assault and attempted assault, no longer distinguished by whether there is an "actual touching," but whether the attacker has "present ability."

A.   Elements

Mnemonic: **Armies Prepare to Attack Intruders**

1. **A**ct
An act, which need not result in injury, but must be more than mere words.

    a. Attempted Battery
    The act may be an actual attempt to injure, or

    b. A Menacing Threat
    A majority of courts also consider a menacing threat designed to induce in a victim a reasonable fear of danger to be an assault.

        i.   Intent
        It is not required that the attacker intend to injure for an act to constitute a menacing threat.

        ii.   A Victim's Fear
        This need not be subjective fear. The threat must be such that a reasonable person would feel some danger. For example, pointing a gun would be assault in a majority of jurisdictions.

2. Apparent **P**resent **A**bility To Injure
   A minority of jurisdictions require that there be no inherent impediment to success of an assault.

3. **I**ntent
   An attacker must have the intent to perform acts that constitute assault.

   a. Statutes
      Because assault is an inchoate crime, many jurisdictions classify assault as a specific intent crime and require knowing or purposeful intent.

   b. Model Penal Code
      Section 211.1 requires purposeful, knowing, or reckless intent, unless a deadly weapon is used, in which case negligent conduct is also culpable.

B.   Attempted Assault
     Attempted assault is designed to encompass conduct that falls short of present ability, but goes beyond mere preparation.

   1. Defined
      Attempted assault is attempted battery *without* present ability.

   2. An Attempt to Attempt
      Because assault is defined as an attempt, the courts are divided as to whether to allow a crime of attempted assault.

   3. Equivocality
      If it is not evident to a reasonable person whether an assaulter's actions are threatening or innocent, there has been no attempted assault. Most jurisdictions that allow attempted assault require a positive act that displays intent.

C. Degrees
Most statutes distinguish between simple and aggravated assault.

1. Simple Assault
At common law, assault was a misdemeanor which encompassed all assaults except those resulting in mayhem.

2. Aggravated Assault
Usually classified as a felony, aggravated assault did not exist at common law. Aggravating factors that result in more severe punishment are based on:

a. Victim's Characteristics
Under most statutes, as well as the Model Penal Code, an assaulter must have knowing or purposeful intent to assault, but need only be reckless as to the characteristics of a victim. Recklessness means that an assaulter should have known that there was a justifiable risk that a victim might be in a special category.

i. Age
A victim is particularly vulnerable due to extreme youth or old age.

ii. Status
A victim is a peace officer on duty.

b. Assaulter's Actions

i. Results
Serious injury is a result.

ii. Means
A deadly weapon is used.

D. When Assault Is Justified
Assault may be justified if it is used in self defense, to defend another, or if the victim has provoked the assault. However, consent of the victim is never a defense to assault. A victim cannot consent to

assault, especially if the victim suffers from a mental or physical weakness.

V.   CHILD ABUSE
(See also, MPC § 3.08)

Child abuse occurs when a person who has a duty of care toward a child exposes them to a foreseeable risk of abuse.

A.   Duty

1. Common Law
Common law has always recognized the duty of a parent toward small children.

2. Statutes
A person has a duty of care toward a child when that person is:

a.   The child's parent or adoptive parent,

b.   The child's legal guardian,

c.   One who has assumed responsibility for the child in the absence of its parent/legal guardian, or

d.   One who has secluded a child from the care of its parent/legal guardian.

B.   Forms of Abuse

1. Neglect
Refusal to provide for the needs of a child or to protect the child from an known abusive person.

2. Physical Abuse
Beatings, physically restraining or disciplining a child for reasons other than the child's welfare.

3. Verbal Abuse
Verbally attacking a child for reasons other than concern for its welfare.

4. Sexual Abuse
Any forced sexual activity with a child or by children.

CASE CLIPS

Regina v. Morgan (1976) KS,
Director of Public Prosecutions v. Morgan (1975) DS

Facts: Ds, one of whom was the victim's husband, had intercourse with a woman who resisted. Ds claimed that they believed the resistance was merely an act.

Issue: Is an honest but unreasonable belief that one has consent a defense to rape?

Rule: One must have the intent to "have sex without the consent of the victim" in order to commit rape. Therefore an honest, but unreasonable belief as to consent negates intent.

Dissent: (Lord Fraser) Belief that another has consented to intercourse should be based on reasonable grounds if it is to be a defense.

Dissent: (Lord Simon) It would not be fair to the victim of a rape to allow the defendant a burden of proof that is lighter than reasonable belief.

Dissent: (Lord Cross) The defendant should be required to use reasonable care to ascertain what facts are relevant to whether his actions are prohibited.

Note: Later that year, Parliament enacted a statute that provided that one may be convicted of rape if one is reckless as to another's consent.

Commonwealth v. Sherry (1982) KS, W

Facts: Ds, doctors, forcibly removed their victim from a party despite her verbal protestations and had intercourse with her. The victim did not try to escape or inform strangers of her plight when the Ds stopped for breakfast during the return trip.

Issue: Must a rape victim physically resist her attackers or attempt to escape in order to prove lack of consent?

Rule: One need not physically resist one's attackers or attempt to escape in order to demonstrate lack of consent to sexual acts. Any resistance which demonstrates that lack of consent is honest and real is enough to show nonconsent.

State v. Rusk (1981) KS, KW, MIB, W

Facts: D was given a ride home by a female acquaintance. D took the woman's car keys and insisted that she come into his apartment. D pulled the woman onto his bed, and lightly choked her when she cried. She agreed to have sex with D because D said he would not harm her if she did.

Issue 1: In the absence of force or threat of force, must one show reasonable fear of imminent and serious bodily harm in order to prove lack of consent to sexual intercourse?

Rule 1: Fear need not be of imminent or serious bodily harm, nor caused by verbal threat. Fear is a legitimate means of establishing nonconsent so long as it is genuine, and reasonably grounded. Reasonableness is a question of fact for a jury to decide.

Issue 2: In the absence of force or threat of force, must one show active resistance in order to prove lack of consent to sexual intercourse?

Rule 2: One does not have to physically resist in order to show lack of consent to sexual intercourse. Resistance need not be active and may involve submission.

Dissent: In the absence of a verbal threat of grievous bodily harm or a display of a weapon which would establish reasonable fear, one should have to show active resistance beyond mere unwillingness in order to prove nonconsent to sexual intercourse.

State in the Interest of M.T.S. (1992) KS

Facts: A seventeen-year-old boy, M.T.S., engaged in nonconsensual sexual penetration of a fifteen-year-old girl. There was no evidence or suggestion that M.T.S. used any unusual or extra force or threats to accomplish the act of penetration.

Issue: Is the element of physical force satisfied simply because the act of penetration is nonconsensual?

Rule: Any act of sexual penetration without the affirmative and freely given permission of the victim is presumed to contain the element of physical force. The victim has no burden to express non-consent.

People v. Evans (1975) KS

Facts: D told a college student that he was a psychologist doing a study on women in singles bars and convinced her to accompany him to a bar and to his apartment. D told her that he could kill her, and how she reminded him of a lost lover. D then grabbed her, and she stayed the night, during which D had sex with her several times.

Issue: May words constitute threat of force in rape, if the speaker does not intend the words to be a threat?

Rule: Words that are perceived as a threat are not sufficient to show threat of force in a rape, unless they are intended by the speaker to be a threat.

People v. Liberta (1984) KS, KW

Facts: D, while legally separated from his wife, attacked and forcibly raped her in the presence of their two and a half year old son.

Issue: May a husband be excluded from prosecution for the rape and/or sodomy of his wife under a marital exemption?

Rule: Marital and gender exceptions must be deleted from statutes prohibiting forcible rape and sodomy. Distinctions violate the Equal Protection Clause unless they are based on a rational difference between classes of people or an overriding government objective.

United States v. Wiley (1974) KS

Note: This is a concurring opinion which discusses the justifications for and against a requirement of corroboration of a rape victim's testimony.

Issue: Must a rape victim's testimony be corroborated?

Rule: A rape victim's testimony must be corroborated in order to protect defendants confronted with fabricated accusations. Independent corroborative evidence is sufficient when it allows a jury to determine beyond a reasonable doubt that the victim's story is not fabricated.

State ex rel. Pope v. Superior Court (1976) KS

Facts: State law allowed the admission of evidence concerning a rape victim's prior sexual activities and lifestyle.

Issue: May evidence of a rape victim's sexual habits be admitted at trial to impeach his/her credibility as a witness?

Rule: Generally, prior sexual activities are inadmissible as irrelevant and distracting to a jury. The exception is prior consensual sexual activity with a defendant.

Concurrence: Evidence as to reputation is questionable at best, and should never be admitted.

State v. DeLawder (1975) KS

Facts: D was charged with carnal knowledge of a fourteen-year-old girl. The trial judged barred questions about the girl's sexual habits.

Issue: Is evidence showing the sexual activity of a rape victim admissible in order to impeach the victim's credibility as a witness?

Rule: The right to effective cross-examination allows for the submission to the jury of any facts which relate to the credibility of a witness.

Government of the Virgin Islands v. Scuito (1980) KS

Facts: D had sexual intercourse with a waitress. The waitress believed D was coercing her and so recited a mantra. D requested a psychiatric examination of the waitress to establish her unstable mental state.

Issue: May a trial judge decline to order a psychiatric examination of the prosecuting witness in a rape trial?

Rule: Psychiatric examination of a rape victim is not permissible if it violates the victim's privacy or leads to trauma or harassment.

In Re M. (1973) L

Facts: D, a thirteen-year-old boy, climbed a fence and threw an object at two police officers. The object caused a small dent in a patrol car.

Issue: Can one be guilty of attempt to commit assault?

Rule: There is no such crime as attempted assault. Assault itself is an attempt to commit battery.

Commonwealth v. Hughes (1979) KW

Facts: D held a butcher knife to the victim's throat, forced her into a car, drove to a secluded spot, raped her at knife point, and returned her to the place of the abduction.

Issue: Must distance of removal and length of time of abduction be substantial in order to satisfy the elements of kidnapping?

Rule: Any movement or length of time that substantially increases risk of harm to a victim or that is beyond that which is incidental to commission of a crime satisfies the distance and time elements of kidnapping.

People v. Barnes (1986) KW

Facts: Marsha paid her neighbor Barnes a visit, seeking to purchase some marijuana. Barnes met her at the front door and invited her into his home. Following Barnes' sexual advances, Marsha expressed her desire to leave. Barnes refused, becoming angry and threatening to strike her. Marsha finally engaged in sexual intercourse with him, exchanging kisses and falling asleep afterward. Marsha testified that she consented because she felt that Barnes would become physically violent had she refused.

Issue: Must the state prove that a victim resisted a sexual assault to secure a rape conviction under California law?

Rule: While the presence of resistance may be probative on the issue of force or nonconsent, its absence may not. Thus, the state need not prove that the victim resisted to obtain a rape conviction.

People v. Williams (1982) W

Facts: D and three other men dragged a woman out of a bar after she refused to have sex with D. They drove her to a house and threatened to hurt her if she did not have sex with them. D, who asserted that the woman freely consented, was barred by a Michigan statute from cross-examining her regarding her prior charge for prostitution and previous sex acts with the defendant.

Issue: Does exclusion of testimony about a rape complainant's past sexual conduct or acts of prostitution violate the Sixth Amendment right to cross examination?

Rule: Testimony about a rape victim's prior sexual conduct or acts of prostitution is not necessarily probative of credibility or consent. Exclusion of such testimony is not a violation of the Sixth Amendment right to cross examination and need not be admitted unless it is directly connected with a material fact of a case.

People v. Adams (1971) DS

Facts: During a prison riot, D seized a guard and led him at knife point to another location within the prison. At all times the victim's location was known by other guards, and D neither attempted to remove the victim from the prison, nor to use the victim to escape. During transport, D threatened to kill the victim if D was fired upon.

Issue: What degree of movement of a victim satisfies the asportation element of kidnapping?

Rule: In order for asportation to satisfy the degree necessary for kidnapping, the victim must be removed from the environment in which he is found. Movement must be more than that which is incidental to the commission of another offense, and must increase the risk of harm to the victim.

Dissent: The crux of the offense of kidnapping should not be movement of a victim but rather involuntariness of seizure and detention. Asportation should be a subsidiary element.

Kizer v. Commonwealth (1984) DS

Facts: D, a sailor, had been separated from his wife for three weeks and had not had sexual relations for six months. After discussing state rape laws with a friend, D forcibly raped his wife because he was "hard up for sex."

Issue: In cases of marital rape, must a wife's intent to terminate the marriage be objectively or subjectively manifested?

Rule: In addition to satisfying the elements of rape, a complainant of marital rape must prove that she has lived apart from her husband, has refrained from engaging in sex with him, and has manifested her intent to end the marriage in a manner that has convinced her husband of her intent.

Dissent: The proper viewpoint should be that of an impartial observer rather than that of the husband.

People v. Olsen (1984) DS

Facts: Ds, the victim's friend and boyfriend, entered the victim's trailer and had sex with her. The victim had engaged in sex with Ds before and had told them that she was sixteen years old. She was actually under fourteen.

Issue: Is reasonable mistake as to the age of a sexual partner a defense to a charge of statutory rape?

Rule: Reasonable mistake as to the age of a sexual partner is not a defense and does not negate criminal intent. A child under the statutory age is incapable of understanding the wrongfulness of his/her actions, and therefore, is incapable of consent and needs special protection.

Dissent: It is cruel and unusual to have strict liability for a crime and not require intentional criminal conduct.

Winfield v. Commonwealth (1983) MIB

Facts: Winfield was indicted for the forcible rape of Nelson. Winfield attempted to proffer testimony concerning the prior sexual conduct of Nelson to show she had a "motive to fabricate" the charges. The court determined the evidence was inadmissible, pursuant to state "rape shield" laws which limit the admission of general reputation evidence.

Issue: Is evidence which seeks to establish the prior sexual conduct of the complainant with persons other than the accused admissible, in light of state "rape shield" provisions?

Rule: Evidence which is relevant to show that the complaining witness had a "motive to fabricate" the charge against the defendant is admissible in a sexual assault case, as long as it shows a pattern of behavior which directly relates to the conduct charged against the defendant.

Dissent: A court considering evidence of this type must determine whether there is a direct correlation between the past sexual conduct and the motive to fabricate that authorizes admission of that conduct.

Commonwealth v. Davis (1980) MIB

Facts: Defendant, while fighting with a man, bit off a piece of his ear. Defendant was convicted of assault with a deadly weapon.

Issue: Can human teeth or body parts be considered dangerous weapons for the purpose of a conviction for assault with a dangerous weapon?

Rule: Body parts alone cannot constitute dangerous weapons for the purpose of an aggravated assault based on their use. For reasons of public policy, and in the absence of legislative action, this type of broadening of the definition of a dangerous weapon is unwarranted.

People v. Cash (1984) MIB

Facts: The complainant told Cash she was seventeen years old, consented to engage in two separate acts of intercourse with Cash, and then called the police. Cash was convicted of statutory rape for having sexual intercourse with a minor under sixteen years of age. Cash asserted that his reasonable mistake of fact as to the complainant's age should be a valid defense.

Issue: May a reasonable mistake of fact as to a complainant's age be a defense to a statutory rape charge?

Rule: The vast majority of states do not recognize the defense of a reasonable mistake of age to a statutory rape charge. The public policy of protecting children from sexual exploitation and harm warrants strict liability for intercourse with minors, regardless of intent. Further, mistake of age defenses, with regard to statutory rape crimes, are not constitutionally mandated.

People v. Nelson (1990) MIB

Facts: Defendant was convicted of sexual assault of a child. Defendant argued that expert testimony regarding "child sexual abuse syndrome" was improperly admitted.

Issue: Should expert testimony pertaining to child sexual abuse syndrome be admissible to aid in the prosecution of an alleged abuser?

Rule: Expert testimony should be admitted if the expert has some knowledge or experience, not common to the world, which will aid the finder of fact in arriving at a determination on the question or issue. The behavioral and psychological characteristics of child sexual abuse victims are proper subjects for expert testimony, but must be limited to rebuttal after the victim's credibility has first been attacked.

Commonwealth v. Burke (1870) MIB
Facts: D was convicted of aiding and assisting the commission of the rape of a woman. The woman had not consented and was too drunk to be capable of consenting.

Issue: In rape, must nonconsent be expressly conveyed?

Rule: "Without her consent" and "against her will" are synonymous; therefore, having sex with a woman who does not, or is in a state where she cannot, directly manifest her consent constitutes rape.

State v. Wheeler (1954) MIB
Facts: D drove past a sixteen-year-old girl whose male friend was trying to rape her, took her from the boy, and drove her further down the road where he raped her himself.

Issue: May a rape victim prove that her attacker took her by force and against her will with uncorroborated testimony?

Rule: When one who seeks to use uncorroborated testimony to prove that a rape occurred against her will, the testimony must not be contradictory, incredible, or inherently improbable.

Chapter 5

HOMICIDE

I. DEFINITION
    (See, MPC § 210.1)

    Homicide is generally defined as the killing of a human being. An act
    resulting in death is always required, unless there is a duty of care, in
    which case an omission may constitute homicide.

    A. Killing
        One kills another by causing a premature end to another's life. Even
        a dying person may be killed if his remaining life span is at all
        shortened.

    B. Human Being
        (See, MPC § 210.0(1))

        1. Beginning
            Most states follow the common law rule that the object of a
            homicide must have been born alive and be viable, so that it is
            capable of an independent existence.

        2. End
            Originally, death was defined as cessation of heart beat and
            breathing. Presently, due to medical advances, death is defined as
            the absence of brain activity.

II. INTENTIONAL HOMICIDE

    A. Generally
        There are two types of intentional homicide: manslaughter and
        murder. Although murder was not graded at common law, most states
        differentiate between first and second degree murder.

        1. Murder
            Murder is the commission of homicide with malice aforethought.
            See also, MPC § 210.2(1)(a). Malice aforethought denotes purpose

and intent, as opposed to accident and mischance. It may be express or implied.

   a. Second Degree Murder
     Until there is proof of an aggravating or mitigating factor, all intentional homicides are classified as second degree murder.

   b. First Degree Murder
     Upon proof of premeditation, second degree murder becomes first degree murder.

  2. Manslaughter
    Manslaughter is intentional homicide committed without malice. Proof of provocation or extreme emotional disturbance reduces intentional homicide from murder to manslaughter.

B.   Distinction between First and Second Degree Murder: Premeditation
Premeditation is a deliberate and planned decision to commit intentional homicide. Premeditation may not be automatically inferred from malice aforethought.

  1. Burden of Proof
    The prosecution must prove the existence of premeditation beyond a reasonable doubt to establish first degree murder.

  2. Time
    Premeditation does not require that a substantial amount of time be spent in forming a decision to kill. Any amount of time which allows for reflection and a conscious choice whether to inflict serious harm is sufficient.

  3. Standard
    A subjective standard that accounts for a defendant's personal characteristics is used in determining the existence of premeditation.

4. Model Penal Code
The Code and many states have rejected premeditation as a basis for grading the severity of a murder. This is based on the concept that the extent of reflection is not indicative of the seriousness of a murder. See, MPC § 210.6.

C. Distinction between Murder and Manslaughter

1. Provocation
A state of provocation is something a reasonable man experiences when he is temporarily deprived of his powers of self-control. However, provocation is not a total defense to an intentional killing because a reasonable person should resist such impulse.

Evidence of provocation reduces an intentional homicide to manslaughter. Provocation indicates that the homicide was committed without malice, because the killing was done in the heat of passion.

a. Burden of Proof

i. Burden of Persuasion
Most statutes treat provocation as an affirmative defense, placing the burden of persuasion beyond a reasonable doubt upon the defendant.

ii. Burden of Production
Other statutes require only that a defendant present evidence of provocation. The burden of persuasion shifts to the prosecution to prove absence of provocation.

b. Standard
The reasonableness of provocation is determined using an objective standard. Thus, rather than focus upon the intensity of the passion provoked in a given defendant, the trier of fact looks to the probable reaction of a reasonable person under the same circumstances.

c. Words Insufficient
At common law, reasonable provocation existed only in certain very narrow circumstances such as an actual physical battery upon the defendant or witnessing a spouse commit adultery. The definition now allows for other provocations, provided they are determined to be objectively reasonable. Words alone are not sufficient provocation for homicide.

d. Cooling Time
A homicide must occur almost immediately after provocation. If sufficient time has passed between the act of provocation and the commission of homicide for a reasonable person to regain self-control and reason, the homicide is murder.

e. Preclusion

   i.   No provocation defense is allowed when the defendant's victim is not the provoker.

   ii. No provocation defense is allowed when the defendant created the provocative situation.

   iii. No provocation defense is allowed when the defendant is mistaken as to the existence of provocation.

2. Extreme Emotional Disturbance ("EED")
Extreme emotional disturbance is the temporary loss of the control and restraint that normally prevents one from committing homicide. See, MPC § 210.3(1)(b).

a. Reasons for Change to EED

   i.   Constitutionality
        Since provocation represents the absence of malice and malice is an element of murder, it is unconstitutional to place any burden of proving the converse of malice on a defendant. Thus, the defense of extreme emotional disturbance replaced the defense of provocation in many states.

ii. Standard

In order to avoid the restrictiveness of an objective standard, the defense of extreme emotional disturbance is evaluated from the viewpoint of a reasonable person in the defendant's situation under the circumstances as the defendant believed them to be. Therefore, the effects of circumstances, such as illness, physical defects, or past personal experiences, may be taken into account.

b. Implications

i. Words

A triggering act is no longer required. Anything that might cause one to lose emotional control, including mere words, may be sufficient.

ii. Cooling Time

Whereas cooling time precludes the provocation defense, it is merely evidentiary for establishing an absence of emotional disturbance. Furthermore, the passage of time may even augment emotional disturbance.

3. Diminished Capacity

Diminished capacity is an entirely subjective defense that takes into account any emotional disorders or idiosyncracies not amounting to insanity, thereby correlating criminal liability more closely with moral culpability.

Only a few states recognize diminished capacity defense because it decreases the incentive to behave in a manner that is acceptable to society.

III. HOMICIDE BY CREATION OF RISK

A. Reckless Murder

(See, MPC § 210.2(1)(b))

When reckless conduct exhibits an extreme or depraved indifference to human life, any death resulting is punishable as murder. Recklessness that does not reach the level of extreme indifference is punishable as manslaughter.

1. Reckless
   Actions that resulted in homicide must have been reckless. Negligent actions are only sufficient culpability manslaughter.

2. Extreme Indifference to Human Life
   Murder by a creation of risk, like all murder, requires the element of malice aforethought; otherwise, the criminal homicide can only be punished as manslaughter. Malice aforethought is implied from extreme indifference to the value of human life.

3. Foreseeable
   The degree of likelihood that death will result from one's actions must be very great, such that a reasonable person could not fail to perceive it.

4. Intent
   Specific intent to kill or harm is not required, only that one consciously disregarded a risk of death. In some jurisdictions, awareness of a risk is implied from a showing of depraved indifference.

B.   Negligent Manslaughter
Involuntary manslaughter due to creation of risk is the accidental killing of a person, contrary to the intention of the parties, during the improper performance of a lawful act. This is not a strict liability offense because culpability requires that the accidental killing occur under circumstances exhibiting gross negligence.

Negligent manslaughter is a lesser included offense of reckless murder, to be invoked only if there is an acquittal for the greater offense.

1. Negligence
   Negligence is a question of fact to be determined in light of all circumstances.

   a. Gross Negligence
      Although tort liability requires only simple negligence toward any risk, criminal liability requires that one be negligent as to a substantial risk of death.

   b. Simple Negligence
      However, when accidental homicide is brought about by an inherently dangerous instrument, only simple negligence rather than gross negligence is required. What constitutes an inherently dangerous instrument is a question of fact, but a gun is almost always considered inherently dangerous.

2. Intent

   a. Objective
      Under the common law and in most jurisdictions, liability is incurred if a reasonable person would have perceived the risk of harm.

   b. Subjective
      For culpability, the Code requires that one knows that one's conduct is life-threatening and that one consciously disregards this risk. However, one need not intend to cause death. See, MPC § 210.3.

3. No Defenses

   a. Contributory Negligence
      Contributory negligence is not a defense to involuntary manslaughter.

   b. Duty of Care
      If one has a duty of care toward another, failure to perceive a risk of harm is not an excuse.

C. Model Penal Code
The Code divides criminal homicide by creation of risk into three categories:

1. Reckless Murder
Reckless murder requires that one act recklessly and evince an extreme indifference to the value of human life.
Felony-murder has been incorporated to a certain extent in reckless murder, because extreme indifference may be implied when one is engaged in a robbery, rape, arson, burglary, kidnapping, or felonious escape. See, MPC § 210.2(1)(b).

2. Reckless Manslaughter
Reckless conduct does not amount to murder when it is not accompanied by extreme indifference to the value of human life. Thus, reckless homicide is punished as manslaughter. See, MPC § 210.3(1)(a).

3. Negligent Manslaughter
Conduct that results in accidental death but which is only negligent rather than reckless in nature is punished as the lesser offense of negligent manslaughter. Misdemeanor-manslaughter has been partially incorporated in negligent manslaughter. See, MPC § 210.4.

IV. HOMICIDE BY COMMISSION OF A CRIME

A. Generally
At common law, culpability for criminal homicide was much more easily established when a death was tied to some unlawful activity. Since one was already morally culpable for the unlawful activity, one should be culpable as well for all criminal results of that activity. Thus, malice aforethought could be inferred from proof of intent to commit a felony. Since a misdemeanor was not as serious an offense as a felony, manslaughter was the offense upon proof of commission of a misdemeanor. However, the Model Penal Code and many jurisdictions, as well as England, have done away with this doctrine of culpability based upon commission of a crime.

B.   Felony-Murder
Most states have statutes that allow for liability for an unintentional homicide that occurs during the perpetration of a felony.

1. Grading

a. Majority
Most states with a felony-murder doctrine distinguish between first and second degree murder according to the seriousness of the felony and the risk factor inherent in the felony. For example, deaths occurring during arson, rape, robbery, burglary, and mayhem are commonly graded as first degree murder.

b. Minority
A few states do not differentiate between first and second degree felony-murder. Rather, a homicide which occurs during a named felony is murder, and a homicide occurring during any other unlawful act, be it an unnamed felony or a misdemeanor, is treated as manslaughter.

2. Limitations
To invoke liability for felony-murder, most states require further proof than simply the commission of a felony.

a. Causation
Most states require a proximate causal relationship between the felony and the homicide. A "but for" relationship is insufficient.

b. Type of Felony

i.   Inherently Dangerous
Some states limit felony-murder convictions to only those homicides that occur during commission of inherently dangerous felonies. An inherently dangerous felony poses a foreseeable danger to human life.

Some of these courts look at the individual case in determining whether the felony is inherently dangerous in a given instance. The others consider felonies in the abstract.

ii. Merger Rule
Most jurisdictions follow the merger rule, which requires the felony to be independent of homicide. Thus, offenses such as assault, battery, and mayhem cannot serve as the underlying felony for a murder conviction because they are included elements of murder.

c. Malice
Most states follow the common law in allowing an inference of malice from the commission of a felony. However, some states require that malice be established independently of the felony, although felonious intent may be evidentiary.

3. Derivative Felony-Murder Liability
It is possible to be liable for a murder that one did not directly cause.

a. Caused by Co-Felon
Under the doctrine of derivative liability, such as that of accomplices and accessories, a felon may be liable under the felony-murder rule for a homicide committed by a co-felon.

i. In Furtherance
Most courts only apply the felony-murder rule to a homicide caused by a co-felon when it is committed in furtherance of the common purpose to perpetrate a felony. Originally, though, a felon could be liable for any murder committed during a felony.

ii. Not in Furtherance
When a co-felon commits homicide, but not in furtherance of the common felonious design, the other felons are not liable under the felony-murder rule.

   b. Caused by Third Party

      i. Previously
          A felon could be liable for any murder committed by
          anyone involved in the felony. This resulted in convictions
          for homicides that were committed by a felony victim or a
          police officer resulting in the death of a co-felon or an
          innocent bystander.

      ii. Presently
          Now, there are limits on felony-murder liability based on
          the acts of a third party.

          (1) Foreseeable
               A homicide must be foreseeable to invoke derivative
               felony-murder liability. Most courts hold that the death
               of a co-felon or an innocent bystander is not a foresee-
               able consequence. Other courts, however, hold that
               these are foreseeable consequences of a felony and
               allow derivative liability.

          (2) Justified
               Most courts do not allow derivative felony-murder
               liability for homicides committed by a felony victim or
               a police officer. Because these people are justified in
               their use of force, the homicide is lawful and there is no
               malice that can be imputed to the felon.

C.   Misdemeanor-Manslaughter
     One may be found guilty of manslaughter for an unintentional
     homicide that occurs during the commission of a non-felonious
     unlawful act.

     As there is no element of mens rea, most statutes require something
     in addition to the commission of a misdemeanor before a criminal is
     held liable.

1. Proximate Cause
   In order to establish liability for involuntary manslaughter, almost all courts require that the offense be the proximate cause of death, rather than just incidental to the homicide.

   In Florida, an exception to the proximate cause rule concerns driving while intoxicated. Once it is established that a defendant was driving while intoxicated, it is irrelevant that the drunkenness was not the proximate cause of death.

2. *Malum In Se*
   In some courts the misdemeanor-manslaughter rule applies only when a non-felonious unlawful activity is *malum in se*, or naturally and obviously wrongful, and not just *malum prohibitum*, or wrongful only because of proscription. However, many courts have explicitly rejected this limitation.

3. Inherently Dangerous
   Some jurisdictions require that the misdemeanor be inherently dangerous, regardless of whether it is *malum in se* or *malum prohibitum*.

4. Amounts to Criminal Negligence
   Some courts require the unlawful conduct to amount to criminal negligence, thereby likening this doctrine to that of creation of risk. See, Ch. 5, III, B.

V. OTHER HOMICIDES

A. Suicide

1. Generally
   Under English common law, suicide was a felony resulting in forfeiture of property and ignominious burial. In America, suicide is not illegal, and only a few states punish attempted suicide.

2. Due to Another's Acts
   If the victim of one's criminal acts commits suicide, one may be culpable for that person's death.

   a. Intentional
      If another's suicide is the natural and probable consequence of one's unlawful and criminal treatment, one may be held culpable for homicide.

   b. Reckless
      Joinder in highly reckless activities is sufficient proximate cause for a finding of culpability for another's self-infliction of a mortal wound.

B. Aiding and Abetting a Suicide
    Aiding and abetting a suicide is differentiated from homicide in that one aids and abets suicide by helping to prepare the way for another's suicide, whereas it is homicide if one actually performs the overt act resulting in death. See, MPC § 210.5.

   1. Grading

      a. Separate Offense
         Some jurisdictions make the aiding and abetting of suicide a separate offense from homicide. This offense may be graded as a misdemeanor or a felony depending on the state.

      b. Included Under Homicide
         Other jurisdictions treat aiding and abetting another's suicide as culpable as murder. Since there can be no consent to murder, there can be no consent to receipt of assistance for suicide.

   2. Nature of Suicide

      a. Joint
         At common law, the survivor of a suicide pact could be held liable for murder. Today, the survivor of a pact where simultaneous suicide is planned by the use of a single, shared

instrumentality can be culpable for aiding and abetting suicide but not homicide.

b. Incitement
In two-thirds of the states, incitement to suicide is not criminal. The remaining states vary greatly in the degree of culpability assigned to incitement to suicide.

C. Right to Die

1. Refusal of Treatment for Oneself
One has a common-law right to refuse treatment for oneself.

2. Refusal of Treatment for Another

a. Previously Competent
In order to refuse treatment for another who is no longer able to personally refuse, there must be clear evidence that the patient would not have wanted continued treatment or had previously decided to refuse treatment in the given situation.

b. Never Competent
When the patient is a child or has always been incompetent, a parent or guardian may consent to treatment and may chose between types of treatment, but may not refuse or remove treatment.

VI. DEATH PENALTY
(See, MPC § 210.6)

A majority of the states administer the death penalty for the most serious of crimes.

A. Policy Considerations

1. Deterrence
The severity of the punishment is a more effective deterrent than the likelihood of the punishment.

2. Irrevocability
The benefits of the punishment outweigh the danger of irrevocably punishing an innocent.

3. Sanctity of Life

a. All Killing is Wrongful
The killing of another human being can be considered wrongful no matter who commits it or to what end.

b. Societal Necessity
Alternately, implementing the death penalty can be looked upon as a society acting in self defense.

B.   Constitutional Requirements
The death penalty is constitutional so long as it conforms to society's evolving standard of decency.

1. First Degree Murder
A death sentence requires that one have intended to take, attempted to take, or actually taken a life. The death penalty has been declared unconstitutional as a punishment for rape and will probably be declared unconstitutional for the punishment of any offense but first degree murder.

2. Review for Proportionality

a. Mitigating Factors
In determining whether the death penalty may be applied, a sentencer must consider *all* mitigating factors that a convict offers.

b. Aggravating Factors
In order to be sentenced to death, the homicide that is being punished must have been committed under aggravated circumstances that outweigh any mitigating circumstances offered by the convict.

3. Discrimination
   A sentence of death is not discriminatory even if it is applied more frequently to members of a certain race, so long as safeguards are implemented to reduce racial bias.

4. Discretion
   The sentencer may not have unguided discretion in sentencing. There must be set rules of guidance to identify mitigating and aggravating factors.

5. Separate Sentencing
   Although the Code and most states require that a convict be given a separate sentencing hearing, most states allow the same jury to sit on both the trial and the sentencing hearing. When a jury trial has been waived and conviction is decided by a judge, the Supreme Court held that it is constitutional for the same judge to hand down a capital sentence.

6. Automatic Appeal
   In many jurisdictions, a death sentence is automatically appealed to determine if such a sentence is sufficiently supported. No action by the defendant is required for this appeal.

CASE CLIPS

Commonwealth v. Carrol (1963) KS

Facts: After a violent argument with his wife, D mulled over her words and the fact that she beat their children. D then shot her while she slept, using a pistol that was on a night table.

Issue: Does the suddenness of an impulse to kill preclude premeditation and reduce first degree murder to second degree murder?

Rule: No impulse is so sudden that it precludes the specific intent to kill which is an element of first degree murder.

People v. Anderson (1968) KS, L, J

Facts: After drinking heavily, D murdered the ten-year-old daughter of the woman with whom he lived by stabbing her more than sixty times.

Issue: What level of premeditation is necessary to sustain a conviction of first degree murder for an intentional killing?

Rule: First degree murder requires prior planning activity, or conduct evincing a motive and a preconceived design.

State v. Thornton (1987) KS

Facts: Thornton was attempting to reconcile with his wife, from whom he had been separated for six weeks. Thornton found his wife in bed with another man, and shot him. Thornton was convicted for murder in the first degree.

Issue: Should a provocation defense reduce a crime from murder to manslaughter if the defendant kills his victim upon finding him in bed with his wife?

Rule: If the passions of a reasonable person would have been inflamed and intensely aroused by the sort of discovery made, then the killing is voluntary manslaughter and not murder. Provocation rulings are very fact specific.

Girouard v. State (1991) KS, W

Facts: D stabbed his wife after she subjected him to a prolonged and vicious verbal assault. The defense argued that Mrs. Girouard's taunts were sufficient to inflame the passions of a reasonable man to strike out and kill, and therefore should mitigate murder to manslaughter.

Issue: Should the traditional circumstances available to mitigate murder to manslaughter be expanded to include verbal provocation?

Rule: A verbal domestic argument is not adequate provocation to mitigate murder.

Note: The court left open the possibility that non-traditional forms of provocation, including words, might justify a conviction of manslaughter under different facts.

Maher v. People (1862) KS

Facts: D, informed that his wife was engaged in an adulterous affair, saw her go into the woods with another man. Still agitated, D entered a saloon a half hour later and shot the man in the ear.

Issue: Can provocation reduce the grading of an intentional killing from murder to manslaughter?

Rule: Provocation that would place a reasonable person under influence of passion and make him act rashly reduces murder to manslaughter.

Dissent: The cause of the provocation should be required to occur in one's presence in order for a legally sufficient passion to be aroused.

People v. Casassa (1980) KS

Facts: D casually dated a woman for six months. When she told D that she did not love him and rejected his gift of wine, he stabbed her in the throat with a steak knife.

Issue: Is extreme emotional disturbance a valid defense when one's actions are caused by mental stress that is the product of delusion rather than external factors?

Rule: The defense of extreme emotional disturbance requires that a defendant be subjectively disturbed and that the disturbance be such that a reasonable person would react in the same manner under circumstances as the defendant believed them to be.

Director of Public Prosecutions v. Camplin (1978) KS

Facts: A fifteen-year-old boy killed a man by splitting his skull with a pan. The boy's defense was that he was provoked by the victim. The judge informed the jury to consider if the alleged provocation was sufficient to make a reasonable man, not a reasonable boy, act as the defendant acted in like circumstances.

Issue: Should the reasonableness of a defendant's actions be judged objectively, by the standards of a reasonable man, or subjectively, by the standards of a reasonable person possessing the defendant's characteristics?

Rule: The reasonableness of a defendant's actions should be judged subjectively, by the actions of a person with the self-control expected of an ordinary person of the same sex and age of the accused, and sharing characteristics of the accused that would affect the gravity of the provocation to him.

Commonwealth v. Welansky (1944) KS, KW, J

Facts: D operated a nightclub in which all the fire doors were blocked, hidden, or locked so that customers could not leave without paying. A bar boy's match ignited the flammable decorations causing a fire that killed many patrons.

Issue: Must one be aware of a risk and commit an intentional act from which injury is a likely result in order to be guilty of manslaughter by wanton or reckless conduct?

Rule: One is guilty of manslaughter by wanton and reckless conduct if one commits an intentional act or omission that a reasonable person would know involved a substantial likelihood of resulting harm.

State v. Williams (1971) KS, KW, J

Facts: Ds, the uneducated, underprivileged parents of a two-year-old, failed to take the child to a doctor for a tooth infection which turned gangrenous. They did not understand that the infection was serious and were afraid that social workers would take the baby because his sickness would lead them to believe that the baby was neglected.

Issue: Can one be culpable for involuntary manslaughter for failure to act when under a duty of care, if one was unaware of a risk to the person to whom he owes a duty?

Rule: If one fails to exercise the care that a reasonable person under similar circumstances would have realized was necessary, one is guilty of negligent manslaughter.

Commonwealth v. Malone (1946) KS, J

Facts: D, a seventeen-year-old, and his friend were at a luncheon counter. D loaded a pistol so that he would have several blank shots and asked his friend to play "Russian Poker." His friend agreed. The gun fired sooner than D expected, killing D's friend by a bullet to the stomach.

Issue: Does recklessness satisfy the specific intent element of murder?

Rule: Acts of gross recklessness from which death may reasonably be anticipated indicate the malice or specific intent to commit murder.

United States v. Fleming (1984) KS

Facts: D, while extremely intoxicated, drove in excess of forty miles over the speed limit, weaving into a lane of oncoming traffic. D lost control on a curve and struck a woman's car, killing her.

Issue: Is intent to injure a necessary element of malice aforethought, which is an element of murder?

Rule: Malice aforethought may be established by conduct that indicates a reckless disregard of a risk of serious bodily harm. It does not require ill will toward another or intent to injure.

Regina v. Serné (1887) KS

Facts: D and an accomplice wilfully set fire to D's home while D's mentally handicapped son was inside. D was in financial difficulty and had recently taken out insurance policies on his home and his son.

Issue: Does the killing of another person by an act done pursuant to commission of a felony constitute murder?

Rule: Any act known to be likely to cause death, done for the purpose of committing a felony, and causing death, constitutes murder.

People v. Phillips (1966) KS, J

Facts: D, a chiropractor, convinced the parents of a young girl to ignore doctors' warnings that it was necessary to remove her cancerous eye. Instead, D convinced them to pay him $700 for treatment to "build up her resistance" to cancer. The girl died.

Issue: May the felony-murder doctrine be applied when a homicide results from a nonviolent felony?

Rule: The felony-murder doctrine is only applicable when a homicide is the result of a felony which is inherently dangerous to human life.

People v. Smith (1984) KS, DS

Facts: D and her husband beat their two-year-old daughter to death because she refused to sit on a couch and eat her snack.

Issue: May an assault that results in death be prosecuted under the felony-murder rule?

Rule: Felony-murder is not applicable when the felony is an integral part of the homicide and the resulting death is included as an aggravated form of the offense charged. This rule may not be abandoned merely because the victim was a child.

State v. Canola (1977) KS, DS

Facts: D and accomplices robbed a jewelry store. The store owner exchanged fire with one of D's accomplices; each killed the other.

Issue: May a felon be prosecuted under the felony-murder rule for the death of an accomplice that was caused by the felony victim?

Rule: The felony-murder rule applies only to homicides that are perpetrated by a felon and/or co-felons in furtherance of a felony.

Concurrence: A felon should bear responsibility for any killing that is the result of the commission of a felony. The only exception to liability should be the killing of a co-felon by a non-felon.

Dissent: Criminal liability should be extended to any death which is proximately caused by, and the reasonably foreseeable result of, acts committed in furtherance of a felony.

Taylor v. Superior Court (1970) KS, W

Facts: D drove a getaway car during the robbery of a liquor store. The store owners shot at D's accomplices, one of whom died.

Issue: May an unarmed felon be prosecuted under a theory of vicarious liability for the homicide of his accomplice by a victim?

Rule: A felon is vicariously responsible for murder if he or an accomplice intentionally commits an act with a conscious disregard for life, and which is likely to cause death, and a victim or a police officer kills in reasonable response to such an act.

Dissent: The implied threat of pointing a gun at a victim is not sufficient provocation to invoke vicarious liability. An express threat does not show a conscious disregard for human life any more than an implied threat.

Gregg v. Georgia (S.Ct. 1976) KS, L

Facts: D, a hitchhiker, robbed and murdered two men who gave him a ride.

Issue: Does the imposition of the death penalty for murder constitute cruel and unusual punishment in violation of the Eighth Amendment?

Rule: (Stewart, J.) The imposition of the death penalty is constitutional where the statutory scheme provides for separate judgment and sentencing, for specific standards by which the trier of fact must consider the circumstances surrounding the crime, and for automatic appeal.

Dissent: (Brennan, J.) The death penalty, like punishment by the rack, is no longer morally tolerable under any circumstances.

Dissent: (Marshall, J.) An informed citizenry would reject the death penalty because it is not the best means of deterrence and retribution.

McCleskey v. Kemp (S.Ct. 1987) KS, KW

Facts: D, a black man, and three accomplices robbed a furniture store. D shot at a white police officer as he entered through the front door in response to a silent alarm.

Issue: Does a statistical survey that shows the disproportionate imposition of the death penalty on black defendants who kill white victims show that the death penalty violates the constitutional guarantees of equal protection and proportional punishment?

Rule: The application of the death penalty is constitutional when there are safeguards implemented to reduce racial bias. A certain amount of discretion in the application of punishment is inevitable and important to benefit convicts whose criminal conduct has occurred under extenuating circumstances.

Dissent: A death sentence should be struck down when there is a significant probability of impermissible considerations.

Dissent: Even with systemic safeguards to guard against discrimination, a state should analyze the constitutionality of the application of the death penalty according to the special circumstances of each case.

Dissent: The Constitution mandates that the death penalty be abolished if it can only be applied discriminately. However, a state would need only to narrowly apply the death penalty to the most serious crimes to avoid discriminatory imposition.

Mullaney v. Wilbur (S.Ct. 1975) L, W

Facts: D killed a man claiming that he attacked the man in a frenzy provoked by the man's homosexual advance.

Issue: Does the Due Process Clause proscribe the requirement that a defendant must prove provocation in order to reduce the degree of the offense?

Rule: (Powell, J.) It is a violation of due process to require a defendant to prove provocation. The prosecution must prove its absence beyond a reasonable doubt, because this absence is an essential element of the offense.

Concurrence: (Rehnquist, J.) A defendant may still be required to prove insanity.

Ex Parte Weems (1984) MIB

Facts: Weems was convicted of murder for the accidental shooting of his friend, Wilson. Weems claimed Wilson was shot accidentally when he tried to put his gun away. The court concluded that Weems had actually tried to kill a man sitting next to Wilson, and used the transferred intent theory to convict.

Issue: What level of intent must be proven to justify a murder conviction based on transferred intent theory?

Rule: An accidental death may support a conviction of murder if "under circumstances manifesting extreme indifference to human life, the defendant recklessly engages in conduct which creates a grave risk of death." Without clear evidence of intent to kill, mere recklessness will not satisfy the burden of proof for murder based on transferred intent theory.

Patterson v. New York (S.Ct. 1977) L, MIB
Facts: D brought a shotgun to the home of his estranged wife. There, D saw his wife standing naked in front of her lover. D killed the lover, and later pled extreme emotional disturbance.
Issue: Is placing on a defendant the burden of proving an affirmative defense beyond a reasonable doubt violative of due process?
Rule: (White, J.) Requiring a defendant to prove an affirmative defense beyond a reasonable doubt does not violate due process. As long as the prosecution must prove all elements of the crime beyond a reasonable doubt, due process has been satisfied. The state cannot be required to rebut in advance every possible affirmative defense.
Dissent: (Powell, J.) This is the same as presuming guilt until proof of innocence. The burden of persuasion of an integral element of the offense is shifted onto the defendant by not mentioning in the definition of the crime that its nonexistence is necessary.

People v. Washington (1976) L
Facts: D shot his homosexual lover as they were riding in a car and arguing over the lover's infidelity and desire to end the relationship.
Issue: Does the use of a reasonable man standard in the evaluation of a heat of passion defense constitute reversible error when applied to a homosexual?
Rule: The reasonable man standard is properly used when applied to a homosexual. Individualized standards of conduct may not be instituted based on special emotional characteristics.

People v. Berry (1976) L, KW, J
Facts: D married a girl half his age. The girl then went to Israel. After she returned, D strangled her with a phone cord. D claimed he was uncontrollably and suddenly enraged by her alternative taunts of infidelity and attempts to sexually arouse him.
Issue: May a heat of passion defense instruction be given if provocation is verbal or the result of a continuous course of conduct?
Rule: The adequacy of provocation must be considered by a jury in light of all circumstances. There is no specific type of provocation required; it

may be verbal and need not occur immediately after a single inflammatory event.

United States v. Brown (1975) L

Facts: D, a prison inmate, became angry after a search of his cell by prison officials and vowed to find the inmate responsible and "send him home in a pine box." D stabbed an inmate and bragged about getting rid of the punk that had annoyed him.

Issue: May premeditation be inferred from one's acts?

Rule: Premeditation may be inferred from one's actions and the totality of the circumstances surrounding the crime.

Hyam v. Director of Public Prosecutions (1974) L, W

Facts: Due to a medical problem, D became unable to have sexual relations with her lover and subsequently grew jealous that he was involved with another woman. D drove to the woman's house and set it on fire, killing the woman's two daughters.

Issue: Is intent to cause grievous bodily harm sufficient evidence to establish malice aforethought, which is necessary to increase an offense from manslaughter to murder?

Rule: Intent to cause grievous bodily harm or knowledge that one's acts are likely to cause such harm is sufficient to establish the requisite intent for murder. Intent may be inferred from one's actions rather than one's subjective thoughts.

Dissent: In order to have the intent to commit murder, one should intend to inflict harm that is more than likely to cause death.

Dissent: Since the death penalty for murder has been abolished, there is no longer a significant difference between murder and manslaughter. Therefore, the two crimes should be combined into a single offense.

Concurrence: Intent to cause grievous harm should amount to malice aforethought whether or not one realizes that one's act may endanger life.

United States v. Escamilla (1972) L

Facts: D, a researcher stationed on a remote arctic island, attempted to prevent the theft of his wine. D's gun was defective and he accidently killed a man with whom he was arguing.

Issue 1: To be guilty of involuntary manslaughter, must one know that his conduct is life-threatening?

Rule 1: To be guilty of involuntary manslaughter, the fact that one's actions are life-threatening must be foreseeable.

Issue 2: In determining whether an act constitutes gross negligence from which manslaughter may be found, should the special circumstances surrounding the commission of the act be considered?

Rule 2: All circumstances surrounding the commission of an act must be considered to determine if there was gross negligence.

State v. Goodseal (1976) L

Facts: D pretended to be a stripper's husband so she would not have to have sex with another man who had paid her. D shot and killed the man, but claimed to have slipped in the snow, accidently firing the gun.

Issue: What is the basis for determining if a felony is inherently dangerous to human life so that it may be a basis for felony-murder?

Rule: The nature of a felony and the circumstances of its commission are relevant factors which must be considered in each case to determine whether a felony is inherently dangerous to human life.

Dissent: The determination as to whether a felony is inherently dangerous to human life should be based upon the felony in the abstract, not the particular facts of a case.

State v. O'Brien (1867) KW

Facts: D, a railroad switchman, failed to perform his duty, causing a passenger train to derail and kill a passenger.

Issue 1: May one be convicted of manslaughter without intent to kill?

Rule 1: Unlike murder, manslaughter does not require intent to kill.

Issue 2: May one be criminally liable for an omission that causes death when in combination with an unexpected event?

Rule 2: One may be culpable for an omission if one has a duty of performance and is found grossly negligent in performing that duty. Negligence is a question for the jury.

United States v. Walker (1977) KW

Facts: D dropped an unlicensed gun in a stairwell. It fired and killed a person.

Issue: Is one guilty of involuntary manslaughter if an unintentional death occurs during the commission of a misdemeanor?

Rule: If a misdemeanor is inherently dangerous and death results, one is guilty of manslaughter.

People v. Stuart (1956) KW, MIB

Facts: D, a pharmacist, filled a prescription for an infant. The bottle of chemicals he used was mislabeled and contained a lethal substance which killed the infant.

Issue: May one be guilty of manslaughter for an unlawful act that was not committed intentionally or negligently?

Rule: One must act with criminal intent or negligence to be guilty of manslaughter. One cannot be held criminally culpable for a reasonable mistake.

Porter v. State (1956) KW

Facts: After failing to observe slow and stop signs, D collided with another car, killing the driver. D was convicted of manslaughter for reckless disregard of life.

Issue: What type of negligence renders one liable for another's death?

Rule: One is criminally liable for negligence of a gross and flagrant character which evinces a reckless disregard for life.

Dissent: Momentary lapses of attention should not legally evince a reckless disregard for human life.

Rule on Rehearing: A momentary lapse of attention or error in judgment is not sufficient negligence to render one criminally liable.

Commonwealth v. McIlwain School Bus Lines (1980) KW, J

Facts: A bus owned by D, bus company, ran over a six-year-old girl who had just exited the bus and was crossing in front of it.

Issue: May a private corporation be held criminally liable for homicide?

Rule: A corporation may be held criminally liable for criminal acts performed by its agents on its behalf, including criminal homicide.

People v. Walker (1965) KW

Facts: The decedent attacked Walker with a knife following an argument. Walker cornered the decedent, knocked him down with a brick, and then killed him.

Issue: When should a killer be convicted of voluntary manslaughter rather than murder?

Rule: Voluntary manslaughter occurs when the killer experiences a sudden, violent impulse of passion that overcomes his reason. There must be a serious and highly provoking injury inflicted upon the person killing, or an attempt to inflict such an injury by the deceased. No delay should be evident between the provocation of the killer and the killing.

Ex Parte Fraley (1910) KW

Facts: D saw a man kill his son. The man was acquitted. Ten months later, D walked up to the man and shot him six times stating "I told you I'd kill you! You killed my boy."

Issue: May the recollection of a past event, after there has been some time for anger to "cool," constitute sufficient provocation to reduce murder to manslaughter?

Rule: A killing committed in revenge for an injury in the past is murder. A day is sufficient cooling time for a reasonable person.

Rowland v. State (1904) KW

Facts: Rowland caught his wife in the act of adultery. Attempting to fire at the adulterer, Rowland missed and killed his wife instead.

Issue 1:   Is an adulterous act by one's spouse sufficient to produce the violent impulse of passion that characterizes manslaughter?

Rule 2:   When a killer is provoked by the sight of a spouse's infidelity, the law will regard his offense as a manslaughter, not a murder.

Issue 2:   Does it matter whether the killer's victim is his spouse or the adulterer?

Rule 2:   An adultery-motivated killing is manslaughter, whether the killer slays his faithless spouse or the adulterer.

Francis v. Franklin (S.Ct. 1985) KW

Facts: D, a prisoner, escaped during a visit to the dentist. When a man slammed a door in D's face, D shot the door, and the bullet passed through the door killing the man.

Issue: Does due process prohibit an instruction that the consequences of one's actions are presumed to be intended unless one can introduce evidence to rebut the presumption?

Rule: (Brennan, J.) A mandatory rebuttable presumption of one's intent to commit criminal acts violates the due process requirement that the prosecution prove every element of an offense beyond a reasonable doubt.

Dissent: While the instruction of rebuttable presumption could be interpreted in an unconstitutional manner if standing alone, there is no danger of this when it is accompanied by an instruction that criminal intention cannot be presumed.

Dissent: The Constitution does not require that every element of a jury charge be examined individually, but that the charge taken as a whole does not shift the burden of proof onto the defendant.

Mayes v. The People (1883) KW

Facts: Mayes came home drunk from a saloon and continued to drink beer from a large glass. Mayes threw the glass of beer at his wife, but the glass struck an oil lamp the wife was holding. Mayes' wife caught on fire and eventually died from the burns. Mayes was convicted of murder, but claimed that he did not intend to injure his wife when he threw the glass.

Issue: Must malice be proven to gain a conviction of murder when the accused acted with extreme recklessness?

Rule: Malice is implied when circumstances show the accused acted with extreme recklessness and in disregard of human life. Throwing a large beer glass at a woman sufficiently manifests malice to render the act murderous if it leads to death.

Pears v. State (1983) KW, J

Facts: D, despite warnings from his passenger and a police officer that he was too drunk to drive, ignored traffic signals, sped, and caused an accident which killed two people.

Issue: May one be convicted of murder when one does not have the intent to harm?

Rule: If one knows that one's conduct may cause serious injury, and persists in that conduct, one exhibits extreme indifference to human life and is guilty of murder by recklessness.

People v. Patterson (1989) KW

Facts: Licerio died after ingesting cocaine provided by Patterson. The California legislature had passed a single statute prohibiting the importation, sale, and administration of many different drugs.

Issue 1: If a statute contains more than one offense, must the entire statute be viewed in the abstract to determine whether a violation is inherently dangerous for the purposes of the felony-murder rule?

Rule 2: Each offense set forth in a statute should be examined separately to determine its inherent dangerousness.

Issue 2: When is a felony inherently dangerous to life in the context of the felony-murder rule?

Rule 2: In the context of the felony-murder rule, a felony is inherently dangerous to life when there is a high probability that its commission will result in death.

United States v. Watson (1985) KW

Facts: Watson was seen by two police officers driving a stolen vehicle and fled into an apartment complex, where he waited for the officers to arrive. One of the officers followed Watson, and upon finding him, the officer pointed his gun at Watson and told him he was under arrest. Watson grabbed the officer, threw him down, and gained control of the officer's weapon. Watson sat on top of the officer and pointed the weapon at his chest. The officer twice repeated to Watson, "It wasn't worth it," before Watson stood up and fired a shot that killed the officer.

Issue: What type of evidence is sufficient to prove premeditation and deliberation?

Rule: Premeditation and deliberation may be inferred from sufficiently probative facts and circumstances. The evidence must be sufficient to persuade, not compel, a reasonable juror to reach a guilty verdict. Although no specific amount of time is necessary, the evidence must demonstrate that the accused did not kill impulsively.

People v. Benjamin (1975) KW

Facts: D argued with a man at a bar and then left. Hours later, when the man left the bar, D approached and shot him four times.

Issue: Does the act of lying in wait evince specific intent to commit murder in the first degree?

Rule: The act of lying in wait coupled with intentional infliction of bodily harm which is likely to cause death shows a state of mind equivalent to premeditation and deliberation, which makes a killing murder in the first degree.

Midgett v. State (1987) MIB

Facts: Midgett was convicted of first degree murder for killing his son. Midgett had physically abused his son for a substantial period of time, and had finally caused his death. Midgett claimed that, in spite of the evidence of prolonged child abuse, a lack of evidence as to premeditation prohibited a finding of first degree murder.

Issue: May evidence of sustained child abuse be sufficient to uphold a conviction for first degree murder of the child, in the absence of evidence as to premeditation?

Rule: In order to sustain a first degree murder conviction, the state must prove that the defendant had the conscious object and formed intention to cause death, and that his actions did not arise out of sudden impulse without reasoning. In the case of prolonged child abuse, it may be inferred that the perpetrator would expect the child to live, and not want or intend him to die. If intent to continue the abuse, but not to kill, is evidenced, a conviction of first degree murder may not stand.

Note: The court found the defendant to be guilty of second-degree murder, which requires the intent to cause serious physical injury.

People v. Stamp (1969) KW, W, J

Facts: D and two accomplices robbed a business at gunpoint. The owner of the business, who had a history of heart disease, suffered a fatal heart attack as a result of the incident.

Issue: Is the felony-murder rule applicable if inherently dangerous conduct is not the sole proximate cause of death, and if the victim's weakened condition is a contributing cause of death?

Rule: The felony-murder rule is applicable to any death which results proximately from the perpetration of a felony which is inherently dangerous to human life. The victim's condition is inapplicable as a mitigating factor.

People v. Gladman (1976) KW

Facts: D robbed a delicatessen and walked to a parking lot. Seeing a police car, D hid under a parked car. When the officer ordered D to put his gun on the hood of the car, D fatally shot the officer.

Issue: What factors are used to determine if one is in "immediate flight" from the commission of a felony?

Rule: The determination that one is in "immediate flight" such that the felony-murder rule may be applied is a question of fact for a jury to decide in light of all the evidence.

People v. Cabaltero (1939) KW

Facts: D, a farm worker, robbed his boss at gunpoint on the day that the boss handled payroll. D's accomplice argued with, and then shot a fellow accomplice who was keeping watch.

Issue: May one be charged under the felony-murder rule for the unplanned actions of an accomplice which result in the death of another accomplice?

Rule: All co-conspirators are guilty of first degree murder under the felony-murder rule for all killings committed by their co-conspirators in the perpetration of a felony.

People v. Hickman (1973) KW

Facts: Ds were running away from police after a burglary attempt. A police officer, thinking he saw a third criminal, fatally shot a plain clothes officer who was chasing Ds.

Issue: May a felon be liable for the killing of a bystander which was committed by a third party in an attempt to apprehend the felon?

Rule: A felon is liable for any death caused by a third party in an attempt to terminate the commission of a felony.

People v. Washington (1965) KW, J

Facts: D and an accomplice attempted to rob a gas station. The station owner shot both men, fatally wounding D's accomplice.

Issue: Is a felon liable for the death of a co-felon by a victim?

Rule: A felon may not be held liable for a death caused by a victim. Malice aforethought cannot be attributable to a felon who does not kill in perpetration of a felony, nor can deterrence be based on a victim's actions.

Dissent: A felon should be liable for killings by victims. This negates the important deterrent effect against the commission of armed felonies during which a risk of killing or of self defense by a victim is reasonably foreseeable.

State v. Goodman (1979) KW

Facts: Victim mistreated his wife. D and the wife's brother drove victim to a secluded spot, cut him, shot him, and threw him in the trunk of D's car. Later, as victim begged for mercy, D shot victim in the head and placed his body on a railroad track so that it would be rendered unrecognizable.

Issue: May a single set of facts be the basis for several aggravating circumstances?

Rule: In a capital case, more than one aggravating circumstance arising from a single set of facts may not be considered. This results in prejudice, as a single issue rephrased several ways will appear to amount to several aggravating factors and create a stronger case for the imposition of the death penalty than the evidence supports.

Tison v. Arizona (S.Ct. 1987) KW

Facts: Raymond, Ricky, and Donald Tison helped their convicted father escape from an Arizona jail. Several days after the escape, the getaway car suffered a blowout, stranding the four Tisons and an accomplice in the desert. Raymond flagged down a passing car, holding the four passengers as captives. Raymond's father, planning on leaving the victims in the desert, instructed his sons to get some water. As they returned, their father and the accomplice brutally murdered the four innocent travelers. Raymond and Ricky were tried, convicted, and sentenced to death under Arizona felony-murder law.

Issue: Does the Eighth Amendment prohibit the death penalty when the defendant's participation in a felony-murder is major but he does not possess an "intent to kill"?

Rule: (O'Connor, J.) The death penalty may be imposed on a defendant whose participation in a felony-murder is major and whose mental state is one of reckless indifference to the value of human life.

Lockett v. Ohio (S.Ct. 1978) KW

Facts: D drove a car in which the robbers of a pawnshop escaped. An accomplice accidently killed the victim.

Issue: In a capital case, does a state's exclusion of evidence about one's level of participation in a killing pursuant to a felony violate the Eighth Amendment?

Rule: In a capital case, the Eighth and Fourteenth Amendments preclude a state legislature from excluding from consideration as a matter of law any evidence that may serve as a mitigating factor.

Eddings v. Oklahoma (S.Ct. 1982) MIB

Facts: D, a juvenile runaway, shot and killed a highway patrol officer who had stopped D's car. In sentencing, the court allowed testimony of aggravating circumstances, but denied evidence of mitigating circumstances. D was sentenced to death.

Issue: Do the Eighth and Fourteenth Amendments prohibit the imposition of the death penalty without consideration of all of mitigating factors presented by a defendant?

Rule: The Eighth and Fourteenth Amendments require that a sentencer must consider as mitigating factors all circumstances and aspects of character that a defendant offers as a basis for a sentence less than death.
Dissent: In considering the imposition of the death penalty, a sentencer must consider all mitigating factors offered by a defendant. However, the sentencer need not accept all proffered factors as facially true.

Enmund v. Florida (S.Ct. 1982) MIB
Facts: A man and woman drove to a house asking for water for an overheated car, then fatally shot and robbed the elderly couple who owned the house. D drove the car in which the murderers escaped, and there was evidence that D masterminded the crime. D was sentenced to death for conspiracy to murder for monetary gain.
Issue: Is the death penalty valid under the Eighth and Fourteenth Amendments for a defendant who neither took, attempted to take, nor intended to take a life?
Rule: Under the Eighth and Fourteenth Amendments, a defendant cannot be sentenced to death solely for participating in a felony in which a person was killed if the defendant did not actually cause or intend to cause the victim's death.
Dissent: The Constitution does not require intent as a requisite for imposition of the death penalty, only that the punishment be proportional to the harm caused and to the defendant's blameworthiness.

United States v. Alexander (1972) W
Facts: Ds fired upon four marines and a female after a staring match and utterance of a racial slur.
Issue: With whom lies the burden of proof of provocation?
Rule: Once evidence of provocation is introduced, the prosecution has the burden of proving beyond a reasonable doubt that it was inadequate to reduce the offense to manslaughter. Provocation is a defense to murder and not an element of manslaughter.

People v. Caruso (1927) W, J
Facts: D, an illiterate immigrant, believed that the doctor's malpractice killed his son. Thinking the doctor was laughing, D killed him.
Issue: What is the standard for determining absence of premeditation and deliberation?

Rule: Absence of premeditation and deliberation is determined using a standard of good-faith, rather than one of reasonableness. If one's state of mind shows that premeditation is impossible, proving that it is a reasonable state of mind is unnecessary.

Commonwealth v. Mazza (1974) W
Facts: A mentally retarded D killed a man, stole his money, hid the body, and used the man's car and credit cards.
Issue: Is there an intermediate level of criminal responsibility between insanity and ordinary responsibility?
Rule: There is no intermediate level of criminal responsibility between insanity and ordinary responsibility. There is no diminished responsibility based on mental retardation.

People v. Wolff (1964) W
Facts: D, a schizophrenic youth, intentionally killed his mother.
Issue: Is duration of time the controlling factor in determining existence of premeditation and deliberation?
Rule: In determining the existence of premeditation and deliberation, the relevant factor is the extent of reflection rather than the duration of time. Mental illness may be considered in ascertaining the extent of reflection.

People v. Poplis (1972) W
Facts: Repeatedly, D brutally beat a three-year-old child. The beatings resulted in the child's death.
Issue: Can recklessness resulting in death be punished as murder?
Rule: Unless accompanied by a depraved indifference to human life, recklessness resulting in death can only be punished as manslaughter.

United States v. Heinlein (1973) W
Facts: Ds wanted to rape a woman. When she slapped one of the Ds, he fatally stabbed her. The other Ds were indicted for felony-murder.
Issue: Is coincidence in point of time and place between a felony and homicide sufficient for conviction under the felony-murder rule?
Rule: Felony-murder requires a homicide to be in furtherance of a felony or within the scope of a common design to commit a felony before a felon can be liable for a co-felon's commission of murder.

Commonwealth Ex Rel. Smith v. Myers (1970) W, MIB

Facts: While D was robbing a market, an off-duty policeman was shot. It was unknown who fired the fatal bullet.

Issue: Can a felon be liable for a homicide that occurs during a felony, regardless of who actually caused the death?

Rule: Under felony-murder doctrine, a felon is culpable for only those homicides caused by him or a co-felon in furtherance of a felony.

Dissent: A felon should be liable for any homicide incident to a felony.

Bell v. Commonwealth (1938) W

Facts: D was driving a standard shift car with only one arm, on the wrong side of the road, at night, and without headlights. One of the two women that D struck died.

Issue: What is necessary to be culpable for negligent manslaughter?

Rule: Culpability for negligent manslaughter requires that the cumulative acts bearing a causal relation to the homicide amount to gross or culpable negligence.

Maryland v. Chapman (1951) W

Facts: D, an Air Force pilot, was forced to abandon his plane. It swerved off course and crashed, killing three people.

Issue: Is simple negligence sufficient for a conviction of involuntary manslaughter?

Rule: Gross negligence, rather than simple negligence, is necessary for conviction of involuntary manslaughter. Homicide as a result of accident, misadventure, or honest error of judgement is not criminal.

Gian-Cursio v. State (1965) W

Facts: Ds, chiropractic physicians, treated a tuberculosis victim with a vegetarian diet and a series of fasting. The patient died.

Issue: Can gross lack of medical competency or gross inattention make a physician liable for manslaughter?

Rule: Death resulting from a physician's gross medical negligence is punishable as manslaughter, even if the medical action or inaction is performed in good-faith.

People v. Magliato (1985) DS

Facts: D and another man got into a verbal war. D cocked his gun, and when startled, pulled the hair trigger killing the other man.

Issue: What is necessary beyond criminal negligence for a conviction of reckless murder?

Rule: In addition to criminal negligence, reckless murder requires a depraved indifference to human life which creates a grave risk of death. Unmotivated wickedness is only indicative of depravity.

Dissent: The threshold for finding depraved indifference should not be so high. Conscious disregard of a grave risk should be sufficient.

State v. Bingham (1985) DS

Facts: D raped and strangled a retarded woman. The strangulation required three to five minutes of continuous pressure.

Issue: Is proof of time to deliberate sufficient to find premeditation?

Rule: Premeditation must be established by proof of actual deliberation and not just proof of sufficient time for deliberation.

Dissent: Lapse of time should be adequate circumstantial evidence to establish premeditation.

People v. Walker (1984) DS

Facts: D, a drug dealer, owed money to his supplier. When pressed for the money, D fatally shot the supplier.

Issue: Must extreme emotional disturbance always be considered for an intentional murder indictment?

Rule: Extreme emotional disturbance is an element of intentional manslaughter and an affirmative defense to intentional murder, yet it can only be considered by the trier of fact when there is sufficient evidence to suggest such a disturbance.

Dissent in Part: Extreme emotional disturbance is a subjective issue which the trier of fact should always be allowed to consider.

People v. Walker (1984) DS

Facts: Memorandum in review of lower court's holding.

Issue: On an intentional murder indictment, must extreme emotional disturbance always be considered?

Rule: Evidence of an actual extreme emotional disturbance is necessary before such a defense may be considered by the trier of fact. A reasonable explanation for an extreme emotional disturbance is irrelevant without first showing that such a disturbance existed.

Gooden v. Commonwealth (1984) DS

Facts: D, a hunter, accidentally shot another hunter.

Issue 1: What level of negligence renders one culpable for accidental homicide?

Rule 1: When one's negligence evinces a reckless disregard for human life, one may be culpable for causing an accidental death.

Issue 2: Is the offense of negligent manslaughter one of strict liability?

Rule 2: Negligent manslaughter is not a strict liability offense. It consists of performing a lawful act in an unlawful manner such that it constitutes criminal negligence.

Dissent: Making one liable for an accident arising in the context of an inherently dangerous activity is equivalent to strict liability.

State v. Aarsvold (1985) DS

Facts: D sold a man cocaine. The buyer died after he injected some into his arm.

Issue: What type of felony is covered by the felony-murder doctrine?

Rule: Felonies that carry the possibility of violence or special risk to life are covered by the felony-murder rule. Actions which are statutorily felonious for other reasons are not covered.

Dissent: The facts of a particular situation, rather than the offense in the abstract, should be considered in determining whether a felonious act is covered by the felony-murder doctrine.

State v. Noren (1985) DS

Facts: While committing a robbery, D hit a drunk on the head, causing him to lose consciousness. The drunk died of asphyxiation due to a prior respiratory problem combined with the loss of consciousness.

Issue: When is a homicide the natural and probable consequence of a felony as required by the felony-murder rule?

Rule: A homicide is the natural and probable consequence of a felony when the felony is the proximate cause of the death or a substantial factor in the death. The felonious conduct must also be inherently or foreseeably dangerous to human life.

State v. Ott (1984) J

Facts: D, slightly emotionally disturbed, intentionally killed his estranged wife when her lover showed up.

Issue: What is the standard for determining extreme emotional disturbance?
Rule: Although an objective standard is used to determine the reasonableness of an action, extreme emotional distress allows for consideration of an actor's personal characteristics, a subjective matter.

People v. Harris (1956) J
Facts: Upon entering a tavern, D was severely beaten by the bouncer for no apparent reason. Later, D returned and shot the bouncer.
Issue: When indicted for intentional murder, may one be convicted of voluntary manslaughter?
Rule: Even when indicted for intentional murder, one may be convicted of voluntary manslaughter if it is shown that one was provoked and had not sufficiently "cooled off."

State v. Snowden (1957) J
Facts: D brutally and sadistically slashed to death a woman he picked up at a bar who insisted he pay for a cab to take her home.
Issue: What constitutes premeditation as required for a conviction of first degree intentional murder?
Rule: Premeditation, required for a first degree murder conviction, is the formation of a deliberate purpose to kill. Since an act of killing may follow this intent as rapidly as successive thoughts of the mind, any lapse of time may be considered in establishing premeditation.

People v. Tilley (1979) J
Facts: D's friend got into a fight with a man. D helped his friend subdue the man and then shot him as he was walking away.
Issue: What type of evidence can support a finding of premeditation?
Rule: Premeditation can be established by such things as the time available for deliberation, the absence of sudden impulse, a series of attacks rather than only one, and the use of deliberate technique.

Holmes v. Director of Public Prosecutions (1946) J
Facts: D's wife told him she had been unfaithful. D immediately and intentionally killed her.
Issue: Is one guilty of manslaughter rather than murder when there is provocation based only on words?

Rule: Mere words, except in circumstances of a most extreme and exceptional nature, are never sufficient provocation to reduce a charge of homicide from murder to manslaughter.

Gibson v. State (1970) J
Facts: While in the back seat of a car, D, a drug addict, grabbed the steering wheel. The car swerved and hit another car, killing the driver.
Issue: What type of actions allow conviction for reckless murder?
Rule: Reckless murder occurs when one's dangerous act, which results in injuries and death, evinces a depraved mind.

People v. Register (1983) J
Facts: D got in a fight at a bar with another man. D shot the man at close range, and then as everyone was leaving, D fatally shot an acquaintance for no apparent reason.
Issue: Is it possible to assert an excuse to negate the reckless murder element of "circumstances evincing a depraved indifference to life"?
Rule: Since the element of "circumstances evincing a depraved indifference to life" goes neither to the mens rea nor the actus reus but rather concerns objective circumstances, it is not subject to negation by excuse.
Dissent: Depraved indifference should be part of mens rea, because when it is coupled with recklessness, it makes one almost as culpable as if one had purposeful intent.

Northington v. State (1981) J
Facts: D allowed her five-month-old daughter to starve.
Issue: For reckless murder, can the extreme indifference to human life be directed solely at one person?
Rule: Reckless murder differs from intentional murder in that reckless murder requires an extreme indifference to human life in general, rather than one aimed at a particular individual.

People v. Aaron (1980) J, MIB
Facts: While committing armed robbery, D killed a person.
Issue: Under the felony-murder rule, is the requirement of malice satisfied by intent to commit a felony?
Rule: Even a murder committed during perpetration of a felony requires the element of malice. The trier of fact must find malice separate from the

intent to commit a felony. That intent may be used as evidence of malicious intent.

Concurrence/Dissent: Rather than impute malice from felonious intent, felony-murder removes the element of malice and requires only a felony and a resultant death. This is why felony-murder should be abolished.

Concurrence: Malice is an element of murder because the statute refers to murder, not just homicide.

People v. Sears (1970) J

Facts: D entered his wife's home with intent to assault. D assaulted his wife and killed his step-daughter. D was indicted for burglary and second-degree felony-murder.

Issue: Does the felony-murder rule apply to all felonies?

Rule: Only felonies which are independent of homicide fall under the felony-murder rule. Assault is an integral part of homicide.

Commonwealth v. Redline (1958) J

Facts: D and a co-felon were fleeing after committing armed robbery. An officer in pursuit fatally shot D's co-felon.

Issue: Under the felony-murder rule, can a felon be convicted for a justifiable killing committed by another?

Rule: A felon cannot be convicted under the felony-murder rule for justifiable homicide committed by another, because although malice can be imputed to a felon, an act of killing may not.

Dissent: In order to protect society, it should not matter who committed the fatal act, once malice is imputed to a felon.

Keeler v. Superior Court (1970) J

Facts: D discovered his estranged wife was pregnant by another man. D kneed her, causing the fetus to be delivered stillborn.

Issue: For purposes of homicide, is a fetus a "human being"?

Rule: To be the subject of homicide, one must be born alive.

Dissent: A viable fetus should be considered a human being for purposes of homicide.

Note: Soon after this opinion, the legislature amended the murder section of the penal code to include the unlawful killing of a fetus.

Locke v. State (1973) L

Facts: Locke entered the apartment of a neighbor, took out a knife, and forced the neighbor to submit to cunnilingus. Locke was charged with committing a "crime against nature."

Issue: Can cunnilingus be considered a "crime against nature"?

Rule: All unnatural copulation with man or beast, including cunnilingus and sodomy, are within the scope of crimes against nature.

Dissent: To hold that cunnilingus is a crime is plain judicial legislation, because neither the common law nor the statute intended to include the act as a crime against nature.

Barber v. Superior Court (1983) J

Facts: Defendant doctors were instructed by the family of a severely brain damaged patient to disconnect the support system and discontinue intravenous nourishment.

Issue: Is it homicide to remove another's life support systems?

Rule: Absent a duty to continue to provide life support, the removal or withholding of such support is not criminal because it is an omission, rather than an affirmative act.

People v. Bonilla (1983) J

Facts: D mortally wounded another, causing brain death. Doctors removed the victim's kidneys and spleen, and then stopped his heart.

Issue: If there are intervening actions that contribute to death, is the original actor still culpable for homicide?

Rule: If one's actions are the direct and operative cause of death because one set in motion the chain of events that ultimately resulted in death, one is properly culpable for the homicide.

Dissent/Concurrence: The original actor should only be liable when a homicide's intervening causes are foreseeable.

Stephenson v. State (1932) J

Facts: D abducted a woman and while on the train chewed her all over. The woman took some poison, got very sick, and died.

Issue: Can one person be culpable for another's suicide?

Rule: If another's suicide is the natural and probable consequence of one's unlawful and criminal treatment, one may be held culpable for that person's death.

Commonwealth v. Atencio (1963) J

Facts: Ds played Russian roulette with a third person. The third person lost.

Issue: Is participation in a highly reckless pursuit sufficient to find culpability for the death of another who joined in the reckless activity?

Rule: Participation in a highly reckless activity resulting in homicide is sufficient proximate cause to find culpability for the death.

In Re Joseph G. (1983) J, MIB

Facts: D and another sixteen-year-old voluntarily decided to drive off a cliff. D drove the car and sustained serious injuries, but his friend died.

Issue: Can a survivor of a genuine suicide pact be held culpable for the murder of the other?

Rule: The survivor of a genuine suicide pact, in which the suicides are undertaken simultaneously by a single instrumentality, can be culpable for aiding and abetting the other's suicide but not for murder.

People v. Warner-Lambert Co. (1980) J

Facts: D, a chewing-gum manufacturer, had a flammable dust floating around the factory. A spark ignited the dust and several people died.

Issue: Is knowledge of a risk alone sufficient for culpability?

Rule: The actual immediate triggering cause that results in homicide must be foreseeable in order to establish culpability based on recklessness or negligence.

Henderson v. Kibbe (S.Ct. 1977) J

Facts: Ds robbed a man and left him by a road, partially dressed, without his glasses, and in the freezing cold. He was fatally struck by a car.

Issue: Is awareness and disregard of a substantial risk sufficient for conviction for reckless homicide?

Rule: One can be culpable for reckless homicide if the ultimate harm is one that should have been foreseen as being reasonably related to one's conduct.

Commonwealth v. Webster (1850) MIB

Facts: D owed a colleague some money. When D was unable to repay the money, the colleague called D names. D became incited, killed his creditor, dismembered him, and burned he body parts.

Issue: May malice aforethought be implied?

Rule: Malice aforethought may be implied when there is proof of commission of a homicide and no evidence of justification or excuse.

Langford v. State (1978) MIB

Facts: D was driving while intoxicated. He swerved and hit another car, killing the other driver.

Issue: What is the mental state of universal malice, as required for reckless murder?

Rule: Universal malice is the purposeful or knowing determination to take life upon slight or insufficient provocation, without knowing or caring who may be the victim.

Dissent: It should be a matter for the jury to decide whether a reckless homicide is of the second degree or the first.

In the Matter of John Storar
Soper v. Storar
Eichner v. Dillon (1981) MIB

Facts 1: Fox was in a vegetative state with no chance of recovery. He had previously stated his opposition to any extraordinary medical life support systems.

Issue 1: Can an incompetent's life-support treatment be discontinued?

Rule 1: An incompetent's life-support treatment can only be discontinued upon clear and convincing evidence of such a desire. This is based upon the common-law right to decline medical treatment.

Facts 2: Storar was retarded and had terminal cancer of the bladder. He did not like the transfusions which temporarily prolonged his life, and his mother wanted them discontinued.

Issue 2: May a parent deprive a child of life sustaining treatment?

Rule 2: Although a parent has the right to consent to a child's medical treatment and to chose between methods of treatment, a parent has no right to deprive a child of life sustaining treatment.

Regina v. Onufrejczyk (1955) MIB

Facts: D's partner disappeared without a trace. D acted quite suspiciously, implicating himself in the possible murder.

Issue: Can a *corpus delicti* be established by circumstantial evidence?

Rule: A *corpus delicti*, which for murder is proof of a criminal death, may be established by circumstantial evidence.

In Re Winship (S.Ct. 1970) MIB

Facts: Not provided.

Issue: What is the standard of proof in criminal cases?

Rule: Because one's liberty and reputation is at stake in a criminal proceeding, the standard of beyond a reasonable doubt is to be used.

Concurrence: Because it is far worse to convict an innocent man than to acquit a guilty man, our society requires a very high standard of proof in criminal cases. This is not as relevant in civil cases.

Sandstrom v. Montana (S.Ct. 1979) MIB

Facts: D confessed to killing a woman, but stated that the killing was not done purposely or knowingly.

Issue: Does allowing an inference of intent violate the constitutional right to due process of law?

Rule: A presumption that either shifts the burden of proof onto a defendant or that is conclusive as to the existence of a criminal element unconstitutionally violates the right to due process of law.

Commonwealth v. Almeida (1949) MIB

Facts: An officer was killed while D perpetrated a felony. It was unknown if a felon or an officer fired the fatal shot.

Issue: Are felons culpable for any death resulting from a shooting that they caused?

Rule: Because a felon's activities are the proximate cause of any death resulting from related activity, he is culpable for the death, regardless of who fired the fatal shots.

Dissent: Culpability for an incidental killing should only exist when a felon *directly* causes the death.

People v. Salas (1972) MIB

Facts: While escaping with the proceeds of an armed robbery, D was stopped by the police. D shot and killed an officer.

Issue: Can a killing committed while fleeing from a robbery be considered a killing in perpetration of a felony?

Rule: Until a robber has reached a place of temporary safety, any killing committed by the felon can be tried under the felony-murder rule because the robbery is still in progress.

Dissent: The additional requirement of scrambling possession should still be necessary to establish continuance of a felony.

State v. Flory (1929) MIB

Facts: D's wife was raped by her father. D went to see the father and killed him.

Issue: How is the issue of cooling time to be determined?

Rule: When determining if there is sufficient cooling time, a jury may take into consideration the facts and details of the particular situation at hand.

Bedder v. Director of Public Prosecutions (1954) MIB

Facts: D, an impotent lad of eighteen, fatally knifed a prostitute when she jeered at him and kicked him in the genitalia.

Issue: What is the standard by which provocation is determined?

Rule: A reasonable-man standard is used in determining the existence of provocation. Although the circumstances of the situation are considered, one's physical characteristics are not to be taken into account.

State v. Horton (1905) MIB

Facts: While poaching turkeys, D killed another man, mistaking him for a wild turkey.

Issue: Does the misdemeanor-manslaughter rule apply to all homicides occurring during non-felonious unlawful activity.

Rule: The misdemeanor-manslaughter rule applies only when the non-felonious but unlawful action is *malum in se*, or naturally evil, and not merely *malum prohibitum*, or just prohibited.

People v. Marshall (1961) MIB

Facts: D gave his car keys to a drunk friend. The friend ran into another car killing himself and the other driver.

Issue: Without any direct causation, can one be convicted of manslaughter for simply having committed a related misdemeanor?

Rule: Criminal guilt is determined by personal fault. Thus, without complicity or direct causation, one is not culpable for manslaughter due solely to commission of a related misdemeanor.

People v. Decina (1956) MIB

Facts: D was an epileptic susceptible to frequent seizures. During a fit, D ran into and killed several young school girls.

Issue: Is knowledge of a risk of harm sufficient for culpability for a resultant death?

Rule: Knowledge of a risk and possible consequences is sufficient for culpability for a resultant death. Intent to kill another or to consciously follow a precise path leading to death is unnecessary for culpability.

Dissent in Part: One cannot be reckless while unconscious, so that if one is unconscious, there should be no culpability. Knowledge of a possible future physical infirmity should be insufficient for culpability.

Commonwealth v. Feinberg (1967) MIB

Facts: D sold Sterno, knowing that his customers were drinking it. When the concentration of methanol increased, D did not warn his customers, and several died of methanol poisoning.

Issue: Is knowledge of a high risk and a failure to warn sufficient to establish criminal negligence for conviction of manslaughter?

Rule: Knowledge of a high risk is sufficient for criminal negligence when combined with a failure to warn, thereby allowing culpability for manslaughter.

Commonwealth v. Konz (1982) MIB

Facts: D's husband was a diabetic, but felt that with the help of prayer, he would not need to administer insulin. He died.

Issue: Is there a legal duty to aid one's spouse, such that culpability can be based on an omission to do so?

Rule: There is only a very limited legal duty to aid one's spouse, such as when the spouse is in an unintentionally helpless condition.

Concurrence: Even when there is a spousal duty to aid, awareness of a risk or a danger to life must accompany an omission for culpability.

Dissent: Deprivation of medical treatment should be considered an affirmative act sufficient for culpability.

State v. Frazier (1936) MIB

Facts: D hit another man, not knowing he was a hemophiliac. The man died several days later.

Issue: Can one be culpable for unintentional manslaughter due to infliction of a wound that is not normally fatal?

Rule: Any non-intentional homicide which is not murder and is not excused or justified is manslaughter, regardless of whether the death is foreseeable. Acceleration of death is sufficient for culpability.

People v. Love (1978) MIB

Facts: When D refused his wife drugs, she started a fight in which she received a severe beating. Her spleen had to be removed, and she developed pneumonia resulting in death a few days later.

Issue: Can one be liable for another's death even if one's acts are not the sole and immediate cause of death?

Rule: Absent any other injury or action related to an injury, a connection between one's actions and the injury of another is sufficient to establish a causal relationship. Thereby, one may be liable for another's death even if one's acts are not the sole and immediate cause of death.

Commonwealth v. Root (1961) MIB

Facts: D was drag racing. His opponent tried to pass on a bridge approach and ran into an oncoming truck, resulting in death.

Issue: Is there still culpability due to proximate cause of death when there is a subsequent intervening act?

Rule: When another's subsequent wrongful act supersedes original conduct, there is no longer sufficient proximate cause for culpability.

Dissent: If one's action is a substantial factor in death and any subsequent action by another is foreseeable, liability should lie.

Chapter 6

CAUSATION AND ATTEMPT

I. CAUSATION
    (See, MPC § 2.03)

In order to impose liability for particular harm, there must be a real connection between the forbidden conduct and the harmful result.

A. Requirements For Liability
    The forbidden conduct must be both a cause in fact (or "but for" cause) of the harm, as well as the proximate cause of the harm.

    1. Cause in Fact
        To be liable for harm it must be shown that the harm would not have occurred but for the criminal conduct.

        Exception: Two Sufficient Causes
        If two individuals perform acts, each of which is sufficient to cause harm, both can be liable for having caused the harm. For example, if two people independently shoot a third person, and the victim dies, and either shot alone would have caused death, in the majority of jurisdictions both people will be liable for causing the death.

    2. Proximate Cause
        The proximate causation test focuses on the strength of the connection between the conduct and the harm. If the link is tenuous or remote, it will be difficult to find one blameworthy. If the connection is more direct, punishment is justified. See also, MPC § 2.03(2).

    3. Criminal and Tort Standards Distinguished
        Unlike tort law, criminal law is largely concerned with moral blameworthiness. Because it imposes harsher penalties such as imprisonment, the criminal law requires a more direct causal connection between action and harm.

B.   Victim Already Weakened – Take Them As You Find Them
Generally, those who inflict harm take their victims as they find them.
If one inflicts harm on someone who is already in a weakened state,
and the harm causes death to occur only a short time sooner than it
would have anyway, the actor is still liable for causing the death.

C.   The Unintended Victim
(See, MPC § 2.03(2))
If a person intends to harm a particular individual, but actually harms
someone else, the intent is transferred and the actor is just as guilty as
though he/she had harmed the intended victim.

D.   Intervening Factors
Intervening factors often contribute to the harmful results of a
defendant's actions. In general, other subsequent acts prevent liability
when they are unforeseeable and completely overwhelm the original
act.

   1. Coincidence
   A completely unforeseeable coincidence that causes harm usually
   breaks the chain of causation. For example, if a person strikes his
   victim, and the victim is struck by lightning and killed while
   walking to the hospital, the person is not liable for causing death.
   However, if the victim gets to the hospital and then dies from poor
   medical care, the actor may be liable unless the care is so improper
   as to be unforeseeable.

   2. Victim's Acts
   An actor may be liable for harm that results from the victim's
   response, if the response is foreseeable. One who threatens harm
   and chases another onto a street where the victim is subsequently
   hit by an oncoming car is liable for the resulting injuries.

3. Another's Acts
When an actor sets off a chain of events resulting in harm, the actor is liable even if acts of a third person contributed, provided the subsequent acts were foreseeable and do not supersede the original act.

    a. Another's Negligence
    If one's acts are the substantial cause of harm, one cannot avoid liability merely because the harm would not have occurred but for the negligence of others.

    b. Harm Already Inflicted
    In some jurisdictions, one is not liable for causing harm if, unbeknownst to the actor, the harm may already have been inflicted by another (i.e., trying to kill a man who has already been killed). One may nonetheless be charged with a lesser offense, such as attempt, if there is a clear criminal intent.

E.   Foreseeable and Reasonable Response
When one commits a wrongful act and a responding citizen is harmed, the original actor is liable for the harm if the response is normal and foreseeable. For example, if an individual starts a fire and a responding fireman is killed due to smoke inhalation, the actor is liable for causing the death.

F.   Joining In Dangerous Behavior
In some jurisdictions, all willing participants in illegal or reckless activity, such as drag racing, are responsible for causing any harmful results. However, a minority of jurisdictions require a more direct causal link than mere participation.

II.   ATTEMPT
(See, MPC § 5.01)
If a person acting with criminal intent takes significant steps towards the commission of a crime but fails to commit the offense, that individual may be guilty of a criminal attempt.

A.   Rationale for Punishing Attempt

    1. No Relief for Unlucky Criminals
    A person attempting a crime should not be able to avoid punishment simply because circumstances prevented completion of the offense.

    2. Proven Menace
    Individuals who attempt to commit crimes have demonstrated their danger to society.

    3. Effective Police Prevention
    Police should be permitted to arrest individuals before a crime is completed in order to prevent harm.

B.   Elements of Attempt

    1. Mens Rea
    Generally, in order to be guilty of attempting a crime, one must specifically intend to commit the substantive offense. More recently, courts have been requiring only that one have the requisite mens rea of the underlying offense. See also MPC § 5.01, Appendix A.

        a. Intended Act Must Be a Crime
        To be guilty of an attempt, it is not enough to show that the defendant intends to break the law. It must be shown that the conduct intended actually violates the law. If one attempts to do something that he believes is illegal, one is not guilty if the attempted act is actually legal.

        b. Ignorance of the Law No Excuse
        One who attempts an illegal act without realizing it is a crime is nonetheless guilty of an attempt, so long as that person specifically intends the act constituting a crime.

        c. Intent to Commit the Particular Crime
        An attempt to commit a particular crime occurs only when the actor specifically intends to commit the particular offense.

Proof that the defendant planned to engage in general criminal conduct is insufficient.

d. Recklessness or Negligence As to the Result
Some crimes only require recklessness or negligence as to the result. For example, one who negligently or recklessly kills another without specifically intending to kill may be guilty of manslaughter.

  i.   Attempting an Unintentional Result
      It would seem impossible to attempt manslaughter; either one intended to kill and is guilty of attempted murder, or one did not intend to kill and thus cannot be guilty of an attempt because there was no specific intent to cause the death of another.

      However, a minority of jurisdictions have held that one may be guilty of attempting a crime requiring recklessness or negligence as to the result, such as attempted involuntary manslaughter, if one intentionally engages in conduct constituting a substantial step towards the offense.

  ii. Rationale
      One whose conduct would have constituted a particular offense but for certain intervention is still blameworthy.

e. Crimes Requiring Reckless or Negligent Conduct
Although rarely prosecuted, it is conceivable that one could be convicted of attempting a reckless or negligent act e.g., attempted reckless driving. One who intends to engage in dangerous conduct and ignores the risk may be guilty of attempting a recklessness crime.

f. Strict Liability Offenses

  i.   Generally
      Although the courts have not grappled with the issue, most commentators hold that it is not possible to attempt a strict

liability crime, unless it is shown that the defendant specifically intended to commit the offense.

ii. Attendant Circumstance Crimes
However, some crimes require an intent to commit a certain act but do not require a mens rea as to certain circumstances. For example, a statutory rape conviction requires an intent to have sex with an underage person, but does not require any state of mind as to the partner's age. To attempt such an offense, one must intend to cause the forbidden result, but need only be reckless or negligent as to the circumstances.

2. Acts Constituting an Attempt

a. Act Required
Guilty thoughts alone are not punishable. In order to be blameworthy one must also take some kind of step towards commission of a crime.

b. Many Standards in Use
Different jurisdictions have employed many different tests in order to determine what kind of preparation or steps constitute a criminal attempt.

   i. The Proximity or Nearness Approach
   Some jurisdictions concentrate on how close a defendant came towards completion of a crime.

   (1) The Holmes Proximity Test
   Preparation can constitute an attempt, if the preparation comes so close to the crime that the intent to commit the crime renders commission highly probable.

   (2) Preparation Not Always Sufficient
   Some states focus on the acts that remain to be done. Thus, if substantial steps have been taken, but many steps remain, the actor will not have come close enough for the behavior to amount to an attempt.

(3)   Chance to Abandon
Some courts hold that an attempt takes place only when there is no longer ample opportunity to abandon the scheme.

ii.   Equivocal Purpose
Though it is not a widely used approach, a court may focus on whether or not behavior shows an unequivocal intent to commit a crime. If this standard is used, a defendant can avoid an attempt conviction by showing that his conduct may have had a legal purpose, as in "I went to my neighbor's house at 2 a.m. to water the plants, not to steal."

iii.   The Model Penal Code Approach
Many jurisdictions follow MPC § 5.01(1)(c), which requires a substantial step that is part of a plan to commit a crime. The Code requires that the conduct be strongly indicative of a criminal intent.

(1)   Distinguished From Proximity Test
Unlike the proximity test, the MPC approach does not require one's acts to come especially close to completion of the crime.

(2)   Distinguished From Equivocal Purpose Test
Though the Code requires the act or acts to be strongly corroborative of criminal intent, it need not be shown that the defendant could only have had a criminal purpose.

C.   Impossibility Defense
A dilemma arises when a defendant is charged with attempting to commit a crime, but actual commission of the crime would not have been possible.

1. Factual Impossibility No Defense
Where facts unbeknownst to an actor make successful completion of an offense impossible, one may still be guilty of an attempt. Examples include one who picks an empty pocket, or one who

tries to shoot another with an unloaded gun. See also, MPC § 5.01(1)(a).

2. Legal Impossibility

   a. Completely Legal Act
One cannot be guilty of an attempt when, although the defendant intended to break the law, the actual act attempted would be legal, even if the facts had been as the defendant believed them to be. For example, one who thinks he is breaking the law by selling Root Beer to minors is not guilty of any offense.

   b. Act Illegal if Facts Were as Actor Believed
At common law, one who erroneously believed he was committing a crime (e.g., the goods he was purchasing were not stolen as he believed), he could not be convicted of an attempt. However, this defense is now rejected in virtually all jurisdictions and by MPC § 5.01(1)(a).

Therefore, one who buys baby powder from an undercover agent, believing it to be cocaine, will be convicted of attempting to possess illegal drugs. Although purchasing baby powder is legal, one cannot avoid liability when a crime would have occurred had the facts been as the defendant believed.

D.   Renunciation and Abandonment
One who has decided to commit a crime and commences preparation may decide at a later point, before actual commission, to abort the plan.

1. Elements

   a. Must be Voluntary
Before considering whether or not the defense of abandonment is valid, all courts require that the abandonment be voluntary. Thus, one who abandons a criminal plan out of fear of being caught in the immediate or near future is still guilty, because such an individual had the clear intent to break the law, has

proven to be dangerous to society, and did not abandon out of a sense of morality.

  b. No Substantial Steps
Some, though not all jurisdictions, require that abandonment occur before any substantial steps are taken.

2. Model Penal Code Approach
According to MPC § 5.01(4), abandonment can be a valid defense, but only if the defendant can show it was complete, voluntary, and not motivated by a fear of being caught or a decision to postpone the crime.

E.   Attempting an Attempt-Like Crime
Some substantive crimes are defined as attempts. For example, assault is often defined as an attempted battery. Although such cases rarely arise, it has generally been held that one may be convicted of attempting an attempt-like crime. Some courts, however, have barred such convictions because they lead to complicated jury instructions and are not necessary for the benefit of society.

III.   SOLICITATION
(See, MPC § 5.02)

Solicitation occurs when one encourages or asks another to commit a crime. If the other person refuses, a solicitation has nonetheless occurred. If the other person accepts, a conspiracy charge will be introduced instead. If the crime actually occurs, the original solicitor will instead be charged as an accomplice to the substantive crime.

1. Rationale
Solicitation is punished because it often leads to danger and people should be protected from instigators.

2. Renunciation
MPC § 5.02(3) permits renunciation as a defense so long as it is voluntary and the solicitor prevents the crime from occurring.

3. Can a Solicitation be an Attempt?
   A solicitation by itself is usually not enough to constitute a criminal attempt.

CASE CLIPS

People v. Acosta (1991) KS
Facts: Acosta, driving a stolen car, led police on a forty-eight mile chase. Two police helicopters, assisting in the chase, collided, killing three people. An expert testified that he had never heard of a midair collision between two police helicopters tracking a ground pursuit, and that the pilot of one of the helicopters broke FAA regulations. Acosta was convicted of murder, but claimed that a collision between helicopters was not a foreseeable result of his conduct, and that the pilot's violation of FAA guidelines was a superseding cause of the deaths.
Issue: What standard of proximate causation should the court use to determine if a defendant's actions proximately caused the harm?
Rule: The "highly extraordinary result" standard should be used. The standard excludes extraordinary results, is simply stated, and allows the trier of fact to determine the issue on the particular facts of the case using common sense. This standard does not involve the defendant's state of mind, but focuses on the objective conditions present when he acts.

People v. Arzon (1978) KS
Facts: D started a fire. In the process of putting out D's fire, a fireman was killed by smoke from a different fire in the same building that D had not started. D was charged with second degree murder.
Issue: Is one liable for all foreseeable harm caused by criminal conduct?
Rule: One is liable for harm which should have been reasonably foreseen as being related to one's acts. It is not necessary that the ultimate harm be intended by the actor or that one's acts be the sole cause of the harm.

People v. Campbell (1983) KS, J
Facts: D supplied a man with a gun and bullets, hoping that he would carry out his intention to commit suicide.
Issue: Is it criminal to incite another to commit suicide?

Rule: In most states it is not criminal to incite suicide. In states that do recognize this crime, there is no unanimity as to severity of punishment. Thus, until a legislature specifically determines a punishment, incitement to suicide is not criminal.

Stephenson v. State (1932) KS

Facts: D abducted a woman, tortured her, and bit her repeatedly. The woman attempted suicide by ingesting poison, but D delayed getting her treatment. She later received care but died due to infection and lack of food and early treatment.

Issue: Is one liable for murder if intervening factors are contributing causes of death?

Rule: One is liable for murder so long as one's criminal acts significantly contribute to the resulting death, even if other causes also contribute to the result.

Commonwealth v. Root (1961) KS, KW

Facts: D accepted another man's challenge to a car race. The other man swerved across the dividing line and was killed by an oncoming truck.

Issue: Is participation in a reckless act sufficient to render one responsible for another's death if other factors intervene?

Rule: In order to be culpable for another's death, one's conduct must have been the direct cause of the death. Superseding intervention breaks the causal link.

Concurrence: One is not liable for another's independent actions.

Dissent: One's conduct should be considered a direct cause of harm if it helps create the dangerous situation.

Note: Recent decisions have sided with the dissent.

State v. McFadden (1982) KS

Facts: McFadden and Sulgrove were drag racing. Sulgrove lost control of his vehicle and struck a third car, resulting in the death of Sulgrove and a six-year old passenger in the third car. McFadden was charged with two counts of involuntary manslaughter, but contended that there was no causation.

Issue: Which proximate cause standard should courts use in criminal trials, the civil standard, or a more stringent "direct causal connection" standard?

Rule: The civil standard of proximate cause is sufficient for a criminal trial. The element of proximate cause, based on the concept of foreseeability, serves the same purpose in both civil and criminal trials: it requires that there be a sufficient causal relationship between a defendant's conduct and a proscribed harm to hold the defendant liable.

Note: Some jurisdictions require the more stringent "direct causal connection" standard.

Commonwealth v. Atencio (1963) KS

Facts: Ds played a game of Russian Roulette with another. Ds took their turns and the gun did not fire. The other was less lucky and died.

Issue: Is one liable for another's death due to participation in a wanton or reckless act?

Rule: One is liable for another's death if one cooperates and helps bring about the deceased's reckless and deathly act.

People v. Kraft (1985) KS

Facts: D, a truck driver, fired shots at the driver of a car that had tried to pass him, then fired at police officers who tried to apprehend him. D had been drinking and smoking marijuana and claimed that he acted out of shock, never intending to hurt anyone.

Issue: To be convicted of attempted murder must one actually intend to kill?

Rule: The offense of attempted murder requires specific intent to commit murder. Knowledge that one's actions may cause death is not enough to warrant a conviction.

Commonwealth v. Peaslee (1901) KS

Facts: D arranged various items in a building so that when ignited, the building and its contents would burn. Later, as he drove towards the building, D changed his mind.

Issue: Can mere preparation amount to an unlawful attempt?

Rule: If preparation comes so near to accomplishment of the act that intent to complete the act makes the crime highly probable, it constitutes a criminal attempt.

State v. Young (1970) KS

Facts: D entered a school building and was convicted of entering a school with intent to disrupt classes. D had been engaged in a sit-in earlier in the day.

Issue: May an otherwise blameless act constitute a criminal attempt?

Rule: A legislature is free to make it an offense to take an otherwise lawful step in furtherance of a hostile end.

McQuirter v. State (1953) KS, KW, J

Facts: A police officer claimed that D, a black man, had followed a woman home and had admitted he planned to rape her. D denied all of the above. The case had a clear racial bias.

Issue: May one be charged with attempting an attempt-like crime?

Rule: One may be guilty of attempting an attempt-like crime so long as the jury is satisfied beyond a reasonable doubt that one intended to commit the crime.

United States v. Jackson (1977) KS, DS

Facts: Ds plotted a bank robbery and obtained weapons and masks, but were arrested before they entered the bank.

Issue: Can preparatory measures constitute a criminal attempt?

Rule: Substantial preparatory steps, if corroborative of criminal purpose, can constitute a criminal attempt.

Note: This is the Model Penal Code approach.

State v. Davis (1928) KS

Facts: D and a married woman wanted the woman's husband killed. D paid an undercover police officer $600 to carry out the plan. When the murder was due to occur, the policeman revealed his identity. D was convicted of attempted murder.

Issue: Does active solicitation of a crime, combined with some preparation, constitute an attempt?

Rule: Mere solicitation does not constitute an attempt, nor do acts of preparation that fail to lead directly or proximately to the commission of the intended crime.

Concurrence: It is unfair to punish one merely for entertaining a criminal impulse.

Dissent: Planning and solicitation should be sufficient proof of attempt.

People v. Jaffe (1906) KS

Facts: D tried to purchase cloth which he mistakenly thought was stolen property. D was convicted of attempting to receive stolen property.

Issue: Can one be guilty of an attempt when, contrary to one's belief, actual commission of the attempted act is not a crime?

Rule: If one attempts an act believing it to be a crime, but the act is actually legal, one may not be convicted of an attempt. It is no crime to attempt that which is legal.

People v. Dlugash (1977) KS, KW, DS, MIB

Facts: D shot a man who had already been shot three times and was dead. D may not have realized the victim was already dead. D was convicted of attempted murder.

Issue: Can one be guilty of attempting a crime if it is factually or legally impossible to accomplish?

Rule: It is no defense to an attempt charge that the crime was factually or legally impossible, if the crime could have been committed had the circumstances been as the defendant believed them to be.

State v. Rose (1973) L

Facts: D accidentally drove his car into a pedestrian. However, D then drove several hundred feet dragging the body under his car. The pedestrian was found dead, but it was unclear if death had been caused by the impact or the subsequent dragging.

Issue: Is one criminally liable for another's death if death was not caused by culpable negligence?

Rule: One is liable for another's death only if it is clear that death was caused by culpable negligence.

Kibbe v. Henderson (1976) L

Facts: Ds robbed a man, and then left him lying drunk, jacketless, and barefoot on the shoulder of an unlit highway. A short time later, the man was hit by a speeding truck and died.

Issue: Is one liable for causing death if other forces are the final cause?

Rule: One is liable for causing harm if the ultimate result is foreseeable to the actor.

Dissent: One should be liable for causing death if one consciously disregards a risk of grave harm, even if unforeseeable factors contribute.

Note: The Supreme Court reversed this decision, holding that one's conduct has caused death if the ultimate harm should have been foreseen as being reasonably related to that conduct.

Regina v. Blaue (1975) L

Facts: D stabbed a female Jehovah's Witness when she rebuffed his sexual overtures. The woman refused emergency surgery because her religion forbade blood transfusions. She died, but would have survived had she accepted a transfusion.

Issue: Is one liable for causing death if the victim's acts intervene?

Rule: One who inflicts harm is liable for the result unless a subsequent cause is so overwhelming as to make the original wound merely part of the history. In addition, those who use violence on others take their victims as they find them.

People v. Harris (1978) L, J

Facts: D had been arguing with a woman about her infidelity. As she drove away, D aimed his gun at her, shooting the car's rear window.

Issue: To be guilty of attempted murder, must one intend to cause death?

Rule: To be guilty of attempted murder, one must intend to kill. It is not enough to show that one intended serious bodily harm.

Note: Courts have disagreed as to whether one may be charged with an attempt to commit crimes such as reckless homicide which do not require intent as to the resulting death.

In Re Smith (1970) L

Facts: D grabbed a woman and ordered her to unlock her car door so they could go somewhere, but the woman escaped. D was charged with attempted kidnapping.

Issue: Does preparation constitute an attempt?

Rule: To amount to an attempt, an act must go further than mere preparation. There must be a clear intent, and it must be such that the crime would occur but for interruption.

Regina v. Eagleton (1855) L

Facts: D, a baker, delivered receipts seeking reimbursement for more bread than he had actually sold.

Issue: What kind of preparatory steps constitute an attempt?

Rule: Once one has committed the last necessary act towards perpetration of a crime, an attempt has occurred.

People v. Rizzo (1927) L, KW, W, J

Facts: Ds knew that a certain man would be carrying a large sum of cash and began to search for him, intending to rob him. They were arrested before they could find him.

Issue: What degree of preparation constitutes a criminal attempt?

Rule: Preparation does not amount to an attempt when substantial steps remain to be taken before the offense is completed.

People v. Orndorff (1968) L

Facts: D drove a man to a bank as part of a scheme to take the man's money. D then decided not to complete the scheme because he was already on parole. He left without taking any money.

Issue: Has an attempt occurred if one abandons a scheme?

Rule: An attempt has not occurred when one abandons a scheme before it reaches its first significant step and numerous potential steps remain before the scheme will succeed.

Commonwealth v. Skipper (1972) L

Facts: D, a prison inmate, smuggled hacksaws into jail by having them hidden inside loaves of bread. The hacksaws were discovered in his cell before he could use them.

Issue: What type of act constitutes an attempt?

Rule: To qualify as an attempt, an act must be sufficiently proximate to the crime such that the scheme cannot be abandoned without a transgression of the law.

People v. Bowen (1968) L

Facts: Ds went to the home of an elderly woman, for whom one of the Ds had previously done odd jobs, for the purpose of stealing from her. As two Ds distracted her, the other Ds searched the home.

Issue: What kind of overt act establishes an attempt?

Rule: To qualify as an attempt, an act must not serve any other purpose besides commission of a crime. If there are other possible explanations for one's acts, an attempt has not occurred.

United States v. Mandujano (1974) L

Facts: D accepted cash from an undercover agent and promised to get the agent some heroin. D left for an hour then returned, claiming he could not find the seller, and returned the money.

Issue: What kind of conduct constitutes an attempt?

Rule: An attempt occurs when one intentionally and knowingly engages in conduct that constitutes a substantial step towards commission of the crime.

Note: This is the MPC approach and is followed by most states.

United States v. Thomas (1962) L

Facts: Ds had sex, or attempted to have sex, with a woman they thought had passed out drunk, but was actually dead.

Issue: May one be guilty of attempting a crime when, due to facts unknown to the actor, the crime could not be committed?

Rule: One is liable for an attempt so long as the crime could have occurred if the circumstances were as the actor reasonably believed them to be.

Dissent: There can be no attempt when the act, if completed, cannot constitute an offense, even if the actor believes an offense is being committed.

Note: The rule follows the MPC, which rejects the impossibility defense.

People v. Staples (1970) L, KW

Facts: D, a mathematician, rented an office above a bank vault and drilled some holes through the floor. However, D took no further steps because he realized stealing from the bank was an absurd idea.

Issue: Can one be guilty of an attempt if one voluntarily abandons his criminal design?

Rule: One is guilty of an attempt if one commits acts causing a sufficient likelihood of commission. It is irrelevant whether one is apprehended or abandons the scheme voluntarily.

Papachristou v. City of Jacksonville (S.Ct. 1972) L

Facts: Ds were engaged in various acts such as loitering. Suspicious police arrested them under a vagrancy ordinance.

Issue: May an ordinance be void due too vagueness?

Rule: An ordinance is void-for-vagueness if it fails to give notice of what conduct is forbidden and invites arbitrary arrests.

In Re M. (1973) L

Facts: D, a thirteen-year-old, threw an object at a police officer, hitting his car. D was charged with attempted assault. Assault is defined as attempted battery.

Issue: Can one attempt an attempt crime?

Rule: One cannot be liable for attempting a crime which is an attempt itself.

People v. Lubow (1971) L, KW, J, MIB

Facts: Ds, diamond dealers, invited a man, to whom one of the Ds owed money, to enter into an illegal scheme to defraud creditors.

Issue: Is one liable simply for soliciting others to commit a crime?

Rule: Mere solicitation is a criminal offense, because it presents a danger to society and people should not be exposed to inducements to commit crimes.

Regina v. Martin Dyos (1979) KW

Facts: Dyos was involved in a scuffle between two groups of youths. Dyos admitted hitting the victim on the head with a brick, inflicting one of the two principal wounds that later caused the young man's death. The cause of the second wound was unknown.

Issue: Must the state prove "but-for" causation in order to secure a murder conviction?

Rule: Before a defendant may be convicted of murder, the state must prove that the death was not caused by another injury.

Regina v. Benge (1865) KW

Facts: D, a foreman on a railroad construction project, misread a schedule, and tracks were not in place when a train came. The resultant accident might have been avoided if the look-out man or the engine driver had been more alert.

Issue: Is one culpable for harm that would not have occurred but for one's action, even if the harm would have been avoided but for others' acts also?

Rule: One is liable if one's negligence is the substantial cause of harm, even if others contributed to the harm.

Commonwealth v. Rhoades (1980) KW

Facts: D started a fire. A responding fireman died due to a combination of cold weather, stress, and smoke inhalation.

Issue: Is one liable for all harm resulting from one's actions?

Rule: One is liable for resulting harm only if one's conduct is the proximate cause of the harm.

United States v. Hamilton (1960) KW, W

Facts: D roughed up a man outside a pool hall. The victim was hospitalized, and later, in a violent fit pulled out his own breathing tubes and died.

Issue: Is one who inflicts injury liable for causing another's death if the death results from ensuing complications?

Rule: If one strikes a blow that is not deadly in itself, but sets in motion a chain of events leading to death, one is guilty of homicide.

State v. Lyerla (1988) KW

Facts: Jensen and Lyerla were travelling in the same direction on an interstate highway. Jensen played games with Lyerla, accelerating when he tried to pass. Annoyed, Lyerla fired his pistol into the truck, killing Jensen but leaving her two friends unscathed. Lyerla was convicted of second degree murder and two counts of attempted reckless homicide.

Issue: May a defendant be convicted of attempted reckless homicide?

Rule: An attempt to commit reckless homicide requires proof that the defendant intended to perpetrate an unintended killing – a logical impossibility. Thus, one cannot be convicted of attempted murder in the second degree.

Dissent: To secure a conviction for attempted second degree murder, the state must merely show that the defendant intended to act with a criminally reckless state of mind.

People v. Murray (1859) KW

Facts: D ran away with his niece and sent for a magistrate to perform a marriage. D was charged with attempting an incestuous marriage.

Issue: Do intention and preparation amount to an attempt?

Rule: A criminal attempt requires more than intention and preparation. Attempt is the direct movement towards commission, manifested by acts that would result in immediate consummation but for outside intervention.

Booth v. State (1964) KW

Facts: A man stole a coat and was arrested, at which time the coat lost its character as stolen property. The police returned the coat to the thief, who gave it to D, telling him it was stolen. D was convicted of attempt to receive stolen property.

Issue: May one be guilty of an attempt if actual commission of the crime is impossible due to circumstances unknown to the defendant?

Rule: One may not be convicted of an attempt when commission is legally impossible, as when the intended act, had it been completed, would not constitute a crime. However, one may be convicted of a crime even though commission is factually impossible, such as attempting to steal from an empty house.

Fine v. State (1952) W

Facts: D had an argument and grabbed a frail old man who had high blood pressure. The man had to be hospitalized, and two months later he died.

Issue: Is one liable for causing death if there is a remote connection between the act and the death?

Rule: One is liable for causing another's death only if the unlawful act is the proximate cause of death. A remote connection between action and death is insufficient to establish a causal connection.

Matter of J.N. (1979) DS

Facts: Ds tried to take an elderly woman's purse, knocking her down and causing her to be hospitalized. Six days later, the woman was taken off life sustaining equipment and died.

Issue: Can medical action be an intervening force relieving one of liability for causing death?

Rule: Only an enormously egregious medical blunder constitutes an intervening force that breaks the chain of causation.

Dissent: When life sustaining equipment is removed, and death results, the original actor should be culpable only if death would have nonetheless resulted within a statutorily determined period.

People v. Scott (1971) DS

Facts: D argued with the occupants of a police patrol car, and then tried to force it off the road. Another police car, chasing D, collided with a bus, and an officer was killed.

Issue: Is one liable for harm if there are other proximate causes besides one's actions?

Rule: Due to the different natures of criminal and tort law, different standards of proximate cause are applied. To be criminally liable, one's act must be grossly negligent and the ensuing harm must be the natural and necessary result.

People v. Krovarz (1985) DS

Facts: D threatened a store clerk with a knife and demanded money, but was then arrested. At trial, D claimed he did not really want the money and only had acted with the hope of being returned to a mental hospital.

Issue: Where an underlying crime requires knowledge, must one have intent to commit the offense to be guilty of an attempt?

Rule: Knowledge as to conduct and circumstances is sufficient proof of potential harm to be deemed a criminal attempt. Specific intent to commit the underlying offense need not be proven.

State v. Latraverse (1982) J

Facts: D had been arrested for selling stolen cars to an undercover policeman. D drove slowly past the officer's home and was driving away when police stopped him and found matches, gasoline, and other items, including a threatening note addressed to the undercover policeman.

Issue: What type of action constitutes an attempt?

Rule: A criminal attempt occurs when, acting with the requisite mens rea of the underlying crime, one takes a substantial step towards commission of the crime. Abandonment of the scheme is a valid defense only if it is complete and voluntary.

United States v. Joyce (1982) J

Facts: D agreed to buy cocaine from an undercover officer and came to a motel with $20,000 cash, but refused to buy it when the undercover officer would not first show D the cocaine.

Issue: What are the required elements of an attempt?

Rule: An attempt occurs when one acting with criminal intent takes a substantial step clearly moving towards commission of a crime. Unambiguous refusal or withdrawal prevents finding such a step.

State v. Brewer (1973) J

Facts: D claimed he intended to rob a store and tried to obtain guns from an undercover police officer.
Issue: What kind of behavior constitutes conspiracy?
Rule: A conspiracy occurs when acting with the intent necessary for the underlying offense, one joins in an agreement to commit a crime. No overt act is required.
Note: Conspiracy is discussed in Chapter 7.

United States v. Everett (1983) J

Facts: D gave an undercover agent a substance that D mistakenly thought was an illegal narcotic.
Issue: Can one be guilty of attempt when completion of the crime is impossible?
Rule: A legislature may choose to punish attempts even when completion of the crime is not possible.

Commonwealth v. Henley (1984) J

Facts: D, a jeweler, purchased gold chains from an informant after being told the chains were stolen.
Issue: Can one be guilty of an attempt when completion of the offense is impossible due to facts unbeknownst to him?
Rule: One who intends to commit a crime and takes all necessary steps is not excused because commission is impossible. One is only excused when the contemplated act is actually legal.

People v. Paluch (1966) MIB

Facts: D offered to cut a man's hair but had no barber's license.
Issue: What level of preparation constitutes an attempt?
Rule: Substantial steps constitute an attempt when they render commission of the crime highly probable.
Dissent: An attempt does not occur until the actor takes steps to prepare the potential victim.

People v. Migliore (1988) MIB

Facts: Migliore and a co-defendant peppered a man's house with gunfire, although none of the bullets fired entered the home. The defendants were aware that the house was occupied, but believed it was another person's house. Defendants were convicted of attempted murder.

Issue 1: What proof is needed to convict a defendant of attempted murder?
Rule 1: To sustain a conviction for attempted murder, the prosecution must prove that defendant had the intent to kill the victim, and took a substantial step towards that result. Specific intent may be shown by surrounding circumstances, including the use of a deadly weapon.
Issue 2: May a defendant be charged with attempted murder if the actual victim is mistakenly thought to be someone else?
Rule 2: Mistaken identity does not negate an intent to kill for the purposes of an attempted murder charge.

United States v. Buffington (1987) MIB
Facts: Defendants were charged with attempted bank robbery. Police officers at the scene of the incident witnessed the defendants driving slowly by the bank, one of them dressed in women's clothing. Upon their arrest, the defendants were found to be armed.
Issue: May a defendant be convicted of an attempt crime if his actions only rise to the level of "mere preparation"?
Rule: Mere preparation does not constitute a substantial step toward the commission of a crime, and is therefore not enough to convict for an attempt crime. A substantial step consists of conduct that is strongly corroborative of the firmness of a defendant's criminal intent. In this case the defendants' actual conduct did not cross the boundary between preparation and attempt.

Thacker v. Commonwealth (1922) MIB
Facts: D was drunk and fired several shots into a tent, but claimed he only wanted to shoot a lantern in the tent and not its occupants.
Issue: To be guilty of an attempt, must one specifically intend the underlying crime?
Rule: To be guilty of attempt, one must specifically intend to commit the underlying crime. Acts that are likely to result in the underlying crime are not enough.

Adams v. Murphy (1981) MIB
Facts: D was charged with attempted perjury.
Issue: Does the crime of attempt apply to *all* crimes?
Rule: There can be no attempt to commit an offense when the actual offense is an attempt to effect a result, as with perjury or solicitation.

Concurrence/Dissent: If a defendant convinces a judge to instruct a jury that attempt is a lesser included offense, he should not then gain dismissal because the crime does not exist.

Dissent: If one intends a crime and commits acts beyond preparation towards commission, one should be guilty of attempt.

Charlton v. Wainwright (1979) MIB

Facts: D worked in a bar and attempted to remove an intoxicated patron who fell down a flight of stairs and died.

Issue: Can one attempt a crime which requires negligence, and not intent, as to the result?

Rule: One may be guilty of attempting a crime involving recklessness or negligence as to the result by intentionally acting with gross carelessness or recklessness.

Chapter 7

GROUP CRIMINALITY

I. ACCOUNTABILITY FOR THE ACTS OF OTHERS
(See, MPC § 2.06)

A. At Common Law

1. Categories of Liability
   Originally at common law there were four categories of liability for a criminal offense.

   a. Principal in the First Degree
   A principal in the first degree is a person who actually commits an offense.

   b. Principal in the Second Degree
   A principal in the second degree or an accomplice, gives aid, counsels, or abets a principal in the first degree in commission of an offense. Technically, a principal in the second degree must be present during the offense, but constructive presence is sometimes sufficient.

   A principal in the second degree is liable to the same extent as a principal in the first degree and can be convicted of an offense even when a principal in the first degree is acquitted.

   c. Accessory Before the Fact
   An accessory before the fact procures, counsels, or commands a principal in the first degree to commit an offense, but is not present physically or constructively at the scene of an offense.

   An accessory before the fact is liable for an offense to the same extent as a principal but cannot be tried without her consent until the conviction of a principal. Furthermore, if a principal is acquitted, an accessory before the fact cannot be convicted.

d. Accessory After the Fact

An accessory after the fact is not involved in the planning or commission of an offense by a principal in the first degree. Instead, knowing that an offense has been committed, the accessory after the fact obstructs justice by harboring or giving aid to the criminal.

An accessory after the fact is liable for a lesser offense than that committed by a principal and cannot be tried before the conviction of a principal. He must be acquitted if the principal is acquitted.

2. Differences Due to Original Offense

All four of these classes-of-offender exist when the original offense is a felony. On the other hand, when the offense is a misdemeanor, one who acts as an accessory before the fact is treated in all respects like a principal. Also, one cannot be an accessory after the fact to a misdemeanor.

3. Statutory Changes

Modern statutes have basically merged the classes of liability, with the exception of accessory after the fact; accessory after the fact is still a lesser offense. The other offenses are punished to the same degree.

B. Mens Rea

1. Intent to Aid

For derivative liability one must intend to aid and abet another in the commission of an offense. This intent must be purposeful. Knowing of another's intent to commit an offense is insufficient. See, MPC § 2.06(3)(a). If one's intent is to spy or to be a detective, the requisite criminal intent is not present and one is not liable for aiding and abetting the commission of an offense.

2. Mens Rea as to Attendant Circumstances

When the offense is one of strict liability, the minimum intent that the aider and abettor to the principal must have is knowledge that the strict liability offense is being committed. Purposeful intent to aid or abet is not necessary.

3. Mens Rea as to Result
   When one purposefully aids and abets another in the commission of an action, it is not necessary that one purposefully intend that action to result in the commission of an offense. The result does not need to be intended, just the action which caused the result. See, MPC § 2.06(4).

4. Departure from the Common Design
   One can only be held derivatively liable for those actions that one counseled a principal to engage in or those actions that were part of a common design. If a principal deviates from the common design in the commission of an offense, an aider and abettor is liable only for those actions for which he gave counsel.

C. Actus Reus
    Presence, prior association, or flight is insufficient for one to be held derivatively liable. One must actually do something, however slight, in advancement of the offense.

1. Exceptions
   Simple presence and non-action are sufficient when there is an affirmative duty to act established either by common law or statute.

2. Continued Course of Action
   One aids and abets an offense when one continues a course of action that aids a principal after one realizes that an offense is being committed. This is so even if one did not know of the principal's intent when one commenced the action.

3. Awareness by Principal
   A principal does not necessarily have to be aware of the aid that is given for the commission of an offense. The aid does not have to change the situation.

D.   Relationship between Liability of Parties

1. Foreseeable or Related Crimes
    Since any act in furtherance of the common design is applicable
    to an accessory, if a felony results in murder, an accessory is liable
    for the murder by the felony-murder rule. Nevertheless, one can-
    not be derivatively liable for an offense greater than that com-
    mitted by the principal.

2. Conviction of Principal

    a. Necessary
        According to some modern statutes, if all other accomplices are
        acquitted, an accessory or accomplice cannot be singly guilty
        by derivation.

    b. Unnecessary
        Other jurisdictions allow for conviction of an accessory even
        when a principal has not been convicted.

        i.   Principal Not Available
             If a crime is shown to have been committed, but conviction
             of a principal is not possible, an accomplice or accessory
             may still be punished.

        ii. Principal Excused or Justified
             If a principal is known and capable of prosecution, but is
             not brought to trial or is acquitted on an excuse or justifica-
             tion, conviction of an accomplice is still possible. This
             allows for prosecution of people who commit crimes
             through the actions of others who are faultless; e.g., duress,
             mental deficiency, lesser evils. See, MPC § 2.06(7).

3. Withdrawal
    Withdrawal from a crime limits one's liability to only those acts
    which were committed up to that point. Physical withdrawal alone
    is insufficient. One must actively remove one's support, commu-
    nicate the withdrawal, or disapprove of the proposed actions, in

order to actually withdraw from the situation. See, MPC §
2.06(6)(c).

4. Exceptions to Accomplice Liability
Occasionally, one who could be held derivatively liable will not
be, due to overriding public policy. For example, a victim of
statutory rape can not be an accomplice to the crime. Therefore, a
secondary party does not necessarily have to be guilty if the
primary party is guilty. See, MPC § 2.06(6)(a).

5. Attempt
According to the common law and modern criminal statutes, one
cannot be guilty of attempting to be an accessory or accomplice.
A crime must be committed before one can be derivatively liable.

6. Vicarious Liability

a. Explained
Derivative liability of an accomplice is not the same as
vicarious liability. Vicarious liability is liability due to one's
relationship to the principal. Derivative liability occurs due to
one's acts as aider and abettor and is dependant on the principal violating the law.

b. No Actus Reus
Vicarious liability allows for liability without a finding of the
proper actus reus. For example, an employer can be liable for
all actions of an employee done within the scope of employment. Also, one can be made vicariously liable for parking and
traffic violations.

7. Accessory after the Fact (Statutory)
An accessory after the fact is any person who harbors, conceals, or
aids an offender, knowing or having reasonable ground to believe
that he has committed the felony, and with the intent that he may
avoid or escape from arrest, trial, conviction, or punishment. The
assistance must be active, and one must know of the person's
criminal status.

II.   LIABILITY WITHIN THE CORPORATE FRAMEWORK

A.   Liability of the Corporate Entity
A corporation can be held criminally liable for criminal acts performed by its agents on its behalf, even if the agent was specifically instructed not to act in such a manner. Otherwise, enforcing criminal statutes aimed at regulating corporate activity would be impractical.

1. Criminal Theory of Respondeat Superior
Three elements are required by the criminal theory of respondeat superior in order to render a corporation liable for the actions of its agents.

   a. Agent Must Commit a Crime
   An illegal act must be committed by an agent with the statutorily required specific intent, which is then directly imputed to the agent's corporation. It is not necessary to show which specific agent committed the act, only that some agent did. Thus, corporations are more easily convicted than individuals. When only knowledge is required for an offense rather than specific intent, the collective knowledge of the employees is sufficient and imputed to the corporation.

   b. Within the Scope of Employment
   Conduct which is authorized, explicitly or implicitly, by the principal or that is similar or incidental to authorized conduct is within the scope of employment. Often, courts will accept actions specifically forbidden by a superior and which occurred despite good-faith prevention efforts by the corporation. An action which is normally outside the scope of employment may be brought within the scope if the action is subsequently approved by a superior.

   c. With Intent to Benefit the Corporation
   As long as an agent intends her actions to benefit the corporation, it can be liable, even if it received no actual benefit. However, the existence or absence of benefit is relevant as evidentiary of an intent to benefit. Again, intent can be inferred if the action is subsequently ratified or approved by a superior

even if there was no prior intent to benefit. This allows for corporate liability for approval rather than commission of criminal conduct.

2. Model Penal Code

The Model Penal Code allows for four types of corporate liability, which are variations of the criminal theory of respondeat superior. See, MPC § 2.07.

a. Traditionally Individual Crimes of Intent

Traditionally individual crimes of intent include those crimes where there is no legislative purpose in making the corporation liable. This includes such crimes as larceny, embezzlement, and manslaughter, which are usually committed by individuals. A corporation is liable only if a high official or board performed, authorized or recklessly tolerated the offense. Only the intent of top officials is imputed to the corporation and not that of subordinated. See, MPC § 2.07(1)(c).

b. Special Crimes of Intent

Special crimes of intent are those which a legislature has plainly intended to impose liability on corporations. When an employee commits an offense within the scope of employment, the corporation may avoid liability by showing that a high managerial agent with supervisorial responsibility acted with due diligence but was still unable to prevent the offense from occurring. See, MPC §§ 2.07(1)(a),(5).

c. Crimes of Strict Liability

When an offense is one of strict liability, a legislative purpose to impose liability on corporations is inferred unless the contrary plainly appears. No evidence of specific intent or intent to benefit the corporation is required, and the defense of due diligence is not available. This category usually covers offenses against the public welfare. See, MPC § 2.07(1)(b).

d. Failure of Regulatory Duties

There is also a small category of offenses based on the failure to discharge a specific duty of affirmative performance imposed by law on a corporation, such as a duty to file a report. This category can be considered a regulatory sub-category of strict liability crimes. See, MPC § 2.07(2)

B. Liability of Corporate Agents
An employer or partner may be liable for strict liability offenses, in a manner similar to that of the corporation. See, MPC § 2.07(6).

1. Knowledge
Knowledge of a strict liability offense may be imputed to an employer or partner when an affirmative duty is placed on that person but is subsequently delegated to an employee or another agent lower in the corporate hierarchy.

2. Act
No personal action is necessary for strict liability offenses. Once an affirmative duty has been established, one is liable for preventing, seeking out, and remedying any violations of that duty, even when the power to do so has been delegated to another.

Nonetheless, only civil penalties such as fines and not criminal penalties such as imprisonment are constitutional when the actions of one are imputed to another. Thus, in the context of corporate agent liability and in absence of an affirmative act, one can only be civilly punished.

III. CONSPIRACY
(See, MPC §§ 5.03, 5.04, and 5.05)

A. Generally

1. Defined
Modern conspiracy is a vague offense. Basically a mental offense, it consists of a meeting of minds with wrongful intent. The object of agreement must be commission of an unlawful act or commission of a legal act by illegal means. See, MPC § 5.03(1).

2. Purpose
Concert of action makes an offense more dangerous to society and harder to prevent than when it is committed singly. The potential for harm is so much greater, that conspirators merit punishment even if the object of agreement is never realized. Therefore, this doctrine fills the gap between derivative liability and principal liability, while also allowing for additional punishment when an offense is actually committed.

3. Development

  a. Uniqueness
  Conspiracy is unique to the common law; it is not found in civil law countries. Rather, they allow for greater punishment when an offense is planned or committed in concert.

  b. Civil and Criminal Conspiracy
  Because civil courts are not required to strictly construe statutes as criminal courts must, the doctrine of civil conspiracy is more expansive than its criminal counterpart. This occasionally carries over into criminal doctrine. Consequently, criminal conspiracy has been more liberally developed than most criminal offenses.

4. Punishment
One may be convicted of conspiracy even if only legal and innocent acts were committed towards execution.

  a. Federal
  Previously, all conspiracy under federal jurisdiction was a felony even if the object offense was a misdemeanor. Now, conspiracy is graded the same as the object offense.

  b. State
  Previously, conspiracy was punished by imprisonment for a set number of years, regardless of the base offense. Now, a third of the states follow MPC § 5.05 and allow the same punishment as for the object crime. The rest fix punishment at some term less than that for the object crime.

5. Liability
Most jurisdictions allow for joint indictment and trial of conspiracy and the substantive offense. Nevertheless, one cannot be convicted and punished for both a substantive crime and conspiracy to commit the substantive crime arising from a single course of conduct. However, one might be convicted of conspiracy to commit an offense even if one committed the offense, because occasionally, this is better prosecutorial strategy.

6. Hearsay Exception
Hearsay evidence is normally presumed inadmissable. However, there is a co-conspirator hearsay exception.

   a. Pre-FRE
   Before the Federal Rules of Evidence, existence of a conspiracy and an alleged conspirator's connection to it had to be established before objection to the testimony could be overruled and the exception put into effect.

   b. Under FRE
   FRE 104(a), however, allows consideration of hearsay testimony in determining if there is a preponderance of evidence establishing a conspiracy and a connection thereto.

7. Withdrawal

   a. Common Law
   Since an overt act was not required for conspiracy at common law, the offense was complete as soon as there was a meeting of the minds with requisite intent. Once an offense was choate, there could be no withdrawal.

   b. Model Penal Code
   Most states follow § 5.03(6) and allow the defense of withdrawal when one renounces criminal purpose and thwarts the success of the conspiracy.

B. Actus Reus

1. Overt Act
An overt act is an act, either lawful or unlawful, performed in furtherance of a conspiratorial objective.

   a. Common Law
   At common law, an agreement, when coupled with wrongful intent, was a sufficient act to constitute conspiracy. Thus, conviction was possible without proof of an overt act.

   b. Statute

      i. Minor Act
      Some states' overt-act requirement is satisfied by minor acts that would be considered equivocal or preparatory under attempt doctrine. Occasionally, when the object offense is serious, such as drug trafficking, an exception to the minor-act rule is allowed.

      ii. Substantial Act
      Other states require a more substantial overt act; a few states even require a substantial step. MPC § 5.03(5) requires only an overt act less than the substantial act required for attempt, making group prosecution easier and enhancing punishment.

2. Agreement

   a. Primary Objective
   Conspiracy requires an agreement to commit an unlawful or criminal act or to commit a lawful act by unlawful or criminal means.

      i. Manifest
      This element consists of a concurrence of wills resulting from agreement. The agreement does not have to expressly state an object to violate the law. Knowledge of the essential nature of the object is sufficient. Specific knowl-

edge of all details or all participants is not required of every co-conspirator.

    ii. Implied
An agreement may be inferred from the circumstances. Although concurrence of action is only evidence of conspiracy, and not equivalent to conspiracy, agreement can be inferred when it appears that the concurrence was not accidental.

b. Secondary Objective
A secondary objective of secrecy is implied only when acts of concealment are done in furtherance of the main criminal objectives of a conspiracy. When done after attainment of the central objectives for the sole purpose of covering up, no secondary objective can be found.

C.   Mens Rea
Knowledge of an agreement does not constitute conspiracy without requisite intent.

1. Prior Standards of Intent as to the Offense

a. Crimmins Doctrine
Under the Crimmins doctrine, knowledge of all attendant circumstances to an offense is required for conviction of conspiracy.

b. Powell Doctrine
The Powell doctrine states that criminal conspiracy must be animated by motive to do wrong. This must be established by independent evidence if the offense is only statutorily proscribed. English courts, the Code, and most states have rejected the Powell doctrine, as an ignorance-of-the-law defense. Since it is not a valid defense to a substantive crime, these jurisdictions do not allow it in conspiracy either.

2. Current Standard of Intent – Feola Doctrine
Feola established that conspiracy to commit a substantive offense cannot exist without at least the degree of criminal intent necessary for the substantive offense itself.

3. When Inferable

   a. Offense is Misdemeanor
   Intent cannot be inferred when the object offense is a misdemeanor. Exceptions are allowed when there is some direct evidence of intent, when there is a special interest associated with the offense, and when the crime is aggravated in nature.

   b. Offense is Felony
   When an object offense is a felony, inference of intent is more easily allowed. This distinction in treatment, based on the grading of the offense, is somewhat contradictory.

   c. Model Penal Code
   The Code does not allow for any inference of intent because the level of culpability is purpose and not just knowledge.

4. Intent to Agree
A conspirator must intentionally enter into an agreement to do an illegal act with the intent to consummate that act. Some courts only require knowledge rather than purpose as the level of culpability.

D.   Number of Conspiracies
Deciding whether there is only one conspiracy or several separate ones involved is the first step in determining extent of liability, propriety of joint prosecution, possible existence of accomplice liability, and admissability of hearsay testimony.

1. "Wheel" Conspiracy

   a. Defined
   A "wheel" conspiracy is one in which several individuals or groups are each involved in a conspiracy limited to themselves

and the central figure. Aside from this mutual relationship to the central "hub," the groups have no knowledge of, interest in, or relationship to the other groups.

b. Treatment
A collection of conspiracies in "wheel" formation is not treated as one large conspiracy. Additional evidence of a relationship between the groups, or "rim," is required for treatment as a single conspiracy.

2. "Chain" Conspiracy

a. Defined
A "chain" conspiracy occurs when several individuals or groups conspire with one or two other groups in order to achieve a step or "link" towards a developing criminal objective. The beginning of a series need not have any relationship to the end except a connection by intermediate progressive agreements.

b. Treatment
A collection of conspiracies in "chain" formation is treated as one large conspiracy, because the success of each group is dependant upon the success of the overall scheme.

3. Duration
Conspiracy continues until achievement of the object, abandonment of the object before commission of an overt act, or arrest. See, MPC § 5.03(7). Although a single conspiratorial agreement may continue for a long period of time, it is not to be treated as multiple conspiracies, even if the agreement is to commit several offenses. The goal of conspiracy statutes is to punish criminal agreements. Therefore, however diverse an agreement's objects, it violates but a single statute. See, MPC § 5.03(3).

E.   Parties

1. Need for Conviction of a Second Party

a. Bilateral Theory
Traditionally, one person alone cannot be convicted of conspiracy, because a meeting of minds with the same requisite intent is a necessary element. Therefore, if only one person has the required intent, all elements of conspiracy have not been met.

   i.   Wharton's Rule
   Wharton's rule states that one cannot be convicted alone of an offense which by its very nature requires cooperative action. Therefore, if all but one of the people who agreed to the criminal objective lacked the requisite intent and are acquitted, then even that one person with the proper intent cannot be convicted of conspiracy.

   ii.   Exceptions
   Most jurisdictions which follow the bilateral theory allow for single conviction when the other parties were excused or not convicted on procedural grounds not amounting to an acquittal.

b. Unilateral Theory
The Code has adopted a unilateral theory of liability which focuses on each individual's culpability. Thus, under MPC §§ 5.03(1) and 5.04(1), it is immaterial that the other parties lacked the requisite intent, have not been convicted, have not been apprehended, are unknown, or have even been acquitted. By 1979, twenty-six states had adopted the Code's unilateral position on conspiracy.

2. Impossibility
   (See, MPC § 5.04)

   a. No Liability
      There is no liability due to impossibility if:

      i.   One cannot commit by statute the offense agreed to,

      ii.   One cannot by statute be liable for the offense agreed to,

      iii. An offense is not yet unlawful and is not committed in an
            unlawful manner, or

      iv.   The object of agreement is inherently impossible.

   b. Liability
      One is liable for conspiracy if:

      i.   The object of agreement is only physically impossible, or

      ii.   One is mistaken as to an elemental fact.

3. Accessorial Liability

   a. Traditionally
      According to the Pinkerton Rule, one conspirator can be liable
      for the criminal actions of a co-conspirator when they are done
      in furtherance of the conspiracy, are within the scope of the
      unlawful project, and are foreseeable or a natural consequence.

   b. Model Penal Code
      The Code, as well as many states, have rejected the traditional
      Pinkerton Rule. They look to the relative individual culpability
      of each conspirator.

4. Joinder
   One who enters into a conspiracy after the original agreement but
   before the achievement of the criminal objective is as culpable as
   the original conspirators.

F.   RICO

1.   Purpose
The Organized Crime Control Act of 1970 sought to eradicate organized crime by strengthening the legal tools used to deal with the unlawful activities of those engaged in organized crime.

2.   Creation
This act created the substantive crime of conducting or participating in the affairs of an enterprise through a pattern of racketeering activity. RICO criminalized a new type of agreement: to participate in an enterprise through a pattern of racketeering activity.

3.   Effect
This new crime allows for a series of events to be tried as a single conspiracy rather than several, as would be required under traditional conspiracy doctrine. Once it can be inferred that each crime was intended to further the affairs of the enterprise, it no longer matters if the offenses are separate and unrelated.

4.   Elements

a.   Agreement
Conviction for RICO requires two agreements:

i.   An agreement to conduct or participate in the affairs of an enterprise, and

ii.   An agreement to the commission of at least two predicate acts.

These may be established by circumstantial evidence, and inferences of knowledge are allowed.

b.   Enterprise
Enterprise is not synonymous with conspiracy. Enterprise is a structured association that exists to maintain operations to achieve an economic goal, which must be definable apart from

the predicate acts which make up the "pattern of racketeering activity." The enterprise may be legitimate or illegitimate.

c. Two Predicate Acts
Two predicate acts are necessary to establish the existence of a pattern of racketeering activity. These two acts must be separate statutory offenses committed by the enterprise.

5. Protection
The Due Process requirement that guilt remain "individual and personal" is still met by RICO even though it touches both insiders and outsiders, including the little fish. Due Process is not violated because it must still be shown that an individual manifested an agreement to participate, directly or indirectly, in an enterprise through the commission of two or more predicate crimes. These evidentiary requirements protect one from unsubstantiated claims.

CASE CLIPS

Hicks v. United States (S.Ct. 1893) KS, L

Facts: Hicks and Rowe both faced Colvert. All were on horseback, and Hicks held a rifle. Hicks removed his hat and said to Colvard, "Take off your hat and die like a man" whereupon Rowe shot and killed Colvard.
Issue 1: If one's statements result in the commission of an offense, is one an accomplice and thus liable as a principal in the offense?
Rule 1: If one makes statements intending to encourage commission of an offense, one is an accomplice. One cannot be an accomplice without intent to encourage or abet the commission of an offense. An intentionally uttered statement does not necessarily indicate intent to aid and abet, even when it has such an effect.
Issue 2: Is one an accomplice if one is present for the purpose of aiding and abetting an offense, but refrains from so doing because it is no longer necessary?
Rule 2: Only if a prior conspiracy exists can one be held liable as an accomplice for an offense committed by another when one is present but finds that it is not necessary to aid and abet.

State v. Gladstone (1970) L
(Cited incorrectly to 1980 in KS)

Facts: Thompson approached D to purchase marijuana. D informed Thompson that he had none for sale, but that Kent probably had some to sell. D gave Thompson Kent's address and drew a map.

Issue: To find complicity, what is the required link between accomplice and the person aided?

Rule: To find complicity, one must do something in association with another for the purpose of committing an offense. There must be counsel, encouragement, or procurement between accomplice and principal. Indicating that another might commit an offense is insufficient for accomplice liability, even if an offense is committed.

Dissent: If one acts knowing he will aid in the commission of a crime by another, one should be liable as an accomplice.

People v. Luparello (1987) KC

Facts: Luparello asked several friends to get information from Martin about the whereabouts of his former lover, "at any cost." Luparello's friends found Martin, and killed him. Luparello was convicted of murder under the theory of aiding and abetting.

Issue: Is an unplanned and unintended act of a co-conspirator chargeable to a defendant under a complicity theory?

Rule: Aiders and abettors are liable for the unplanned and unintended acts of co-conspirators. Aiders and abettors are responsible for the criminal harms they have naturally, probably, and foreseeably put into motion.

State v. McVey (1926) KS, L

Facts: D, worked on a steam ship. The principals allowed a boiler to build up too much steam. It blew, and several people died. D was charged as an accessory for counseling them to disregard the danger and to so act.

Issue: Can one be an accessory to manslaughter even though manslaughter is involuntary, unpremeditated, and unintentional?

Rule: One can be an accessory to manslaughter. An accessory to manslaughter aids, counsels, or procures another to commit an unlawful act or a lawful act in a grossly negligent manner resulting in homicide. Although the death is unintentional, if the aid is intentional and voluntary, one is an accessory to manslaughter.

Muench v. Israel (1983) L

Facts: Ds were charged with first degree murder. Ds sought to introduce expert psychiatric testimony to demonstrate that they lacked the mental capacity to form a specific intent.

Issue: Is a personality disorder probative of an ability to form specific intent?

Rule: Psychiatric testimony may be irrelevant in determining whether one can form the requisite intent, and thus can be excluded.

Dissent: Expert testimony may be relevant to determining one's mens rea.

People v. Abbott (1981) KS

Facts: D, was drag racing with Abbott. Abbott's car ran into another car, killing its passengers.

Issue: Can one be an accomplice to criminally negligent homicide?

Rule: An accomplice to criminally negligent homicide shares the requisite culpable mental state with a principal and intentionally aids in the commission of a negligent act which results in death.

Wilcox v. Jeffery (1951) KS

Facts: An American gave a concert in England in violation of the Aliens Order. D paid to attend the concert and wrote an article about the performance.

Issue: Is mere presence at the commission of an offense sufficient evidence of aiding and abetting?

Rule: Intentionally being present at, taking part in, concurring with, or encouraging any illegal act is sufficient action for accomplice liability; a "but for" causal link is not required.

Concurrence: Presence at only the legal portions of a partly illegal event and intentional absence from the illegal portions is not criminal.

State v. Hayes (1891) KS

Facts: D asked Hill to join in burglarizing a store. Hill went along with intent to get D arrested. D helped Hill enter the store, but did not enter himself.

Issue: Can one be an accessory to the acts of another when the other does not have the necessary intent?

Rule: Even with felonious intent, one cannot be an accessory if the principal does not also have felonious intent, because all elements of an offense must exist before they can be imputed to another.

Blond's Criminal Law   221

New York Central & Hudson River Railroad Co.
v. United States (S.Ct. 1909) KS

Facts: Pomeroy was an assistant traffic manager for D. Pomeroy paid rebates to sugar merchants to keep them from switching to water transportation. Pomeroy was convicted for payment of rebates.

Issue: Is it constitutional to impute to a corporation the commission of criminal offenses executed by its officers and agents?

Rule: It is constitutional to convict a corporation of a crime committed by an agent or officer. Acts committed within an agent's scope of authority benefit the corporation. If one of those acts involves the commission of an offense, the corporation can be liable, even if the specific act is prohibited by the corporation.

United States v. Hilton Hotels Corp. (1972) KS, KW

Facts: One of D's purchasing agents participated in a joint refusal to deal, which he had been specifically instructed not to take part in. A joint refusal to deal is a *per se* violation of the Sherman Act.

Issue: Can a corporation be liable for an offense committed by an agent against the corporation's specific instructions?

Rule: Although not expressly stated in the Sherman Act, a corporation can be liable for its agents' acts when they are within the scope of their authority, even when done against company orders.

Commonwealth v. Beneficial Finance Co. (1971) KS, L

Facts: Two men who worked for two of D's subsidiaries bribed members of the Small Loans Regulatory Board to get high maximum-interest rates set on certain loans.

Issue: For corporate liability, must an offense be performed, authorized, or tolerated by high-level employees?

Rule: It is not necessary for a high-level corporate employee to perform, authorize, or tolerate criminal actions in order for the corporation to be held liable as a principal. A corporation that gives an employee enough authority to handle the particular business involved can be liable for any criminal action committed by that employee whether or not her position is high-level.

State v. Ford Motor Co. (1979) KS

Facts: Three women were killed by incineration when their car, a Pinto manufactured by D, was rear-ended.

Issue: Can a corporation be convicted of reckless homicide?

Rule: (No opinion, just a newspaper article.) Although it appears that a corporation can be convicted of homicide for the specific acts of an agent, no jury has yet convicted a corporation for reckless homicide based on knowledge of a product defect.

Gordon v. United States (1954) KS

Facts: In violation of the Defense Production Act, some of Ds' employees made sales without collecting the required down payment.

Issue: Is a partner's or employee's knowledge of or participation in illegal actions attributable to another partner or employer?

Rule: A partner's or employee's knowledge of or participation in illegal actions that affect public welfare can be imputed to an employer or partner, because one is liable for compliance with a public welfare duty even when it is delegated to another.

Dissent: When knowledge or intent is required, it should be proven rather than imputed. Otherwise, the result is violation of the common law principle that the sins of one shall not be visited upon another simply because the one is the agent of the other.

United States v. Park (S.Ct. 1975) KS, L

Facts: Some of Acme Markets' warehouses were rodent infested. D, Acme's president, was informed of these violations. Although the problem got better, it was not resolved.

Issue: In matters affecting public welfare, may one be held accountable for statutory violations without a showing of wrongful action?

Rule: Those in responsible relation to a public danger have a duty to prevent and remedy violations. Failure to meet this duty results in personal liability, even absent some active wrongdoing. However, powerlessness is a possible defense.

Dissent: To be culpable one should have to engage in wrongful conduct amounting at least to common-law negligence.

United States v. MacDonald & Watson Waste Oil Co. (1991) KC

Facts: MacDonald, a contaminated waste disposal service, violated a regulation by disposing of solid waste at a site without a permit. D'Allesandro, president of MacDonald, was convicted of the crime on the basis that he was a responsible corporate officer who was in a position to ensure compliance with the regulation. D'Allesandro had no personal knowledge of criminal activity.

Issue: Can a corporate officer be held criminally liable even if he had no personal knowledge of criminal activity?

Rule: A corporate officer must have knowledge of criminal activity to be held liable; being a responsible corporate officer is not enough. However, knowledge can be proven through circumstantial evidence or willful blindness.

Krulewitch v. United States (S.Ct. 1949) KS, J

Facts: D and a cohort transported a woman from New York to Miami for the purpose of prostitution. The woman gave hearsay testimony as to a statement made by the cohort weeks after the trip.

Issue: In every conspiracy, is there a continuing subsidiary objective?

Rule: There is not a general continuing subsidiary objective of preventing detection and punishment inherent in every conspiracy. Admissability of hearsay testimony is limited to statements made in furtherance of the objectives of the conspiracy charged.

Concurrence: The boundaries of the conspiracy doctrine have been stretched too far already. A further expansion to include a continuing subsidiary objective is not merited.

Pinkerton v. United States (S.Ct. 1946) KS, L, J

Facts: D and his brother conspired to deal in whiskey, and other illicit things. While D was in jail, D's brother committed tax fraud.

Issue: Is a conspirator liable for all substantive crimes committed by a co-conspirator?

Rule: A conspirator is liable for all substantive crimes committed by any other conspirator when they are in furtherance of the conspiracy, fall within the scope of the unlawful project, and are foreseeable.

Dissent in Part: Without evidence of counsel or knowledge of a co-conspirator's act, there should be no liability.

Interstate Circuit, Inc. v. United States (S.Ct. 1939) KC

Facts: Interstate, a movie theater chain, was convicted of a conspiracy in violation of the Sherman Anti-Trust Act. Interstate entered into agreements with eight independent movie distributors concerning the terms for Interstate's continued exhibition of each distributor's films. To prove a conspiracy, the Government had to establish that each of the eight distributors had an agreement with one another. The Government had no proof that the distributors communicated with one another, but the

Government possessed a letter that showed that each distributor had knowledge that the other distributors would enter into the same deal. On the basis of this letter, the trial court found that each distributor had agreed to conspire with one another to take uniform action on the Interstate proposals in violation of the Sherman Act.

Issue: Can a conspiracy be proven by showing that each party knew of the other parties' actions, even if there was no express agreement?

Rule: (Stone, J.) Conspiracy can be proven by showing that each party knew that concerted action was contemplated and invited, and that each party adhered to the scheme and participated in it.

United States v. Alvarez (1980), (1981) KS

Facts: D loaded appliances on a plane that was to import marijuana and said he would help unload the plane on its return from Colombia.

Issue: Is assisting others with a legal act involved in a criminal venture sufficient evidence to show one joined in the conspiracy?

Panel Decision: Not every act of a third person which assists in the accomplishment of the conspirators' objective is sufficient to demonstrate concurrence in that agreement.

Rule: (En Banc Decision) Knowledge of criminal conduct combined with some assistance is sufficient to find joinder in a conspiracy.

Dissent: Joinder should require more than commission of a legal act.

People v. Lauria (1967) KS, L, KW, DS, J

Facts: D operated an answering service which he knew was used by several prostitutes in the line of business.

Issue: If one knows that one's goods or services are to be used for criminal purposes, is one part of a conspiracy to further an illegal enterprise?

Rule: Knowing that one's services or goods are being used for criminal purposes does not establish intent to participate in a misdemeanor. Direct evidence of such intent or an inference of intent to participate based on a special interest or the aggravated nature of the crime is necessary to find conspiratorial intent.

Kotteakos v. United States (S.Ct. 1946) KS, L

Facts: Thirty-two people in different groups dealt individually with one man who acquired loans for them using fraudulent applications.

Issue: Can a wheel conspiracy, where a central figure deals individually with two or more people or groups, be treated as one conspiracy?

Rule: When a group of people are related to each other only through their mutual agreements with one central conspirator, proof of knowledge of a comprehensive conspiracy is necessary for treatment as a single conspiracy.

United States v. Bruno (1939) KS, L

Facts: Ds were involved in a drug scheme. Smugglers imported drugs to New York, middlemen distributed to retailers in New York and Texas, who then sold to addicts. There was no cooperation or communication between retailers.

Issue: Can a chain conspiracy be treated as one conspiracy even when the chain separates?

Rule: When the success of one group's criminal activity is dependant upon the success of a whole chain of criminal activity, the entire scheme can be considered one conspiracy.

Gebardi v. United States (S.Ct. 1932) KS, J, MIB

Facts: Ds, a man and a woman not married to each other, traveled from one state to another in order to have sex.

Issue: If one cannot be guilty of a given substantive offense, can one nonetheless be liable for conspiracy to commit the offense?

Rule: One cannot be convicted of conspiracy to commit an offense which one cannot be personally convicted of committing.

Note: One person alone cannot be convicted of conspiracy. Thus, if all but one of the defendants is acquitted of conspiracy, the one must be acquitted as well.

Garcia v. State (1979) KS

Facts: D wanted her husband dead. D contacted a man who was a police informant. The informant set up a contract for D.

Issue: Can one be convicted of conspiracy when the only other conspirator only feigns acquiescence in the agreement?

Rule: Under the unilateral theory of conspiracy, rather than the traditional bilateral theory, one can be convicted of conspiracy even if the other conspirator only feigns agreement.

United States v. Elliott (1978) KS

Facts: Ds engaged in repeated illegal activity organized by one man. Ds did not work in concert and did not know of each other.

Issue: When events only allow for a finding of several conspiracies under traditional conspiracy doctrine, is it still possible to find one conspiracy under RICO?

Rule: RICO created the substantive offense of conducting or participating in an enterprise through racketeering activity. Participation in this enterprise is sufficient to find a single conspiracy under RICO, even if one's illegal activity is distinct and unrelated to that of other members of the enterprise.

Braverman v. United States (S.Ct. 1942) L, MIB

Facts: Ds were bootleggers who violated several provisions of the Internal Revenue laws as per one continuing agreement.

Issue: May a single continuing agreement to commit several criminal offenses be punished as several conspiracies?

Rule: A single agreement, even one that involves several offenses, can only be punished as one conspiracy. Conspiracy is a crime to punish agreement, not criminal acts, which are punished separately.

United States v. James (1976) L

Facts: The FBI came to arrest a fugitive at the headquarters of the Republic of New Africa. Ds opened fire as they were trained to do.

Issue: Must a conspiracy involve an express agreement, and must a conspirator know of all of the details or phases of a conspiracy?

Rule: An agreement can be inferred from the circumstances, and knowledge of all details and phases of a conspiracy is unnecessary.

State v. St. Christopher (1975) L

Facts: D approached his cousin about murdering D's mother. The cousin feigned to agree to the plan and informed the police.

Issue: Can one be convicted of conspiracy even if the other conspirator only feigns agreement to the plan?

Rule: Traditionally, one cannot be convicted of conspiracy without a bona fide co-conspirator, but the new view holds such a conviction valid.

United States v. Chagra (1986) L

Facts: D was indicted for conspiracy to commit second-degree murder, which requires malice aforethought but not premeditation.

Issue: Can there be an agreement to conspire without premeditation?

Rule: Conspiracy requires an agreement to accomplish a criminal offense and the offense's specific intent. Generally, these two states of mind collapse into one, but they can be analyzed individually. Thus, an agreement to commit a specific-intent crime can be established without proving premeditation.

Shaw v. Director of Public Prosecutions (1961) L, MIB

Facts: D published a directory wherein prostitutes advertised.

Issue: Does the offense of conspiracy to corrupt public morals exist?

Rule: It is within the scope of the common law to create offenses such as corruption of public morals in order to protect the safety, order, and moral welfare of the state.

Dissent: The doctrine of conspiracy should not be extended so far in the creation of new unlawful acts.

Concurrence: The right to expand the doctrine of conspiracy is valid. If the people did not think so, a jury would never convict one of an offense which overstepped the boundaries of the common law.

Ventimiglia v. United States (1957) L

Facts: Ds paid a union official to issue their employees "working cards." The Taft-Hartly Act forbids such action if the official is a representative of any of Ds' employees, which he was not.

Issue: Can there be a conviction for conspiracy even though the criminal object of the agreement is impossible to achieve?

Rule: There can be no conspiracy when the object of an agreement is inherently impossible. However, conspiracy can exist if the object of an agreement is only physically impossible.

United States v. Michelena-Orovio (1983) L

Facts: D was a seaman found on a Colombian ship bound for the U.S. laden with twelve tons of marijuana.

Issue: Can knowledge of a conspiracy and joinder therein be inferred from participation in one part of an illegal scheme?

Rule: Knowledge of and joinder in a conspiracy can be inferred from participation in one part of an illegal scheme when the act participated in suggests that one relies on and expects further illegal acts to proceed from one's own act; that the act is minor is not important.

Dissent: One who conspires to import drugs does not necessarily conspire to possess with intent to distribute. Participation in the one should not automatically infer participation in the other.

Grunewald v. United States (S.Ct. 1957) L

Facts: Ds conspired to evade taxes, which had a three-year statute of limitations. The main objectives were attained more than three years before the indictment, but acts of concealment were performed within three years of the indictment.

Issue: Are acts of concealing the existence of a conspiracy sufficient to imply a secondary element of secrecy to the agreement?

Rule: A secondary element of secrecy cannot be inferred from acts of concealment done after the attainment of a conspiracy's main objectives. However, acts of concealment done in furtherance of the main criminal objectives of a conspiracy are sufficient for an inference of a secondary element.

Iannelli v. United States (S.Ct. 1975) L, MIB

Facts: Ds violated several federal gambling statutes.

Issue: May one be convicted for both a substantive crime and conspiracy to commit that crime?

Rule: One may be convicted of both a substantive crime and conspiracy to commit that crime when legislative intent so suggests, thus superseding Wharton's Rule. Wharton's Rule applies when an offense is only committed by two people and when conspiracy to so act does not pose a significant threat to the public.

Dissent: It is double jeopardy to convict one of a substantive crime and of conspiracy to so act. Also, punishment for a substantive crime adequately satisfies social concerns.

United States v. Turkette (S.Ct. 1981) L, J, MIB

Facts: D headed a group of individuals associated in fact for the purpose of trafficking drugs, committing arson, bribery, etc. D and his group also committed acts of racketeering.

Issue: Under RICO, does "enterprise" encompass both legitimate and illegitimate enterprises?

Rule: RICO statutory language does not limit the scope of "enterprise" to only infiltration of legitimate enterprises.

United States v. Feola (S.Ct. 1975) L, J, MIB

Facts: Ds planned to swindle or rob heroin dealers. The dealers were actually undercover agents. Ds assaulted the agents.

Issue: Can conspiracy require a higher mens rea than the substantive crime conspired to?

Rule: Where certain knowledge is not needed for conviction of a substantive offense requiring a mens rea, such knowledge is not required for a conviction of conspiring to commit that offense.

Dissent: Although this principal is correct, the substantive crime should require a higher mens rea.

Bailey v. United States (1969) L, J

Facts: An unidentified man robbed another. D was present at the robbery, had a slight prior association with the robber, and fled when the robbery was over. The robber was never caught or identified.

Issue: Is presence alone sufficient for derivative liability?

Rule: Participation of some sort is necessary for derivative liability. Prior association or flight, alone or combined with presence, is still insufficient for liability.

Dissent: A combination of prior association, presence, and flight should be enough to find derivative liability.

State v. Grebe (1970) L

Facts: D, D's son, and D's dog got in a fight with the neighbors. D's son fatally wounded one of them.

Issue: Is derivative liability dependant upon intentional action?

Rule: To be held liable for aiding and abetting, one's actions need to be intended to aid or abet another. Simple knowledge of another's intent to commit an offense is insufficient for derivative liability.

Dissent: Knowledge of another's unlawful intent should be sufficient to find the existence of intentional aiding and abetting.

People v. Marshall (1961) L, J

Facts: Knowing that his friend was drunk, D gave him the use of D's car. While D was at home in bed, the friend ran head on into another car, killing himself and the other driver.

Issue: Is knowledge of actions resulting in a criminal offense necessary for derivative liability?

Rule: Derivative liability requires complicity in the misconduct. There can be no complicity in the misconduct without knowledge of the actions which result in an offense.

United States v. Carter (1971) L

Facts: D aided and abetted another in the robbery of a cab driver. The other man shot and killed the cab driver before taking the money.

Issue: Can one be liable for murder when one's acts only amount to aiding the commission of a non-lethal felony?

Rule: If one is found derivatively liable for a felony, and if a victim dies in furtherance of the felony, one can also be liable for murder by the felony-murder doctrine.

Concurrence/Dissent: Liability under the felony-murder rule should not lie unless a killing is committed in furtherance of a common design or plan between principal and accomplice.

People v. Kessler (1974) L, J

Facts: D sat in the car while his companions entered a tavern to commit burglary. One of D's companions shot and wounded the tavern owner with a gun he picked up during the burglary.

Issue: Can one be liable for the acts of an accomplice which one did not intend to occur?

Rule: When one aids another in the planning or commission of an offense, one is liable for any conduct of that person which is in furtherance of the planned and intended act.

Dissent: An accessory's liability should extend only to the commission of the planned acts.

People v. Taylor (1974) L

Facts: D sat in the car while his accomplices committed robbery, during which one of the accomplices was murdered.

Issue: Can one be liable for an offense when all of one's accomplices have been acquitted?

Rule: If one's accomplices are acquitted on a charge because an element of the offense cannot be proved, the court can be collaterally estopped from finding one liable for that offense.

United States v. Bryan (1973) L

Facts: D aided the commission of larceny. The principal was acquitted because he was only an innocent dupe. The lower court still held that larceny had been committed and that D was an accessory.

Issue: Must a principal be convicted in order find another liable as aider and abettor?

Rule: Conviction of a principal is not necessary for accomplice liability when there is proof that the offense occurred.

Dissent: An exception should be when one is charged with aiding and abetting a specific principal, who is subsequently acquitted.

State v. Thomas (1976) L

Facts: D saw another boy's gun and was invited to go up onto the roof to shoot police. D went up onto the roof, D left the roof, and the other boy fatally shot a police officer.

Issue: Is withdrawal from an offense without more sufficient to prevent a finding of derivative liability?

Rule: Mere withdrawal from an offense is inadequate to avoid liability. One needs to communicate one's withdrawal, show disapproval as to the common design, or actively remove one's support.

Queen v. Tyrrell (1893) L

Facts: D aided and abetted a man in obtaining unlawful carnal knowledge of her while she was under age.

Issue: Is it possible to aid and abet one's own statutory rape?

Rule: It is legally impossible to aid and abet one's own statutory rape. These statutes exist to protect young women, and it is contrary to the statute's intent to punish those it is designed to protect.

Concurrence: Rape statutes make no mention of the victim being an accomplice to the offense.

State v. Beaudry (1985) L, DS

Facts: D was the designated agent for a corporate license to sell alcohol. D's employee kept D's tavern open later than statutorily allowed for the purpose of entertaining two friends.

Issue: Can an employer be vicariously liable for the illegal actions of an employee?

Rule: An employer is vicariously liable for an employee's illegal acts committed within the scope of employment which extends to all job-related activities, employer-permitted actions, and acts close in nature to permitted activities. Absence of sanction or prohibition by an employer does not preclude vicarious liability.

Dissent: Actions not permitted or prohibited by the employer should be outside the scope of employment.

City of Missoula v. Shea (1983) L

Facts: D received sixty parking violations over two years.

Issue: Is a *prima facie* presumption of liability upon proof of illegal parking and ownership violative of the Due Process Clause?

Rule: It is unconstitutional to make a car owner *prima-facie* liable just because her vehicle is illegally parked. This shifts the burden of persuasion, contradicting presumption of innocence. However, it is constitutional to impose vicarious liability with traffic violations.

Dissent: A rebuttable *prima facie* establishment of liability is not unconstitutional and is good public policy.

Concurrence in the Dissent: Specific intent is not an element of traffic and parking misdemeanors.

Stephens v. State (1987) L

Facts: A friend came to stay at D's home. The friend committed robbery, told D, and stayed another night. The police arrived, and D denied knowledge of the robbery.

Issue 1: Is one who falsely denies knowledge of a crime or allows an offender to stay in one's home an accessory after the fact?

Rule 1: Denial of knowledge and permitting an offender to stay in one's home is insufficient affirmative action to make one an accessory after the fact. Mere passive actions are insufficient.

Issue 2: Is self-motivated intent sufficient to establish liability as an accessory after the fact?

Rule 2: Self-motivated intent is insufficient to establish intent to hinder, prevent, or delay apprehension of an offender. Actions must be done with intent to aid or be likely to aid an offender.

United States v. Magness (1972) L

Facts: D rented a motel room for a fugitive. Days later, the FBI approached D and informed D of the warrant for the fugitive's arrest.

Issue: Does harboring or concealing an offender without knowledge of the offense constitute the crime of accessory after the fact?

Rule: Actions of harboring or concealment without knowledge of another's crime do not constitute accessory after the fact.

Holland v. State (1974) L, MIB

Facts: D, city manager, discovered that an employee was growing marijuana. D informed the captain of police and confronted the employee, who resigned. D and the captain decided to handle the situation as an internal affair.

Issue: Is failure report a felony to the authorities a crime?

Rule: It is not a crime to fail to report a felony. Long ago at common law the offense of misprision of felony existed, but its purpose is now obsolete and incompatible with present American law.

Pace v. State (1967) KW

Facts: D was driving a car with Rootes in the back seat. D picked up a hitchhiker, whom Rootes robbed while in the car.

Issue: Is mere presence at the scene of a crime sufficient for liability as an accessory before the fact?

Rule: Presence without anything else is insufficient to establish accessorial liability. There must be some form, however slight, of affirmative conduct to find the existence of a common design or purpose which was aided or abetted.

State v. Ochoa (1937) KW

Facts: Ds participated in a violent riot involving the police and resulting in the death of the sheriff.

Issue 1: Must felonious intent be formed before commission of an offense in order to be guilty of aiding and abetting?

Rule 1: One does not need to share in a common design prior to commission of an offense in order to aid and abet that offense. Realizing that an offense is being committed and continuing to engage in conduct which aids that offense imputes the required intent.

Issue 2: Can one be charged with both commission of an offense and aiding and abetting the same offense?

Rule 2: One can be charged with commission of an offense as well as with aiding and abetting an offense, although one can only be convicted of one or the other. This is not prejudicial, because there is no difference at law between one who aids and abets an offense and one who commits an offense.

State v. Tally (1894) KW

Facts: D's relatives rode to the next town to kill Ross. D telegraphed to the next town to prevent delivery of a previous telegram warning Ross of D's relatives. D's relatives killed Ross, probably before he would have been able to get any telegram.

Issue: Can one be liable for aiding and abetting, even if one's aid is of no actual use to the principal committing the offense?
Rule: If one's aid puts a victim at any disadvantage, even one that doesn't materially change the situation, one has aided and abetted the offense. This is true even if the person who commits the offense or the victim is unaware of the aid.
Dissent: It should be shown that the aid actually caused a disadvantage which would have changed the situation.

Wilson v. People (1939) KW

Facts: D helped Pierce burglarize a drugstore so as to get Pierce arrested. D thought this would enable him to retrieve his watch, which D thought Pierce stole.
Issue: Can one be an accomplice for assisting another to commit an offense if one's intent is only to act as a detective or spy?
Rule: One who acts as a feigned accomplice in order to trap another is not liable because an accessory must share the principal's intent.

People v. Beeman (1984) KW

Facts: D gave friends information which they used in perpetrating a robbery. D knew of their intent but did not want to be involved.
Issue: To be guilty of aiding and abetting, is knowledge of a principal's intent sufficient or must one have criminal intent?
Rule: An accomplice must not only have knowledge of the principal's intent, but must also intend to commit, encourage, or facilitate the commission of an offense.

Ex Parte Marley (1946) KW

Facts: D's employee gave insufficient weight to a woman buying meat in violation of a statute on weights and measures. D was not present during the transaction and did not instruct the employee to so act.
Issue: Can an employer be liable for illegal actions of an employee?
Rule: An employer can be liable for strict liability offenses committed by an employee even when not present during the offense and without knowledge, in order to protect the public when proof of intent is almost impossible to show. Valid defenses are that an employee's actions were accidental or were mistaken.
Dissent: No considerations of public policy merit a departure from the rule that criminal intent is a necessary element of a crime.

State v. Verive (1981) KW

Facts: Woodall hired Verive to beat up Galvin, a scheduled witness in an upcoming trial. Verive was charged with conspiracy to dissuade a witness and attempt to dissuade a witness.

Issue: May a person be convicted of both an attempt to commit a crime and conspiracy to commit that same crime?

Rule: Attempt and conspiracy are separate and distinct offenses. Conspiracy requires an agreement, while attempt requires an act beyond mere preparation. One may be charged with and convicted of both.

Callanan v. United States (S.Ct. 1961) KW

Facts: D was convicted of both conspiracy and the substantive offense, resulting in a sentence longer than the maximum allowed under the substantive offense.

Issue: Can one be punished cumulatively for both conspiracy to commit an offense and the offense itself?

Rule: One can be punished cumulatively for both conspiracy and the completed offense since the detrimental nature of conspiracy is distinct from that of the object of a conspiracy.

Griffin v. State (1970) KW

Facts: A policeman went to investigate a car accident. D, the driver started to attack the officer. A fight ensued involving the onlookers.

Issue: Can a conspiratorial agreement be proven by circumstantial evidence?

Rule: A conspiratorial agreement can be found when evidence, even of a circumstantial nature, establishes a concert of action with common intent and object.

United States v. Diaz (1988) KW

Facts: Diaz was apprehended by drug enforcement agents during an attempted drug deal. Peirallo, another dealer involved in the transaction, was convicted of carrying a firearm under a separate statute. As a result, Diaz' sentence was increased by five years.

Issue: Is a conspirator liable for crimes committed by a co-conspirator?

Rule: A party to a continuing conspiracy may be liable for substantive offenses committed by a co-conspirator in furtherance of the conspiracy.

United States v. Spock (1969) KW

Facts: Ds wrote and signed an anti-Vietnam document advocating the violation of the Universal Military Training and Service Act.

Issue: Does a politically active group's counsel and offer of aid to those who will commit an illegal act constitute conspiracy?

Rule: An agreement can be inferred from political statements when evidence suggests concerted activity towards the commission of an offense, rather than just parallel conduct. Specific intent to adhere to the illegal acts advocated must also be found.

Dissent: Action in the political and public forum should be protected by the First Amendment. Such acts do not threaten the public in the way that normal conspiracies do.

United States v. Fox (1942) KW

Facts: D pleaded guilty to conspiracy and testified against the co-conspirators. The prosecution ended up entering a *nolle prosequi.*

Issue: Can one be guilty of conspiracy if no co-conspirator is found guilty as well?

Rule: If all co-conspirators are acquitted, one may not be singly convicted for conspiracy. However, if the co-conspirators are just not found guilty (as with a motion of *nolle prosequi*), one can be singly guilty of conspiracy.

United States v. Indelicato (1989) KW

Facts: Indelicato was charged with murdering three reputed organized crime leaders at a New York Italian restaurant. RICO, the statute governing organized crime prosecutions, required the Government to prove the existence of a "pattern of racketeering activity."

Issue: If multiple acts are committed simultaneously as part of a single criminal transaction, does this establish a "pattern of racketeering activity" within the meaning of RICO?

Rule: If there are similarities between certain acts with respect to victim, methodology, goal, etc., and if there is evidence of a threat of continuation of racketeering activity, the acts may constitute a "pattern" under RICO even though they are nearly simultaneous.

United States v. Neapolitan (1986) KW

Facts: Neapolitan, a minor player in an auto-theft ring, was indicted on five counts of mail fraud and one count of racketeering conspiracy under

RICO. Neapolitan was acquitted of all the mail fraud counts, but was convicted of the RICO conspiracy.

Issue: May a person be convicted of a RICO conspiracy if he has not agreed to personally commit the crimes prohibited by the statute?

Rule: The Government may convict a person under RICO if he joins a conspiracy, the goal of which is the conduct of or participation in the affairs of an enterprise through a pattern of racketeering activity. The conspiracy section of RICO does not require the Government to prove that a defendant agreed to personally commit the requisite acts.

United States v. Falcone (1940) W
Facts: Ds sold sugar, yeast, and cans to bootleggers.

Issue: Are sellers of legal goods conspirators when they know their goods are being put to illegal uses?

Rule: A seller's knowledge of illegal use of his goods is insufficient to render him a conspirator. A seller must promote the illegal venture, have a stake in the venture, or know of the conspiracy.

Direct Sales Co. v. United States (S.Ct. 1943) W
Facts: D sold a small-town doctor huge quantities of morphine at reduced prices for many years.

Issue: Can sellers of restricted goods be conspirators solely due to knowledge of illegal use of their products?

Rule: Legal sellers of restricted goods can be guilty of conspiracy when knowledge is inferable from volume, frequency, and prolonged repetition of sales and when there is unlawful intent to further a buyer's illegal project.

Commonwealth v. Dyer (1923) W, MIB
(Cited incorrectly to 1922 in W)
Facts: Ds allegedly conspired to create a monopoly in fresh fish.

Issue: Must the object of a conspiracy's agreement be criminal?

Rule: The object of a conspiracy can either be criminal or unlawful. Unlawful acts are not statutorily criminal but in the context of a concerted agreement can be criminally punished due to an injurious effect on the public interest.

United States v. Brown (1985) DS
Facts: D told a heroin dealer that the buyer, actually an undercover cop, looked okay and that the dealer should sell to the agent.

Issue: Can presence and knowledge of a crime be sufficient to find participation in a conspiracy?

Rule: Mere presence and knowledge of a crime is insufficient to prove joinder in a conspiracy, but when combined with circumstantial evidence suggesting agreement, a conspiracy can be found.

Dissent: Without proof of an agreement or at least of a stake in the outcome of an illegal activity, one should not be found a conspirator.

United States v. Jackson (1982) DS

Facts: Ds separately hired an arsonist to burn different buildings. The two Ds had separate motives, and their "jobs" were unrelated.

Issue: Are similar purposes and a common link sufficient evidence of a single conspiracy?

Rule: In order to find one conspiracy rather than several, there must be a common aim or purpose among those involved; a common link or similar purposes alone is insufficient.

Regle v. State (1970) DS

Facts: D conspired to rob a restaurant with an undercover agent, an informer, an insane man, and another who received a *nolle prosequi*.

Issue: Can one be the only one convicted for a conspiracy?

Rule: The essence of conspiracy is a mental confederation between two people. Therefore, if only one person has the requisite intent, a conspiracy cannot exist. However, one can be convicted alone for conspiracy, when a co-conspirator had the requisite intent, but for various reasons was not prosecuted and/or found guilty.

United States v.
United States Gypsum Co. (S.Ct. 1978) DS

Facts: Over the telephone, Ds exchanged current and future price information on gypsum board, used in construction.

Issue: Can a conviction for conspiracy lie without a finding of intent?

Rule: Even in the context of anti-trust litigation, a conspiracy cannot be found without proof of mens rea. Moreover, the level of culpability required in anti-trust cases is knowledge.

Concurrence/Dissent: There is not a great difference between requiring a mens rea of knowledge and allowing an inference of intent from causal effects.

Concurrence/Dissent: The required level of culpability should be purpose and not just knowledge.

United States v. Sutherland (1981) DS, J

Facts: One D, a judge, worked separately and at different times with the other two Ds to fix traffic tickets.

Issue 1: In RICO, can the agreement and the requisite two acts of racketeering be shown through circumstantial evidence?

Rule 1: In a RICO trial the two acts of racketeering and the agreement can be established through circumstantial evidence.

Issue 2: May two separate conspiracies be tried as one "enterprise conspiracy" under RICO?

Rule 2: Multiple pre-RICO conspiracies can only be joined as one "enterprise conspiracy" when there is an agreement to commit a substantive RICO offense; this agreement may be established by circumstantial evidence.

State v. Walden (1981) DS

Facts: D watched and did nothing while Hoskins assaulted D's son.

Issue: Is mere presence enough for accomplice liability?

Rule: Generally, presence alone is insufficient for accomplice liability. An exception occurs when one is a friend of the principal and one's presence is encouraging. If one's presence alone amounts to aid or communication of encouragement, then one can be held liable. This liability is not based upon a failed duty to prevent an offense, although such a duty can be considered as circumstantial evidence.

State v. Walden (1982) DS

Facts: (Appeal from the lower court.)

Issue: Is one's presence and failure to act when one is under an affirmative duty sufficient to establish accessorial liability?

Rule: The common-law affirmative duty of parents to their children as well as statutory affirmative duties allows for accessory liability for presence alone. These duties are more than circumstantial evidence that one's presence amounts to communication of encouragement.

State v. Smith (1984) DS

Facts: Ds robbed a store. One used fear as inducement, and the other used a hammer. Both were convicted of armed robbery.

Issue: In robbery, is the use of a deadly weapon by one principal applicable to others, making all guilty of armed robbery?

Rule: The use of a deadly weapon in perpetrating a robbery is only applicable to an accomplice if he aided or counseled the use of the deadly weapon.

Dissent: An accomplice's failure to say anything about the use of a deadly weapon should, without more, make its use imputable.

United States v. Alvarez (1985) DS

Facts: Ds were part of a conspiracy to effect a drug deal. During a bust, a federal agent was killed, as well as the dealer who shot him.

Issue: Can co-conspirators be liable for homicide when it is not the object of the agreement?

Rule: Co-conspirators can be held liable for all reasonably foreseeable results of an agreement, even if a result is homicide. Inquiry into the individual culpability of a particular co-conspirator is unnecessary.

State v. Chism (1983) DS

Facts: D and his lover Duke saw D's one-legged uncle, Lloyd, stab his ex-wife several times. Lloyd put her body in Duke's car and told the boys to drive him to the forest. D and Duke then dropped off Lloyd and the body. Hours later, D told police where the body was.

Issue: What are the necessary elements of accessory after the fact?

Rule: Accessory after the fact requires completion of a felony, knowledge of the felony, giving of aid to the felon, and intent that the felon will avoid or escape arrest, trial, conviction, or punishment.

Dissent: Failure to act is not proof of intent to aid. Affirmative actions to show purposeful aiding of a felon should be required.

United States v. Peltz (1970) J

Facts: D used information from an SEC employee for monetary benefit. The government lost nothing tangible due to D's acts.

Issue 1: Can circumstantial evidence prove an agreement's existence?

Rule 1: Testimony establishing a working relationship is sufficient to rationally conclude that an agreement exists.

Issue 2: Must the object of a conspiracy be statutorily criminal?

Rule 2: Even an act that is not punishable as a substantive offense by itself can be the object of a conspiracy.

People v. Foster (1983) J, MIB

Facts: With the object of robbing an old man's home, D entered into an agreement with a police informer.

Issue: Can one be guilty of conspiracy absent another's intent to enter into agreement?

Rule: The bilateral theory of conspiracy requires two people and a sharing of intent. It is the applicable standard absent a clear intent to adopt the unilateral theory of conspiracy.

McDonald v. United States (1937) J

Facts: Kidnappers received marked bills in ransom. D exchanged the marked bills for clean ones, but was not part of the kidnapping.

Issue: If one enters into a conspiracy after it has started, is one liable for the acts committed prior to entry?

Rule: When one enters into a pre-existing conspiracy prior to the achievement of its object, one can be liable for all acts and offenses of the conspiracy, committed either before or after joinder.

State v. Parker (1968) J

Facts: Larry gave D and two others a ride in his car. One of the passengers robbed and assaulted Larry while D looked on.

Issue: Can mere presence make one guilty of aiding and abetting?

Rule: Presence at an offense one knows is taking place and lack of objection can suggest one is an accessory through approval of the action.

Merrell v. United States (S.Ct. 1983) J

Facts: D was convicted for cleaning and serving coffee in an illegal gambling parlor. He was not involved in the gambling operation.

Issue: Must an accomplice's actions be necessary to the illegal activity or merely helpful?

Rule: (Petition for writ of certiorari denied.)

Dissent: (White, J.) Though lower courts have held that helpful actions to illegal activity are sufficient for complicity, others hold that liability requires one's actions be necessary.

United States v. Licavoli (1984) J

Facts: Ds were mobsters who committed murder and bribery. Some were previously tried for these substantive offenses.

Issue: What is the nature of the predicate acts required by RICO?

Rule: Under RICO, murder is a predicate act. Conspiracy to commit and commission of an offense can both be predicate acts. Acquittal or conviction for an offense does not preclude use as a predicate act.

Concurrence: Although these principals go against normal rules of construction, RICO is a unique and special offense which needs to be given broad application and interpretation.

Commonwealth v. Benesch (1935) MIB

Facts: Ds conspired to sell unapproved securities.

Issue: When an offense is only *malum prohibitum*, can one be convicted of conspiracy without proof of an intent to do wrong?

Rule: When an act is not in itself wrong, but only *malum prohibitum*, wrongful intent must be shown. This does not create the necessity of proving wrongful intent for conviction of such substantive crimes, rather only when they are the object of conspiracy.

United States v. Dege (S.Ct. 1960) MIB

Facts: Ds, husband and wife, were indicted for conspiracy to illicitly bring goods into the U.S. with intent to defraud the government.

Issue: Can a husband and wife alone be convicted of conspiracy?

Rule: A husband and wife alone can be convicted of conspiracy because they are no longer regarded as one person by the law.

Dissent: A statute must be construed according to its intent at the time of enactment, in which case the husband-wife doctrine is valid. There are also policy reasons for keeping the doctrine.

United States v. Falcone (S.Ct. 1940) MIB

Facts: Ds sold sugar, yeast, and cans to bootleggers.

Issue: Is a seller of goods who knows that they will be put to illicit use a co-conspirator?

Rule: Conviction for conspiracy cannot rest on proof of knowingly supplying an illicit offender alone. Without proof of participation in or knowledge of a conspiracy, a supplier is not a co-conspirator.

Note: This is an affirmation of the Court of Appeals for the Second Circuit's opinion of this case. See, Ch. 7, above.

Jeffers v. United States (S.Ct. 1977) MIB

Facts: D headed a drug distribution ring in Gary, Indiana.

Issue: Is conspiracy to distribute drugs a lesser included offense of conducting a continuing criminal enterprise to violate the drug laws?
Rule: Conspiracy to distribute drugs is a lesser included offense of conducting a continuing criminal enterprise to violate drug laws. Therefore, upon conviction for the lesser offense, the Double Jeopardy Clause precludes trial for the greater, except under certain exceptions.
Dissent: A defendant's failure to alert a prosecutor of the possibility that one offense may be a lesser included offense should not be one of the exceptions to the Double Jeopardy Clause.

State v. Moretti
State v. Schmidt (1967) MIB
Facts: Ds conspired to perform an abortion on an undercover agent who was not actually pregnant.
Issue: Can there be conviction for conspiracy where attainment of the unlawful object is inherently impossible?
Rule: There can be no conviction for conspiracy when achievement of the object of the agreement is inherently impossible. However, if the object is only factually impossible in a given situation, a conviction will lie. Non-pregnancy is a factual impossibility to abortion.
Dissent: It is inherently impossible to perform an abortion on a non-pregnant woman.

United States v. Garguilo (1962) MIB
Facts: D, Macchia, accompanied Garguilo several times while Garguilo was engaged in counterfeiting.
Issue: Does mere presence and knowledge of an offense make one an accomplice?
Rule: Presence and knowledge alone are insufficient for complicity. Some evidence of aiding the offense is necessary.
Concurrence/Dissent: Although knowledge of an offense alone is insufficient for aiding and abetting, presence of a friend is adequate encouragement to support such a finding.

United States v. Peoni (1938) MIB
Facts: D sold counterfeit bills to Regno, who sold them to Dorsey; all three knew the bills were fake. Dorsey was arrested for possession.
Issue: If one's original act has as its natural consequence the commission of a criminal offense, can one be held an accessory?

Rule: Once one's connection with an act is over, one cannot be held criminally liable for any consequences. One is not liable for knowledge that eventually one's goods may be unlawfully used.

Standefer v. United States (S.Ct. 1980) MIB

Facts: D gave an IRS agent several vacation trips. The agent was acquitted on some of the counts, but D was convicted on all counts.

Issue: Can an accessory be convicted when the principal in the first degree is acquitted?

Rule: Statutory liability now allows for conviction of an accessory if the principal is acquitted.

People v. Zierlion (1959) MIB

Facts: Four men went to steal a safe. Finding it too heavy to remove, they went for help. They returned with D and were arrested.

Issue: Can an accessory after the fact be convicted as a principal in the original offense?

Rule: If one's intent is to be an accessory after the fact, and one lacks the additional intent to commit the original offense, one can only be liable for accessory after the fact.

Dissent: When an offense is incomplete, one who joins in order to complete the offense should be just as liable as one who aided and abetted from the commencement of the offense.

Commonwealth v. McIlwain School Bus Lines, Inc. (1980) MIB

Facts: One of D's cars ran over a child.

Issue: May a corporation be criminally liable for homicide by vehicle?

Rule: An absolute-liability criminal statute allows for an assumption of legislative purpose to impose liability on a corporation unless the contrary plainly appears. Thus, a corporation can be held criminally liable for homicide by vehicle.

Chapter 8

JUSTIFICATION AND EXCUSE

I. INTRODUCTION

A. Generally
A person will sometimes violate the letter of the law, but defend his actions on the basis that the conduct was justified or excusable.

B. Justification and Excuse Distinguished
Justification is the claim that a technically illegal action was actually the proper thing to do in a given situation. One who makes an excuse admits that the act violated the law, but asserts that the actor is not to blame because an ordinary person faced with similar circumstances would have done the same thing.

II. USE OF FORCE FOR SELF-DEFENSE

A. When Force Is Permitted
The use of force is permitted when it is necessary as a means of protection against the use of unlawful force by another. One may only use the amount of force necessary to protect against the threatened unlawful harm. See, MPC § 3.04.

B. Exceptions

1. Resisting Arrest
Force may not be used to resist an arrest, even if the arrest is unlawful.

2. Trespasser
Force may not be used by a trespasser who is being forcibly evicted, unless the trespasser is threatened with death or serious harm.

3. Original Aggressor
One may not use force if he or she wrongfully caused the confrontation.

C.   Use of Deadly Force

1. Model Penal Code
   According to MPC § 3.04, the use of deadly force is permitted when the actor believes it necessary to protect against death, serious bodily harm, kidnapping or rape.

2. Objective and Subjective Standards
   The courts have widely differed on what standard should be applied to determine if a person's belief in the need to use deadly force was justified.

   a. The Objective Standard
      The majority of courts require a person to show that the belief in the need to use deadly force was reasonable.

      i.   Pure Objectivity
           Under a purely objective test, the use of deadly force is justified if a reasonable person in the same immediate situation as the defendant would have believed such action was necessary.

      ii. Flexible Objectivity
           Some courts ask how a reasonable person would have reacted, if that reasonable person were of the same size as the particular defendant, or of the same sex, or had undergone prior experiences that the defendant had experienced.

   b. The Subjective Standard
      A minority of jurisdictions use the subjective standard. Under this test, the actor needs only to demonstrate that he or she genuinely believed the use deadly force was necessary, regardless of what a reasonable person in the same situation would have believed.

3. The Duty to Retreat
   The courts are divided as to whether a victim is ever under a duty to retreat from an attacker. In some jurisdictions, the use of deadly

force is forbidden when an individual can safely retreat. See, MPC § 3.04.

a. One is obliged to retreat only if he *knows* he can do so in *complete* safety.

b. One is never required to retreat from one's own home.

D. Protecting Others
Force may be used when it is reasonably necessary to protect another against unlawful bodily harm. This is subject to the same limitations as the use of force to protect oneself.

1. Mistaken Intervenor
There are divergent views on punishing an individual who mistakenly intervenes; e.g., someone who defends a third party against an undercover police officer.

a. At Own Risk
In some jurisdictions one intervenes at one's own risk, and an intervenor will be punished if his assumptions turn out to be mistaken.

b. Permitted If Reasonable Belief
In other states, intervention is excused so long as the actor reasonably believes it is necessary to prevent unlawful harm.

2. Model Penal Code
According to MPC § 3.05 the belief in the need to intervene must be reasonable, and the intervenor may not use excessive force.

E. Protecting Property
A reasonable amount of non-deadly force may be used to prevent unlawful interference with property. See, MPC § 3.06.

1. Deadly Force
Deadly force may not be used solely for the protection of property because life is more valuable than property.

    a. In One's Home
    Some states hold that deadly force may be used in the defense of one's home if there is a reasonable belief that the intruder intends to commit a felony.

    b. Limitations
    Other jurisdictions limit the use of deadly force to instances where there is a reasonable fear of certain specifically delineated dangerous felonies.

  2. Deadly Mechanical Devices
  Most jurisdictions now bar the use of deadly mechanical devices for the protection of property since the devices pose a menace to innocent intruders such as police officers.

F.   Law Enforcement
A law enforcement officer may use any reasonable force necessary to carry out an arrest. See, MPC § 3.07.

  1. Deadly Force
  A law enforcement officer may not use deadly force in making an arrest unless it is necessary to prevent death or serious bodily harm.

  2. Fleeing Felon
  Deadly force may not be used to stop one who is fleeing from a non-dangerous felony unless the suspect poses an immediate threat of death or serious harm.

III.   DURESS

The defense of duress may be employed if threats by a third party against a defendant or member of his family created a reasonable fear of imminent death or serious bodily harm. See, MPC § 2.09.

A.   Not a Defense For Murder
Generally, duress is not a permissible defense for the killing of an innocent person.

B.   Imminence Requirement Relaxed
A few jurisdictions have softened the imminence requirement, instead asking if a reasonable person would have been able to resist the threats made to the defendant.

IV.   NECESSITY

Criminal actions may be excused on the grounds that they were necessary in order to prevent a greater harm. This is discussed in MPC § 3.02. However, the defense is not available in some situations:

A.   Never an Excuse for Killing
One may not kill an innocent person to save one's own life.

B.   Not Available if at Fault
The defendant must not have brought about the circumstances which caused the criminal act to be necessary.

C.   Not a Means of Protest
One may not use the necessity defense for criminal acts, such as sit-ins, aimed at blocking a governmental policy.

V.   ENTRAPMENT

The entrapment defense may be used when a criminal act would not have occurred but for the trickery, persuasion or fraud of a law enforcement official.

A.   Majority Rule
The majority of jurisdictions hold that the entrapment defense is valid only if it can be shown that the government's actions implanted the criminal design in the defendant's mind. In these jurisdictions, the government need only show that the defendant was predisposed to committing the crime in order to defeat the entrapment defense.

B.   Minority Rule
A minority of jurisdictions only require the defendant to show that a reasonable person would have succumbed to the government's

inducements. Under this approach, adopted by MPC § 2.13, it does not matter if the defendant had a predisposition towards the crime.

VI. INTOXICATION AND ADDICTION

A.   Voluntary Intoxication
Voluntary intoxication is available as a defense in some jurisdictions if one can show that the intoxication prevented him from forming the requisite intent. In other jurisdictions, no distinction is made between general and specific intent crimes, and thus voluntary intoxication is never a defense. See also, MPC § 2.08.

1.   General Intent Crimes
The common law and most jurisdictions today do not allow voluntary intoxication as an excuse for general intent crimes.

   a.   No Escaping Liability
   The decision to get drunk is usually a conscious one, and people should not use it as a tool to escape liability.

   b.   Drinking as a Reckless Act
   The act of getting drunk can be viewed as reckless in and of itself, and thus the defendant will have the requisite mens rea for all crimes except those requiring a specific intent.

   c.   Protecting the Public
   Society has a strong interest in being protected from individuals who intentionally get drunk and lose all inhibitions.

2.   Specific Intent Crimes
Voluntary intoxication in some states is a valid defense to a specific intent crime.

   a.   Incapable of Intent
   The intoxication defense will work if the defendant can show he was so drunk he was unable to form the specific intent required for conviction.

Example: If D is drunk and randomly fires a shot at his neighbor, D cannot be charged with "assault with intent to kill" if he was too drunk to have formed such an intent.

    b. "But for Intoxication" Irrelevant
If a defendant admits to having the requisite intent, it is not a valid defense to argue that one would not have had the intent but for the intoxication.

B.   Involuntary Intoxication

    1. May be a Defense
Involuntary intoxication can be a complete defense, if the defendant can show:

    a. The intoxication took place under duress, or

    b. The intoxication was the unforeseeable side-effect of a medically prescribed drug.

    2. Stronger Effect No Defense
A defendant will not be excused by showing that an intoxicating substance had an effect that was stronger than anticipated.

C.   Addiction
Addiction to a narcotic will not excuse criminal conduct.

    1. Addiction not a Crime
A state may not declare addiction a crime in and of itself.

    2. Addiction not a Defense
If addiction were a valid defense, then addicts could commit all kinds of crimes in the pursuit of drugs.

    3. Protecting Society
Society has a right to be protected from the acts resulting from other people's chemical dependencies.

VII. INSANITY

A.   Not Guilty by Insanity
One may avoid liability for criminal acts by asserting that he or she was insane at the time of the crime.

1. Fairness
It is unfair to punish people for acts that result from mental illness.

2. No Deterrence
Punishing insane people does not have a deterrent effect, as it is difficult to deter acts resulting from mental illness.

B.   Standards to Determine Insanity
Different jurisdictions employ different tests for determining if a defendant is legally insane.

1. The M'naghten Test
Under the M'naghten test, to establish a valid insanity defense, one must prove that due to mental illness, one:

a. Did not know the nature and quality of the act, or,

b. If one did know the nature and quality of the act, one still did not know the act was wrong.

2. The Model Penal Code Approach
Under MPC § 4.01, one is not guilty by reason of insanity if one:

a. Lacks the ability to appreciate the wrongfulness of the conduct, or,

b. Lacks the ability to conform one's conduct to the requirements of the law.

3. Comparison of M'Naghten Test and Model Penal Code
The MPC standard is less strict than the M'Naghten test, as it allows the insanity defense to be used by individuals who realize their acts are wrong, but nonetheless cannot abide by the law.

4. Recent Trends
Widespread dissatisfaction over the not guilty by insanity verdict in the trial of John Hinckley, the man who attempted to kill President Reagan, has led to a re-evaluation of the insanity defense. The trend is now towards stricter standards.

VIII. AUTOMATISM

Criminal acts may be excused if they are a reflex or convulsion and beyond the actor's control. See, MPC § 2.01. See also, Ch. 3.

A. Not Culpable
One is not blameworthy for such acts because:

1. It is unfair to punish acts that are automatic and hence not intentional.

2. Acts that are automatic or reflexive cannot be controlled and hence cannot be deterred.

B. No Commitment
Unlike insanity, this defense does not result in commitment to a mental institution.

IX. DIMINISHED CAPACITY

Although not legally insane, one may nonetheless have a diminished mental capacity and thus be unable to form the requisite intent for a particular crime. See, MPC § 4.02

A. Lesser Charge
A successful use of the diminished capacity defense may lead to a conviction on a lesser charge, but rarely leads to complete acquittal.

B.   Limited Availability.
Many jurisdictions have rejected the diminished capacity defense entirely. These states bar the use of any expert psychiatric evidence except in insanity cases.

CASE CLIPS

United States v. Peterson (1973) KS

Facts: Not provided.
Issue: When is killing justified as a means of self-defense?
Rule: The right of self-defense arises out of necessity. There must be a threat of death or serious harm that is actual or apparent. A threat must be unlawful and immediate, and one must believe there is serious danger. That belief must be reasonable by an objective standard.

People v. Goetz (1986) KS, MIB

Facts: Four young thugs on a subway car surrounded D and asked for money. D, believing he was in danger of serious harm, shot and wounded the four youths.
Issue: In self-defense cases, must a belief in the need for deadly force meet an objective (i.e., reasonableness) standard?
Rule: The use of deadly force is permitted only if a reasonable person under the same circumstances and situation would have found it necessary. Circumstances such as one's prior experiences and physical characteristics may be considered.

Commonwealth v. Kendrick (1966) W

Facts: D was having an affair with another's wife, and went to the other man's house to tell him. Before D got in the house, the man attacked D with a fireplace poker. D stabbed and killed the man and was convicted of murder.
Issue: Is one who kills in self-defense guilty of manslaughter or murder?
Rule: If one's means of defending oneself are excessive, and death results, one is guilty of manslaughter.

State v. Kelly (1984) KS, W

Facts: D's husband had subjected her to violent beatings for several years. Shortly after a violent dispute, D saw her husband charging towards her. She stabbed him with a pair of scissors, and he died.

Issue: Is expert testimony on battered woman's syndrome admissible when self-defense is asserted?

Rule: Expert testimony on battered woman's syndrome may be relevant in determining whether one reasonably believes the use of force is necessary and justifiable.

State v. Norman (1989) KS

Facts: Norman shot her husband as he slept. Norman was mentally and physically abused by her husband for twenty five years: she was beaten up, burned with cigarettes and hot coffee, made to eat pet food from a bowl on the floor, and forced into prostitution. Norman presented evidence that she exhibited battered wife syndrome and claimed perfect self-defense, but was convicted of voluntary manslaughter.

Issue: Can a woman who suffers from battered wife syndrome claim self-defense if she kills her husband when not faced with an imminent threat of death or great bodily harm?

Rule: Self-defense is not a justification unless the defendant believes that she faces imminent death or great bodily harm. Battered wife syndrome does not relax the requirement that the threat be imminent.

State v. Abbott (1961) KS

Facts: D was involved in a heated confrontation with his neighbors in their common driveway. The neighbor brandished a hatchet. D might have been able to safely return to his home, but continued to fight. D's neighbors were injured.

Issue: Can self-defense be asserted when the defendant could have safely retreated?

Rule: The use of *deadly* force is not justifiable when an opportunity to retreat is at hand. One is required to retreat only if he *knows* he can do so with *complete* safety. One is not required to retreat if doing so will cause risk of injury.

United States v. Peterson (1973) KS, L

Facts: A trespasser was leaving D's property, when D retrieved a pistol and threatened to shoot the trespasser "if you move." The trespasser then took out a wrench and approached the D, who shot and killed him.

Issue: Is one's use of deadly force permitted as self-defense if one's actions contributed to the danger?

Rule: Defensive killing is not justified when the danger can be avoided. The right to kill in self defense is only available to those free from fault and not those who incite the danger.

State v. Hodges (1986) L

Facts: D's husband frequently beat her over many years. D had just endured another beating, and with her husband yelling at her, she shot and killed him.

Issue: Is an objective or subjective standard used when battered woman syndrome is involved in a self-defense claim?

Rule: When battered woman syndrome is an issue, a subjective standard is used in determining whether one's belief in a need to assert self-defense is reasonable, and expert testimony is allowed.

Commonwealth v. Martin (1976) L, W

Facts: D, a prisoner, stabbed a corrections officer who was restraining another prisoner. D claimed he acted because he believed the other prisoner was in grave danger.

Issue: Can force be justifiable as a means of protecting others?

Rule: Intervening protective force is justified if a reasonable person would consider it necessary, and if the party actually in danger would be justified in using such force.

Crawford v. State (1963) W

Facts: D shot and killed a man who had robbed D once before and had just forced his way into D's home.

Issue: Is deadly force permissible to repel an attack on one's dwelling?

Rule: Deadly force may be used to repel an assault on one's dwelling if there is a reasonable apprehension that the assailant intends to commit a felony or inflict serious harm.

Law v. State (1974) L

Facts: D was inside his home and heard noises. He thought that burglars were present, but in fact it was two police officers. D fired several shots through the door and hit two officers.

Issue: When is a killing justifiable as a necessary means of preventing a crime?

Rule: Deadly force may be used to prevent a felony such as murder, robbery, burglary, rape or arson only if the force is a necessity. Apprehension of a felony must be reasonable, and the preventative force used may not be excessive.

Bishop v. State (1987) L

Facts: D set up a trap gun in his home that could shoot intruders while D was at work. An intruder was shot and killed.

Issue: Can a deadly automatic device be used to prevent unlawful entry?

Rule: Though one is sometimes justified in using deadly force to prevent unlawful entry, mechanical devices endanger firemen, police officers, and curious children, and their use is not justified.

Dissent: Use of deadly mechanical devices should be permitted if there is a reasonable expectation of a felony, and a felony was actually intended by the victim.

Kohler v. Commonwealth (1973) L

Facts: D admitted purchasing heroin, but claimed he did so to assist police officers seeking information on illicit drug traffic.

Issue: When a justification is asserted, must affirmative instructions on that specific defense be given?

Rule: Concrete instructions as to the specific justification asserted are to be given.

People v. Ceballos (1974) KS, KW, J

Facts: D set up a spring gun in his garage. While D was away, an intruder was shot and injured.

Issue: May one employ a device that uses deadly force in one's absence, if one would have been justified in using such force if present?

Rule: Deadly force may not be used solely for the protection of property. Therefore, a device of deadly force may not be used in one's absence because robbery only poses a threat of death or serious harm if one is present.

Durham v. State (1927) KS

Facts: D, a law officer, was trying to a arrest a suspect. The suspect resisted and began hitting D with an oar. D shot the suspect in the arm.
Issue: How much force may a law officer use in making an arrest?
Rule: If a suspect resists arrest, an officer may use whatever force is necessary to overcome such resistance.

People v. La Voie (1964) KW

Facts: La Voie's automobile was intentionally hit from behind and pushed across an intersection. Four intoxicated men emerged from the vehicle, threatening La Voie and advancing rapidly. La Voie shot and killed one of the men.
Issue: When may a person justifiably use deadly force in self-defense?
Rule: If a person reasonably believes that he is in imminent danger of being killed or receiving great bodily harm, he may defend himself with the use of deadly force if necessary.

State v. Leidholm (1983) KW, DS, J

Facts: D, who was frequently beaten by her husband, killed him in his sleep after one such beating.
Issue: Is the validity of a self-defense justification measured by an objective or subjective standard?
Rule: A subjective standard is used in determining the validity of a self-defense justification. Accordingly, self-defense is permissible if the circumstances caused one to believe force was necessary to defend herself.
Note: There is wide disagreement on whether an objective or subjective standard of reasonableness should be used in self-defense cases.

Tennessee v. Garner (S.Ct. 1985) KS, L, KW, W, MIB

Facts: A police officer shot and killed an unarmed suspect fleeing from a burglary.
Issue: May deadly force be used to apprehend an apparently unarmed suspected felon?
Rule: (White, J.) Use of deadly force is not justified to prevent the escape of a felon who poses no immediate threat.
Dissent: (O'Connor, J.) Burglary often involves violence, and deadly force should be permitted as a last resort to prevent burglary suspects from escaping.

People v. Curtis (1969) L
Facts: D engaged in a violent struggle with a police officer who was trying to arrest him. D felt the arrest was baseless and unlawful.
Issue: May a suspect forcibly resist an unlawful arrest?
Rule: Physical resistance can invite grave harm and is not a permissible or effective means of dealing with an unlawful arrest.
However, there is a right to reasonably resist excessive force.

People v. Ball (1973) L
Facts: D, a teacher, punished a student by paddling. The student was badly bruised. D was convicted of battery.
Issue: When is a teacher's discipline of a student unlawful?
Rule: A teacher may punish a student so long as the discipline is not wanton or malicious.
Dissent: To protect children's welfare, any unreasonable punishment should be deemed criminal, not simply malicious punishments.

Director of Public Prosecutions v. Lynch (1975) L
Dir. of Public Prosecutions for Northern Ireland v. Lynch (1975) KW
Facts: D was ordered to drive three armed gunmen. D thought he would be killed if he did not follow the orders. The gunmen then committed a murder.
Issue: Is duress a permissible excuse for being an accomplice to murder?
Rule: Although it is not available to one who actually kills an innocent person, duress is an excuse for one who aids and abets a murder. One might help in the various preparatory steps with the reasonable hope that a crime will not be completed.
Concurrence 1: It should always be left to a jury to determine the validity of a claim of duress.
Dissent 1: Duress is not an excuse for one who actually murders and should also be unavailable to one who aids and abets a murder.
Dissent 2: One should not be allowed to kill to save one's own life.
Concurrence 2: Duress should be permitted even in murder cases because the criminal law should not require that one be a hero and sacrifice one's own life.

State v. Warshow (1979) L, KW
(Cited incorrectly to 1980 in KW)

Facts: Ds blocked access to a nuclear power plant which they believed was very dangerous. Ds asserted a necessity defense.

Issue: What level of danger creates sufficient necessity to excuse an offense?

Rule: The necessity defense requires that the emergency arise without the fault of the actor, the emergency be imminent, the act be the only way to avoid injury, and the seriousness of the emergency outweigh the criminal wrong. Imminent means threatening to occur immediately.

Concurrence: The availability of the necessity defense is precluded when a legislative choice has been made as to the values at issue.

Dissent: When a necessity defense is made, the fact that all other alternatives had been exhausted should be considered.

State v. Garoutte (1964) L

Facts: D, who admitted he drove negligently and caused another's death, compensated the victim's family. The family then asked that no criminal charges be filed against D.

Issue: Can criminal charges be dropped upon compensation of an injured party?

Rule: Pending statutory change, misdemeanor charges may be dismissed when an injured party has been compensated.

Note: The court in this case seemed unsatisfied with the result and urged the legislature to take proper action to prevent similar results.

United States v. Hillsman (1975) KS

Facts: Ds fired shots at two undercover officers. Ds believed the officers were felons, and claimed they were only trying to make a citizen's arrest.

Issue: May one use force to carry out a citizen's arrest?

Rule: A private citizen has the right to arrest one who is believed to have committed a felony in the citizen's presence, but only if the felony was in fact committed. Unlike a police officer, a private citizen acts at his own peril.

Concurrence: One should not be criminally liable for conduct one believes is lawful and socially desirable.

People v. Unger (1977) KS, KW

Facts: D escaped from prison after receiving numerous threats from other prisoners.

Issue: When is otherwise illegal conduct justifiable as a necessity?

Rule: Conduct that would otherwise be criminal may be justifiable in circumstances where the conduct is necessary to avoid a greater public or private injury. One must be without blame in bringing about the circumstances.

Dissent: When one escapes from prison, the necessity defense should only be permitted if the escapee makes an effort to contact authorities after the escape.

United States v. Bailey (S.Ct. 1980) MIB

Facts: Defendants escaped from prison and were convicted for escape from federal custody. On appeal, defendants claimed that due to various threats and beatings received while inside the prison, they had no choice but to escape. The defendants did not attempt to surrender to the authorities after escaping.

Issue: When may an inmate who has escaped prison use a necessity or duress defense to avoid criminal sanctions for the escape?

Rule: (Rehnquist, J.) A criminal defendant charged with escape may claim duress or necessity only upon a showing of a bona fide effort to surrender or return to custody as soon as the claimed duress or necessity has lost its coercive force.

Dissent: (Blackmun, J.) If an escape was originally justified, it is too much to demand that a defendant return to prison in order to justify their departure. An escapee should at least be permitted to present evidence to the jury that the harm resulting from a return to custody would outweigh the harm of his continued absence.

United States v. Schoon (1992) KS

Facts: Defendants entered the IRS building in Tucson where they chanted "keep America's tax dollars out of El Salvador," splashed simulated blood on the walls and floor, and generally obstructed the office's operation. Defendants were arrested for obstructing activities of the IRS. They argued a necessity defense, claiming that their actions were necessary to remedy the conditions in El Salvador.

Issue: Is the necessity defense applicable to cases involving indirect civil disobedience?

Rule: The necessity defense can never be used in cases involving indirect civil disobedience. To invoke the necessity defense, defendants must show that: (1) they were faced with a choice of evils and chose the lesser evil; (2) they acted to prevent imminent harm; (3) they reasonably anticipated a direct causal relationship between their conduct and the harm to be averted; and (4) they had no legal alternative to violating the law. This test can never be satisfied in indirect civil disobedience cases.

Regina v. Dudley and Stephens (1884) KS
The Queen v. Dudley and Stephens (1884) KW

Facts: Ds were stranded at sea, and on the verge of starvation. Ds killed another castaway and fed off his remains in order to survive.
Issue: May one kill an innocent person if it is necessary to survive?
Rule: However strong the temptation may be, one cannot decide that one's own life is more valuable than that of another innocent individual. Thus one cannot kill an innocent person even if it is necessary for survival.

Cruzan v. Director, Missouri Dept. of Health (S.Ct. 1989) KS, MIB

Facts: Cruzan, brain dead from a car accident, was kept alive on a life support system. Cruzan's family wanted to honor her wishes and have the system turned off. The Supreme Court of Missouri denied the request because there was no clear and convincing evidence of Cruzan's wishes to withdraw treatment.
Issue: Does a state law requiring clear and convincing evidence of an incompetent's wishes to withdraw treatment violate the incompetent's constitutional rights?
Rule: (Rehnquist, C.J.) A person's right to refuse medical treatment must be balanced with the state's interest in the protection and preservation of human life. Thus, the state's procedural requirement designed to protect and preserve human life is constitutional.
Concurrence: (Scalia, J.) Federal courts have no business in this field. The State has always had the power to prevent suicide.

People v. Kevorkian (1994) KS

Facts: Dr. Kevorkian was prosecuted for providing several people with the physical means to commit suicide. Kevorkian argued that the Michigan statute under which he was prosecuted violated the Due Process Clause because the right to commit suicide is a fundamental liberty interest. He also argued that assistance is part of this protected interest.

Issue: Does the Due Process Clause protect a right to commit and/or assist suicide?

Rule: The Due Process Clause does not protect a right to commit or assist suicide. Suicide has always been disapproved by society, and was often criminalized. The right to refuse treatment is different from the right to commit suicide because committing suicide is an affirmative act to end a life, but refusing treatment is a passive act that lets nature run its course.

Note: The dissents stress that the government interest in preventing a terminally ill patient from ending his suffering is weak, and the failure to recognize a right to suicide based on its historical proscription, is unsuitable for the fast-moving progression of the modern world.

State v. Toscano (1977) KS

Facts: D falsified insurance claims, but claimed he was under duress because a creditor had threatened to harm D and his wife.

Issue: Is an objective or subjective standard used when one claims duress as an excuse for one's actions?

Rule: For a crime to be excused due to duress, a threat of harm must be such that an ordinary person would be unable to resist. One's situation and physical characteristics, but not one's temperament, can be considered.

Regina v. Kingston (1994) KS

Facts: Penn wanted to blackmail Kingston. Penn lured a fifteen-year-old boy to his flat, drugged him, and then invited Kingston to sexually abuse the boy. Kingston claimed that he too was drugged by Penn, and although the act was intentional, the intent arose out of circumstances for which he was blameless.

Issue: Does intoxication, secretly induced by another, negate the mens rea needed to be convicted of a crime if the defendant would not have committed the crime when sober?

Rule: Intoxication, even secretly induced by another, is no excuse. Absence of moral fault is not sufficient to negate mens rea. To allow intoxication to be a defense, numerous witnesses would have to show, given the defendant's personality and susceptibilities, that the drug was really the cause of the offense.

Roberts v. People (1870) KS

Facts: D was drunk and fired shots at another. D was charged with assault with intent to murder.

Issue: May one be convicted of a crime committed while too drunk to have full control of all of his faculties?
Rule: One must have the requisite intent to be convicted of a crime. However, asserting that the requisite intent would not have existed but for the intoxication is not a valid excuse.

People v. Hood (1969) KS

Facts: D, intoxicated, shot and injured a police officer who was trying to arrest him. D was charged with assault with a deadly weapon and assault with intent to murder.
Issue: May one be charged with a general intent crime if one was under the influence of alcohol?
Rule: Evidence of intoxication should not be considered when one is charged with a general intent crime. An intoxicated person is capable of intending a simple act such as striking another.

Pate v. Robinson (Sup. Ct. 1966) L, J

Facts: D had severe mental problems. One night he shot and killed his wife.
Issue: Must a hearing be held to determine if one is competent to stand trial?
Rule: There is a constitutional right to receive an adequate hearing to determine one's competency to stand trial.
Dissent: One's courtroom behavior can demonstrate competency to stand trial, and thus a competency hearing should not be necessary in all cases.

Jackson v. Indiana (Sup. Ct. 1972) L, W

Facts: D was charged with robbery. He was found not competent to stand trial and was committed to a mental hospital.
Issue: Can one be committed to a mental facility, in the same manner as one found not guilty by insanity, as the result of a pre-trial competency hearing?
Rule: Indefinite commitment of a criminal defendant, without a criminal trial, is a deprivation of equal protection and violates due process. Once it is determined one will never be able to stand trial, one must either be released or the state must institute civil commitment hearings.

M'Naghten's Case (1843) KS, W
Daniel M'Naghten's Case (1843) L, MIB
Facts: D shot and killed the secretary of the prime minister. D claimed insanity as a defense.
Issue: What is the proper standard for acquittal on the basis of insanity?
Rule: To establish a valid insanity defense, it must be proven that either one did not know the nature and quality of the act, or one did not know that the act was wrong.

State v. Crenshaw (1983) KS, DS
Facts: D suspected his wife of having an affair. D stabbed and beheaded her, believing his religion compelled him to do so. D claimed the insanity defense.
Issue: Under the M'Naghten "right-from-wrong" test, must one who claims the insanity defense realize his acts were morally wrong?
Rule: Showing that one knew society considered an act to be wrong defeats a defense of insanity. It is irrelevant that one may have personally considered the act morally proper, because then all defendants could claim they believed their actions were morally proper.
Dissent: One should not be punished for an act that one believed was morally proper.

United States v. Lyons (1984) KS, J
Facts: D, who was addicited to pain killers, was charged with buying drugs. D claimed insanity on grounds of inability to conform to the law.
Rule: The defense of duress or necessity in an escape case requires a bona fide effort to surrender or to return to custody once the threatened harm is gone.
Concurrence: Although an escapee should be required to contact authorities in order to assert necessity, the poor condition of prisons should not be ignored.
Dissent: It is unfair to require a prisoner to return to the dangerous place that necessitated the escape.

State v. Green (1982) KS
Facts: D killed a police officer. D exhibited insane behavior throughout his life, though he behaved normally at the time of his arrest.
Issue: Can the insanity defense succeed if there is evidence that one has on occasion acted normally?

266 Justification and Excuse

Rule: To defeat the insanity defense, it must be shown that the defendant has exhibited behavior consistent with sanity, and also behavior inconsistent with insanity. It is not enough to show that one has occasionally exhibited normal behavior, as most insane people have periods of normalcy.

State v. Strasburg (1910) KS

Facts: Strasburg was convicted of first degree assault. Strasburg argued that a statute prohibiting the insanity defense violated the Washington State Constitution because it deprived him of due process.

Issue: Is there a constitutional right to an insanity defense?

Rule: Defendants in Washington state have a constitutional right to prove that they were insane at the time of the crime. The sanity of the accused is as much a substantive fact, used to determine guilt, as whether the defendant physically committed the act. If the defendant was insane at the time of the commission of the act, the act was legally not the defendant's act.

State v. Korell (1984) KS, MIB

Facts: Korell, traumatized while serving in Vietnam, developed severe psychological problems, including paranoia. Korell, believing that his former boss was trying to kill him, broke into his former boss' home and shot at him. The court did not allow Korell to present an independent insanity defense because Montana had abolished its use. Instead, Korell could only present evidence of mental defect to prove that he did not have the state of mind that is an element of the crime.

Issue: Is there a fundamental right to an insanity defense?

Rule: There is no fundamental right to an insanity defense in Montana, although Montana law allows testimony of mental condition that could cast doubt on a defendant's state of mind. The legislature made a conscious decision to hold individuals who act with a proven criminal state of mind accountable for their acts, regardless of motivation or mental condition.

State v. Guido (1963) KS

Facts: Guido shot her abusive husband immediately after she considered taking her own life. Guido claimed temporary insanity. She was examined by two court-appointed psychiatrists who reported that Guido was legally sane when she committed the crime. When Guido's attorney read the report he realized that the psychiatrists misunderstood the legal definition of insanity, and after he spoke with the psychiatrists they changed their report to read that Guido's state at the time of the crime did constitute a disease within the legal rule. The prosecutor claimed fraud, and Guido was convicted.

Issue: What constitutes a "disease of the mind," as required by the M'Naghten rule?

Rule: Mental disease as a legal concept means that at the time of the act, the accused was laboring under a defect of reason that prevented him from knowing either the nature and quality of the act, or that the act was wrong. The assumption is that some wrongdoers are sick while others are bad, and that it is immoral to stigmatize the sick. Thus, the question of who is insane is an ethical question that the law must decide, not a medical question.

Note: The court stated that it had simply described the problem of what constitutes a disease of the mind, not answered it, to show that there is room for dispute, and the psychiatrists did not act fraudulently by changing their report.

State v. Jones (1983) KS, J

Facts: D was charged with armed assault. At trial, the judge entered a plea of not guilty by reason of insanity, even though D did not wish to make this plea.

Issue: May a court enter an insanity plea on behalf of a defendant even if the defendant objects?

Rule: Any competent defendant has the right to refuse an insanity plea, as long as the defendant is competent to make, and does make, an intelligent and voluntary waiver.

United States v. Freeman (1966) J

Facts: D, a drug addict, was charged with selling narcotics. D claimed he could not be convicted because at the time of the act he did not have the capacity and will to be criminally liable.

Issue: Should people be held criminally liable if, though they realize the wrongfulness of their conduct, they are still unable to conform their behavior to the law?

Rule: A person is not responsible for criminal conduct if, as a result of mental disease, he cannot appreciate the wrongfulness of his conduct, or cannot conform his conduct to the law.

Concurrence: Standards of insanity are likely to change as new medical discoveries are made.

Note: This is the Model Penal Code approach.

United States v. Brawner (1972) KS

Facts: Not provided.

Issue: Can evidence of a defendant's mental state at the time of the crime be introduced to show that the defendant could not have formed the requisite intent to commit a crime?

Rule: Evidence of an abnormal mental condition, short of insanity, can be submitted in order to negate a defendant's intent. This diminished mental capacity does not excuse the crime, although it may show that the defendant could not form the required mental state (e.g., specific intent) required to be found guilty of the crime.

State v. Wilcox (1982) KS

Facts: Wilcox, a semi-retarded, schizophrenic, dyslexic, suffering from organic brain syndrome, was charged with aggravated felony murder and aggravated burglary, charges requiring a purpose to commit a felony. The judge disallowed evidence to show that Wilcox's specific intent was negated by his mental condition.

Issue: Can expert psychiatric evidence of a defendant's mental state be introduced to show an incapacity to form the requisite specific intent to commit a crime?

Rule: The partial defense of diminished capacity is not a valid defense, and consequently, a defendant may not offer expert psychiatric testimony to show that he lacked the mental capacity to form the specific mental state required. The insanity defense adequately safeguards the rights of the insane. The court specifically rejected the rule in Brawner.

Robinson v. California (S.Ct. 1962) KS, MIB

Facts: A California statute made it illegal to "be addicted to narcotics." D was arrested for having needle marks on his arms, although he was not under the influence of any drugs at the time of his arrest.

Issue: Does a statute that criminalizes the status of being a narcotics addict violate the Due Process Clause of the Fourteenth Amendment?

Rule: A law that makes the disease of narcotics addiction a criminal offense constitutes cruel and unusual punishment under the Eighth and Fourteenth Amendments.

Dissent: The statute is part of a program to control narcotism through prevention and cure. It does not punish the addict who has progressed past the volitional stage, but punishes habitual use. Therefore California's policy does not violate the Eighth or Fourteenth Amendments.

State v. Stasio (1979) DS

Facts: D attempted to rob a bartender. D claimed he was too drunk to have formed an intent to rob.

Issue: Can criminal offenses requiring specific intent be excused due to voluntary intoxication?

Rule: Voluntary intoxication does not excuse criminal conduct regardless of the offense charged, unless it disproves premeditation when the charge is murder. Society must be protected from dangerous conduct, and those who voluntarily become intoxicated should not escape responsibility for their actions.

Concurrence: One avoids liability only when so intoxicated as to be unable to think or control one's mind.

Concurrence in result and dissenting: If due to intoxication one cannot form the intent that is an element of a crime, one should not be treated similarly as those who willfully commit the same act.

Powell v. Texas (S.Ct. 1968) KS, W

Facts: D was convicted of being drunk in a public place. The trial court ruled that being a chronic alcoholic was not a defense.

Issue: Does a statute prohibiting public drunkenness constitute cruel and unusual punishment when applied to a chronic alcoholic?

Rule: (Marshall, J.) A statute prohibiting public drunkenness does not constitute cruel and unusual punishment if it applies to the defendant's act of being in public, rather than to his status as an alcoholic.

Dissent: (Fortas, J.) Intoxication is a condition symptomatic of the disease of alcoholism, not an act, and therefore criminal penalization violates the Eighth Amendment.

United States v. Moore (1973) KS,L, MIB

Facts: Moore, convicted for possessing heroin, claimed that he was not responsible for possessing the drug because his addiction caused him to lose the power of self-control.

Issue: Is drug addiction a defense for the crime of possession of illegal substances?

Rule: Drug addiction is not a defense for the possession of illegal drugs. This defense would weaken important policies that deal with the peculiar nature of the problem of drug traffic.

Concurrence: The elements for criminal responsibility (a voluntary act and a mental state) are fulfilled in the offense of knowing possession of a prohibited article.

Director of Public Prosecutions v. Majewski (1976) L
Facts: D was charged with assault but claimed he had mixed alcohol and medication the night of the incident, and thus had no recollection of the incident.
Issue: Can self-induced intoxication excuse criminal acts?
Rule: Getting drunk is a reckless act that is voluntarily undertaken and does not excuse general intent crimes. Intoxication can only exculpate specific intent crimes.

City of Minneapolis v. Altimus (1976) L
Facts: D caused a car accident, tried to leave the scene, and later assaulted a police officer. Several days earlier, a doctor had prescribed valium to D for a back problem, and D claimed his actions were caused by the drug.
Issue: Can one avoid liability by claiming involuntary intoxication?
Rule: One can avoid liability by showing an unexpected intoxication caused by a medically prescribed drug which caused temporary insanity.
Concurrence: Involuntary intoxication is a valid defense if one lacks the capacity to either appreciate the criminality of his acts or conform his conduct to the law.

State v. Q.D. (1984) L
Facts: D, an eleven-year-old boy, was charged with trespass.
Issue: Can a statutory presumption that a child is incapable of committing a crime be rebutted?
Rule: A statutory presumption that a child under a certain age is incapable of committing a crime can be rebutted by clear and convincing evidence that the child understood the act and knew it was wrong.

Smith v. State (1980) KW
Facts: Smith, an army private, commandeered a vehicle at gunpoint and left the base after being notified of his impending discharge. After being cornered by the police, Smith shot and severely wounded an officer. Two psychiatrists supported Smith's insanity claim, while one declared him fit to stand trial. The trial court accepted the latter's analysis and sentenced Smith to fifteen years in prison.

Issue 1: What burden of proof must the state bear to overcome an insanity defense?

Rule 1: Once the affirmative defense of insanity is introduced, the burden is on the state to prove sanity beyond a reasonable doubt.

Issue 2: May a trial court adopt the findings of one medical expert over the contrary findings of a greater number of medical experts?

Rule 2: A trial court is free to make its own conclusions regarding both lay and expert testimony.

State v. Maik (1972) KW

Facts: Maik confessed to stabbing his best friend sixty-six times with a hunting knife. Psychiatric examination revealed that drug use or stress caused the defendant to become psychotic sometime before the murder. Maik had not been under the influence of any drugs when the murder occurred.

Issue: May a defendant plead insanity if his psychosis was triggered by voluntary drug use?

Rule: If voluntary intoxication results in a fixed state of insanity after the immediate influence of an intoxicant has passed, a defendant may use this mental illness as an affirmative defense.

United States v. Pohlot (1987) KW

Facts: Pohlot plotted to have his wife killed during bitter divorce proceedings. Turned in by a government informer, Pohlot claimed that the murder plot was a weak attempt on his part to fight back against his wife's abusive treatment.

Issue: May evidence of mental illness be used to negate a statutory element of mens rea under the Insanity Defense Reform Act of 1984?

Rule: Mental disease or defect is admissible whenever it is relevant to prove that the defendant did or did not have a state of mind that is an element of the offense. Evidence used in this manner is not meant to establish that the defendant lacked the *capacity* to form the required mens rea, and thus is not barred by the Insanity Defense Reform Act.

Fersner v. United States (1984) DS

Facts: D saw a man fighting with a woman. Fearing she was in serious danger, D intervened by killing the man with repeated hatchet blows to the head.

Issue: When may force be used in defense of a third party?

Rule: One may use force when it is reasonably necessary to protect another. Reasonableness is based upon the facts as perceived by the intervenor. One may not use excessive force.

State v. Nelson (1983) DS

Facts: D held two people hostage whom he believed had stolen his property. D wanted to get the property back and claimed justification on the grounds of "defense of property."
Issue: Is one justified in using force to defend property?
Rule: One may use reasonable force to prevent criminal interference with property, but may not use force to recover property at a later time.

United States v. Russell (S.Ct. 1973) DS, J, MIB

Facts: D was arrested for selling drugs to an undercover agent. The agent supplied D with certain legal ingredients which were needed to manufacture the drug.
Issue: Is the defense of entrapment available simply because the government participates in the criminal enterprise?
Rule: (Rehnquist, J.) The defense of entrapment is limited in its availability. Entrapment is viable only when the government's deception actually implants the criminal design in the mind of the defendant.
Dissent: (Douglas, J.) One should not be blamed for a crime that was instigated by government officials.
Dissent: (Stewart, J.) When the entrapment defense is asserted, predisposition should be irrelevant. The focus should be on the government's behavior.

United States v. Pollard (1959) DS

Facts: D, a police officer, committed many robberies. D claimed that since the murder of his wife and daughter, he has had an irresistible impulse to break the law.
Issue: Can one be acquitted by reason of insanity because a criminal act was caused by an irresistible impulse?
Rule: The irresistible impulse defense fails when one's behavior shows planning or premeditation.

Johnson v. State (1982) DS

Facts: D participated in a rape and murder. D claimed lack of sufficient mental capacity to form the requisite intent to commit fist degree murder.

Issue: Can one be acquitted on grounds of diminished capacity to form the requisite intent?

Rule: The diminished capacity defense is not available when a state legislature has determined that insanity is the only means of avoiding criminal liability.

Dissent: Whether one is capable of forming a requisite intent is a question of fact, and any evidence bearing upon that question should be admitted.

People v. Wetmore (1978) J

Facts: D was charged with burglary, but claimed that he lacked the specific intent required for conviction due to mental illness.

Issue: May evidence of mental condition show a lack of specific intent?

Rule: If a crime requires specific intent, one who because of mental disease or defect lacks that intent cannot be guilty of that crime.

Werner v. State (1986) MIB

Facts: Werner pointed a gun at the driver of a vehicle, who subsequently provoked Werner by daring him to shoot. Werner shot and killed the driver, for which he was convicted of murder. At trial, evidence was excluded as to the state of mind of the defendant at the time of the shooting. The evidence would have been used to prove that the defendant suffered from Holocaust syndrome, stemming from his family's internment in a concentration camp.

Issue: May evidence as to the defendant's state of mind be excluded as irrelevant if the evidence does not concern a statutorily accepted defense?

Rule: Self-defense statutes permit the use of force only when a person reasonably believes the force to be immediately necessary. Evidence which would merely establish a defendant's susceptibility to violence is immaterial with respect to a claim of self-defense, and is properly excluded.

Dissent: Any relevant facts and circumstances going to show the condition of the mind of the accused at the time of the offense is admissible evidence.

Fulcher v. Wyoming (1981) J
Fulcher v. State (1981) MIB

Facts: While drunk, D was arrested for disturbing the peace. In the prison cell D beat up another prisoner. D claimed unconsciousness at the time of the beating due to an earlier concussion.

Issue: Is the defense of unconsciousness different from the insanity defense?

Rule: Unconsciousness, or automatism, is a defense distinct from insanity.

Concurrence: Unconsciousness comes under the defense of mental illness or deficiency.

State v. Reese (1978) J

Facts: D escaped from prison after another prisoner threatened to kill D.

Issue: Can escaping from prison be justified as a necessity?

Rule: Necessity is a valid defense for escaping from prison only if a prisoner flees from an intolerable immediate situation and immediately surrenders after the escape. The state has the burden of disproving the necessity defense.

Dissent: Requiring a prisoner to surrender is unrealistic and unwarranted.

United States v. Contento-Pachon (1984) J

Facts: D smuggled drugs into the U.S. after threats were made on his wife and young son. D asserted both necessity and duress.

Issue: When does one use the duress defense, as compared to the necessity defense?

Rule: Duress is asserted when there is an immediate and realistic fear of death or serious bodily injury and there is no reasonable opportunity to escape. Necessity is invoked when one acts for the benefit of the general welfare or to achieve a greater good.

People v. Carradine (1972) J

Facts: D witnessed a homicide but refused to testify because she feared she would be killed. D was charged with contempt.

Issue: Is duress a valid excuse for refusing to testify?

Rule: Duress is not a valid excuse for refusing to testify as the state offers protection and relocation. Justice cannot be administered unless citizens cooperate.

Sigma Reproductive Health Center v. State (1983) J

Facts: D was convicted of trespass after occupying the reception area of an abortion clinic. D claimed the acts were necessary to protect the unborn.

Issue: May offenses committed during protest actions be defended as necessary?

Rule: The necessity defense is not available when there is an alternative means of protest. In addition, necessity is a valid defense only when there is an immediate risk of harm and the illegal act will actually stop the threatened harm.

State v. Simon (1982) J

Facts: D, an elderly and disturbed man, fired shots at a neighbor whom D feared for no apparent reason.
Issue: Is an objective or subjective standard used to determine the validity of a self-defense claim?
Rule: An objective standard is used in determining self-defense justification. A person is justified in using force only if a reasonable person in the same situation would find it necessary to defend against unlawful force.

State v. Wanrow (1977) J

Facts: D, a small woman on crutches, was in the midst of an argument with a large drunken man whom she suspected of molesting her daughter. Startled when she discovered him standing behind her, D shot and killed him.
Issue: In assessing the danger faced by a person who uses self-defense, must one only consider the immediate circumstances?
Rule: When determining if an individual had a valid reason for acting in self-defense, a subjective standard should be applied. All the facts and circumstances known to that individual, as well as the individual's physical characteristics may be considered.
Note: There is sharp disagreement on the degree of subjectivity that should be used in self-defense cases.

Martin v. Ohio (S.Ct. 1987) MIB

Facts: Martin was charged with murder after she shot and killed her husband. She pled self-defense, but was found guilty. Martin further argued that the Ohio rule that places the burden of proof on the defendant as to the elements of self-defense was a violation of the Due Process Clause.
Issue: Does the Due Process Clause of the Fourteenth Amendment forbid placing the burden of proving self-defense on the defendant?
Rule: (White, J.) As long as the jury instruction clearly conveys that all evidence presented, including that related to self-defense, must be considered in deciding the state's sufficiency of proof as to the elements of the crime, a state is entitled to place the burden of proof for self-defense on the defendant.

Dissent: (Powell, J.) A state has no authority to shift the burden of proof to the defendant if: (1) the factor at issue makes a substantial difference in punishment and stigma or (2) the factor was historically significant. Under this analysis, it is impermissible to require the accused to prove self-defense, as its proof is decisive to the result of the case, and is historically a primary justification for conduct.

Jahnke v. State (1984) J

Facts: D, a sixteen-year-old boy, had been abused by his father for many years. D's father left after a violent altercation. When D's father returned, D shot and killed him.

Issue: May one kill in self-defense because the deceased's prior behavior caused fear of serious harm or death?

Rule: One may not kill just because one reaches the subjective conclusion that another's prior acts lead to a fear of death or serious harm. Such killings are characteristic of anarchy.

Concurrence: One may not take the law into one's own hands, and later justify the action by maligning the deceased victim.

Dissent: Expert testimony should be admitted to demonstrate that battered children reasonably believe they are in imminent danger.

Dissent: In self-defense cases, it is important that jurors be carefully screened to ensure they recognize that self-defense is a valid justification for homicide.

State v. Goodseal (1971) J

Facts: D, a prostitute, agreed to sleep with a man. D and the man disagreed on price. The man then tried to force himself upon D, and D shot and killed him.

Issue: May one kill in order to prevent sexual assault?

Rule: One is entitled to kill in order to prevent sexual assault, but a jury may convict a person of murder if the jury feels the killing was actually motivated by anger, punishment, or vengeance.

Shuck v. State (1975) J

Facts: D and several others were engaged in a fistfight. D went to retrieve a baseball bat to help one of his allies in the fight. D ended up striking and killing one of the combatants.

Issue: May one use deadly force to defend against non-deadly force?

Rule: One may not use deadly force to defend against non-deadly force. However, murder charges may be reduced to manslaughter if the action was a hot-blooded response to the provocation of mutual combat, or if there was an honest but mistaken belief in the need to use deadly force.

People v. Guenther (1987) MIB

Facts: The defendant, upon viewing an altercation on his property, began firing at those involved. The charges were dismissed pursuant to a state statute which provided immunity from criminal prosecution for the occupant of a dwelling who uses physical force against an intruder.

Issue 1: In a criminal trial, which party has the burden of proving statutory immunity for purposes of a motion to dismiss.

Rule 1: The burden of proof necessary to obtain a dismissal based on statutory immunity rests upon the defendant. The extraordinary protection this type of statute gives, as well the greater wealth of information accessible to the defendant, makes this a reasonable allocation of the burden.

Issue 2: What is the standard of proof applicable to a motion to dismiss based on statutory immunity?

Rule 2: The defendant seeking statutory immunity must establish by a preponderance of evidence that: (1) another person made an unlawful entry; (2) he had a reasonable belief that a crime was committed or intended to be committed; (3) he had a reasonable belief that the intruder would use physical force; and (4) he used force against the actual intruder.

Note: This type of statute does not portray the majority view in the United States.

State v. Gallagher (1983) J

Facts: D physically resisted when a policeman made an unlawful warrantless entry into D's home and tried to arrest D.

Issue: May one resist an unlawful arrest?

Rule: There are circumstances where the unlawful and warrantless intrusion into a home creates a privilege to resist.

Concurrence: There is no crime of interference with a police officer when the officer is acting illegally.

Garner v. Memphis Police Department (1983) J

Facts: A police officer shot and killed an unarmed suspect fleeing from a burglary.

Issue: May deadly force be used by the police to apprehend an apparently unarmed suspected felon?

Rule: The use of deadly force to apprehend a fleeing suspect is justified only if the suspect has committed a violent crime or if there is probable cause to believe the suspect is armed or likely to endanger others.

Note: This decision was affirmed by the Supreme Court.

Commonwealth v. Klein (1977) J

Facts: D shot two burglars who were fleeing from D's store.

Issue: May a citizen use deadly force to effect a citizen's arrest?

Rule: A private citizen may not use deadly force to arrest a suspect when the crime concerns property and there is no threat of death or bodily harm.

Note: The defendant in this case was nonetheless acquitted, because this was the first case in the state to deal with this issue and the law could not be applied retroactively.

People v. Samuels (1967) J

Facts: D directed and starred in his own porno films. D was charged with assault because one film showed him whipping and bruising another man. D claimed the other man consented to the beating.

Issue: Is consent of a victim an absolute defense to assault?

Rule: Consent is a valid defense to assault only if the bodily harm is not serious or it is a foreseeable hazard incident to lawful athletic contests. The law prohibits assault in order to prevent people from injuring others, even if there is consent.

People v. Onofre (1980) J

Facts: Ds engaged in acts of oral sodomy. A statute declared that any act of consensual sodomy was a crime.

Issue: May a statute regulate private, cloistered, noncommercial sexual conduct between consenting adults?

Rule: A statute that regulates private, cloistered, noncommercial sexual conduct of consenting adults violates the constitutional right to privacy.

Note: The Supreme Court later ruled in Bowers v. Hardwick that there is no constitutional right to engage in consensual sodomy.

People v. Barraza (1979) J

Facts: D helped an undercover police officer purchase heroine after the officer repeatedly asked D for such help. D claimed entrapment.

Issue: What degree of undercover police action will constitute entrapment?

Rule: Entrapment occurs when police action induces a normally law abiding citizen to commit a crime out of friendship or sympathy, or makes a crime unusually attractive. The entrapment defense requires an objective standard focusing on police conduct.

United States v. Gamble (1984) J

Facts: Undercover government officials undertook an elaborate scheme to get D to help fill out fraudulent insurance claims.

Issue: What level of undercover police conduct violates due process?

Rule: A violation of due process occurs when government agents' involvement is of a tenor which shocks the conscience.

State v. Kennamore (1980) MIB

Facts: D was on a camping trip when another man hit him over the head with a bottle. D shot and killed the other man.

Issue: Is there a duty to retreat before using force in self-defense?

Rule: One has a duty to retreat, so long as it can be done safely, in order to avert the necessity of using deadly force.

Dissent: One should only have a duty to retreat when there is ample time and a safe and effective avenue is available.

Hampton v. United States (S.Ct. 1976) MIB

Facts: D purchased drugs supplied by a government informant and then resold them to government agents. D was convicted of heroin distribution.

Issue: Does government activity constitute entrapment even when one is predisposed to commit the crime?

Rule: A predisposition to committing a particular crime precludes the use of the defense of entrapment.

Dissent: If law enforcement conduct deliberately entices someone to commit a crime and the crime is the product of government creativity, a conviction should be barred under the entrapment defense. A predisposition should not matter.

Mathews v. United States (S.Ct. 1988) MIB

Facts: Mathews was convicted of accepting a bribe. At trial, Mathews moved to raise an entrapment defense, but the motion was denied because Mathews would not admit to all of the elements of the offense charged.

Issue: May a defendant in a federal criminal prosecution raise an entrapment defense if he denies commission of the crime?

Rule: (Rehnquist, C.J.) A defendant in a criminal prosecution is entitled to an entrapment defense, even if he denies one or more elements of the crime charged, if there is sufficient evidence from which a reasonable jury could find entrapment.

Concurrence: (Scalia, J.) The defense of entrapment will rarely be inconsistent with a defense on the merits. If a genuine inconsistency exists, the defendant's lack of credibility which would result from his testimony will serve to protect the interests of justice.

Dissent: (White, J.) Entrapment is a limited defense, because a defendant cannot both claim that he did not commit a crime, and that if he did, he was tricked into it. Allowing such inconsistency invites perjury, and results in increased confusion among jurors.

United States v. Kelly (1983) MIB

Facts: The FBI set up a fake organization and engaged in a variety of activities as part of the famed Abscam investigation. D, a Congressman, initially rejected a bribe, but later accepted cash payments in exchange for his influence.

Issue: May a person be convicted of a crime when the government creates an unusually strong temptation?

Rule: If the government merely provides an opportunity to commit a crime, no entrapment occurs, and conviction for a subsequent crime does not violate due process.

Concurrence: Although scam operations may be unwholesome, the Supreme Court has not yet defined what kind of government conduct is outrageous. Until then, such action is not entrapment.

United States v. Murphy (1985) MIB

Facts: The FBI manufactured sham criminal cases as part of "Operation Greylord," an investigation of the Chicago courts. D, a judge, thought the cases were real, and dismissed charges in many of these cases in exchange for cash payments. D claimed there was no real crime because the cases were fake.

Issue: May one be convicted for participating in a crime which is really only a government decoy?

Rule: One can be convicted of a crime, even if it is part of a government decoy. All undercover operations necessarily involve government decoys.

Even if an operation is fake and never comes to fruition, the government can use bait to root out corruption.

United States v. Jacobson (1990) MIB

Facts: Jacobson was convicted for receiving child pornography through the mail. The government had made Jacobson the subject of 5 undercover sting operations, after procuring his name from the mailing list of a reputed pornography dealer. The arrest came after Jacobson ordered a sexually explicit magazine depicting children which was offered to him by government agents. Jacobson claimed that the government lacked a basis for making him the target of an undercover operation.

Issue: When is it appropriate to make a party the focus of a criminal undercover operation?

Rule: The government must have a reasonable suspicion, based on "articulable facts," that a crime has occurred or is likely to occur before targeting an individual for an investigation. Without evidence of a target's predisposition to criminal behavior, a sting operation is illegal as a form of entrapment.

Dissent: Due process does not require an objective suspicion of probable cause to create a legitimate right to perform a criminal investigation. Law enforcement officials are entitled to draw inferences based on available information to choose the subjects of their investigations.

State v. St. Clair (1953) MIB

Facts: D aided two others in a holdup after the others threatened to kill D, D's wife, and D's son if D did not help them.

Issue: Is coercion or duress a valid excuse for a criminal act?

Rule: Duress is an excuse if the criminal act is induced by a well grounded fear of imminent death or serious harm.

United States v. Calley (1973) MIB

Facts: D, a soldier, killed 22 unarmed women and children during a mission in Vietnam. D claimed he acted under orders of his superior.

Issue: Are criminal acts excused when committed in response to the orders of a superior?

Rule: The excuse of superior orders is not available when a person of ordinary sense and understanding would realize the order was unlawful.

Dissent: Soldiers are taught to follow orders, and a person should only be punished for following orders if virtually everyone would realize the order was unlawful. One's particular intelligence and experience should also be considered.

State v. Monahan (1954) MIB

Facts: D, a fifteen-year-old boy, participated in a robbery with his father during which the father killed two persons.

Issue: May a juvenile be tried as an adult for a severe felony?

Rule: If legislation bars children under a certain age from being tried as adults, the legislation applies, regardless of the severity of the offense charged.

Dissent: Children of sixteen can distinguish right from wrong and should be held accountable for their acts.

Dissent: Punishment is necessary to deter juvenile crime.

People v. Guillett (1955) MIB

Facts: D was drunk and invited a woman to his home. D tried to rape her. D was charged with assault with intent to rape.

Issue: When intent is an element of a crime, can intoxication be a defense?

Rule: When a crime requires specific intent, the crime cannot be committed when the intent does not exist. Intoxication can negate the existence of specific intent.

Fisher v. United States (S.Ct. 1945) MIB

Facts: D, a library janitor, strangled and stabbed to death a librarian. D was convicted of deliberate and premeditated murder.

Issue: Can one's psychological makeup be considered when determining the existence of deliberation and premeditation?

Rule: Mental deficiency is not a necessary factor in determining if one's acts were deliberate and premeditated and thus psychological makeup need not be considered.

Dissent: Premeditation does not occur when one's act is a reflex to a stimulus.

Dissent: Since there are degrees between sanity and insanity, medical evidence that shows a defendant incapable of deliberation and premeditation should be considered.

Knights v. State (1899) MIB

Facts: D was charged with arson and wished to plead not guilty by reason of insanity.

Issue: Which party has the burden of proof after a defendant enters an insanity plea?

Rule: The law presumes sanity, but once a plea of insanity is made, the burden shifts to the state to prove the defendant is sane.

People v. Wood (1962) MIB

Facts: D brutally murdered two people. D claimed he was insane and had acted under religious delusions.

Issue: Is a belief that one's acts are morally right sufficient for an acquittal on grounds of insanity?

Rule: One's acts are not excused simply because one believes they were proper. One is culpable if one realizes the acts are against the law and against community standards.

People v. Wolff (1964) MIB

Facts: D, a fifteen-year-old boy, killed his mother by hitting her repeatedly with an ax handle. All four psychiatrists who testified stated D was insane, but the jury convicted D of murder.

Issue: Must a jury accept expert psychiatric testimony when determining sanity?

Rule: Jurors are not required to accept the opinions of psychiatric witnesses. Trial is by jury, not by experts.

Holloway v. United States (1945) MIB

Facts: D, a former mental patient, raped two women. D claimed insanity.

Issue: May a jury find one guilty even if expert psychiatric testimony states one is insane?

Rule: A jury may draw its own conclusion as to one's sanity and culpability, even if the conclusion conflicts with expert psychiatric opinion.

Chapter 9

THEFT OFFENSES

I.   LARCENY

Larceny is the only common law theft offense. It is generally defined as the trespassory taking and asportation of property from the possession of another with intent to permanently deprive the owner of that property.

Mnemonic: **TAPPIN'**

A.   <u>T</u>respassory Taking
A trespassory taking is a taking without consent of the person in possession or the owner. If there is either consent to the taking or some type of delivery of the property, larceny is not possible.

B.   <u>A</u>sportation
Asportation is the carrying away or removal of property. Only infrequently is this element important, because courts accept almost any movement, however slight, as sufficient for purposes of larceny.

C.   <u>P</u>roperty
(See, MPC § 223.0(6))
Originally, under common law, the only property subject to theft was transferable goods and wares; this did not include real property such as land, because land is not physically transferable. Since then, some courts have extended the scope of property to include anything of value, such as sex and information. Most courts, though, do not recognize lines of credit or loan guarantees as things of value. Real property is still not considered property.

D. **P**ossession
Property taken must be in the possession of another. One cannot commit larceny by taking that which one already possesses. Custody does not amount to possession.

1. Physical Possession
Physical possession is the state of being physically in control of property. The exertion of control over the property is physical in nature.

2. Constructive Possession
Although one person may have property in his possession, the possession becomes mere custody in the eyes of the law if another person has or acquires constructive possession of the same property. Constructive possession is a legal creation given to the person to whom the property belongs, but who does not have physical possession.

Constructive possession occurs most often in the employee/employer context as when an employee receives possession of property from a third party in the name of the employer.

E. **In**tent
One must have the intent to permanently deprive the owner of property at the time of taking.

1. Non-Felonious Intents
If one's intent at the time of taking possession is not to permanently deprive another of his property, then larceny has not been committed. However, if one's intent becomes felonious after the taking, then larceny has occurred.

Some examples of non-felonious intent are:

a. Intent to temporarily deprive,

b. Intent to repay,

c. Claim of right, (see, MPC § 223.1(3)), and

d. Belief that property is abandoned (see, MPC § 223.5).

2. Mistake Resulting in Excuse
    In most instances any mistaken belief, even a good-faith mistaken belief, will suffice for an excuse. In some courts, though, a mistaken belief that property is abandoned must be reasonable.

II.   EMBEZZLEMENT

A.   Origins
    A problem with common law larceny is that it does not cover people who are in lawful possession of another's property and who then convert the property to their own ends. Such actions became more prevalent in the 19th century, because employers allowed employees to receive money or other property from customers or clients. Since the property was in the possession of the employee, the employee could not be convicted of larceny if she were to feloniously convert it. In response to this gap in the law, England enacted the first embezzlement statutes. At first, only certain categories of people were subject to these statutes, but over time they were expanded and generalized.

B.   Elements
    Generally, embezzlement is defined by statute as fraudulent conversion by one who is already in lawful possession of another's property.

Mnemonic: **COIN POP**

1. Conversion
    Conversion is the receipt of and the withholding or applying of another's property. It has also been defined as acting upon property in such a way that undermines a trust which is the foundation of an owner's willing transfer of possession.

2. **Int**ent
Embezzlement requires a conversion of property with felonious intent; intent to convert another's property to one's own or a third party's use and benefit. Embezzlement is a completed offense as soon as property is converted with felonious intent.

  a. Intent to Repay
Intent to repay does not negate felonious intent, because embezzlement's specific intent does not include permanent deprivation.

  b. Claim of Right
Claim of right does negate felonious intent because one does not intend to take from the possession of another. Rather, one believes that the property is one's own and that the other person only has custody of the property.

3. **Po**ssession

  a. Lawful
Embezzlement requires lawful possession of property, either physical or constructive. If one converts property to which one only has custody while another has constructive possession, one commits larceny, not embezzlement.

  b. By Bailee
One may be in lawful possession due to a bailment. When there is a bailment and subsequent conversion with felonious intent by a bailee, the offense is larceny by bailee.

A bailment is an agreement between two parties by which the owner temporarily gives another possession of property; bailment can be established contractually or statutorily. It is also possible to have a constructive bailment, as when one takes the property of another without felonious intent to convert.

c. Unlawful
If one has acquired possession unlawfully, e.g., by stealing or some other criminal offense, one cannot be guilty of embezzlement, but may be found guilty of the original offense by which possession was obtained.

4. Property
In general, property which is subject to larceny is also subject to embezzlement; see, Ch. 9, I, C. Even if property is acquired through credit or borrowing, there can be no fraudulent conversion and embezzlement unless the property belongs to another.

III. FALSE PRETENSES
(See, MPC § 223.3)

False pretenses is generally defined by statute as the making of false representations, knowing that they are false, with intent to thereby deceive and cause transfer of title to property.

Mnemonic: **FAKING IT**

A. False Representations
Originally, false statements had to concern a present or past material fact; false promises were not punishable. Some courts now accept false statements as to future facts when the statements are made knowingly and with intent to deceive.

B. Knowing
It is necessary to show that one knew or should have reasonably known that the representations one made were false. False statements or promises made unknowingly are not punishable.

C. Intent to Defraud
One must have the intent to deceive through the use of false representations. An intent to repay or restore will *not* negate intent to deceive, because this offense is complete when title passes due to deception.

D. Title
False pretenses is concerned with the transfer of title rather than possession. If title has not passed due to a material false representation, the offense of false pretenses has not been committed.

1. Transfer of Possession Due to Fraud
In general, if fraud is used to induce voluntary transfer of possession but not title, possession does not transfer. One is then guilty of larceny by trick rather than embezzlement.

2. Transfer for Special Purposes
Although title to money usually passes with possession, if money is to be used for a specific purpose, possession passes, but title does not pass until the specific purpose is completed. Thus, if fraud is used in an inducement to a transfer of money for special purposes, possession does not transfer either, and one is guilty of larceny by trick instead of false pretenses.

IV. THEFT
(See, MPC § 223.1(1))
Strict procedural and historical differences inherent in larceny, embezzlement, and false pretenses prevent them from overlapping and result in gaps between them. Moreover, if one shows that the offense committed is different from the offense charged, a court must reverse on procedural grounds. In order to resolve some of these problems, as well as others, certain states have statutorily consolidated the various offenses against property into the single offense of theft.

V. ROBBERY
(See, MPC § 222)
Robbery is a common law felony which is an aggravated form of larceny and is defined as the use of force or threat of imminent force during a larcenous taking of property from the owner.

Mnemonic: **FLOW**

A. Force or Threat of Imminent Force
A use of force or threat of imminent force must occur before or during a taking. Once property has been taken and theft is complete, any

subsequent use of force or threat only constitutes assault or battery. Some courts have ruled that a taking is not necessarily complete as soon as one has the property in one's physical possession; thus, in some cases a use of force in fleeing from another or in escaping from a room will result in a conviction of robbery.

B.   Larceny
The underlying element of robbery is larceny, and the use of force is simply an aggravating factor. Because larceny requires intent to permanently deprive, some courts allow the good-faith defenses found in larceny. Other courts only allow these defenses when they are reasonable. Finally, because robbery is such an extreme form of theft in that it includes a use of force, some courts do not require a showing of intent. This results in precluding any defenses based on a claim of right or an intent to repay or restore.

C.   Owner
Robbery is also distinguished from larceny in that one must take physical possession from the owner. Thus, while the owner's presence is not required for a taking in larceny, there can be no robbery without the owner being present.

VI. EXTORTION
(See, MPC § 223.4)
Extortion is another aggravated form of larceny. Extortion differs from robbery in that property is acquired through a use of non-physical threats. Some courts distinguish extortion from blackmail; when the victim is a public official these courts call the offense extortion, and when the victim is a private citizen, the offense is blackmail.

A.   Threat
Any threat of a non-physical nature is within the scope of extortion.

1. Public Exposure
Frequently, the threat is that of public exposure. Even if the information one threatens to reveal is true, one can still be guilty of extortion.

2. Criminal Prosecution

The courts are divided as to whether it is extortion to threaten an embezzler or thief with prosecution if that person fails to restore the property taken. It is definitely extortion if one demands a greater amount than that which was taken by the criminal; however, the law is unclear when one demands only that which was originally taken.

B. Larceny

Although larceny is the basis for extortion and one of the elements of larceny is intent, certain extortion statutes do not allow good-faith excuses because of the extreme nature of the offense of extortion.

VII. BURGLARY

(See, MPC § 221)

At common law, burglary was defined as a breaking and entering of the dwelling of another under cover of night with intent to commit a felony within. The offense of burglary was created to protect the safety and security of the home.

Mnemonic: **BEDOUIN**

A. **B**reaking and **E**ntering

Common law required a use of force to gain entry and this constituted breaking. Most modern statutes only require entry with felonious intent; even entry into a public place with intent to commit a felony will meet this requirement.

B. **D**welling

At common law, dwelling signified more than just residences. This term applied to any outbuildings associated with and near a main residence, with occupancy of a structure as the important factor. Statutory changes enlarged the scope of coverage to include any edifice designed for the habitation of men or animals or for the shelter of property; dwellings need not be completely enclosed and may be a public place.

C.   **O**f Another
One cannot commit burglary by breaking into and entering one's own home with intent to commit a felony. Burglary requires that the building be that of another person.

D.   **U**nder Cover of Night
Although at common law it was important for the breaking to occur at night, most statutes have removed this requirement. Many statutes, however, grade the offense differently when entry occurs at night.

E.   **In**tent
Entry must be accompanied with intent to commit a felony. The intended felony does not have to actually occur, but it is additional evidence helping to establish intent.

VIII.   RECEIVING STOLEN PROPERTY
(See, MPC § 223.6)

Receiving stolen property is generally defined as buying or acquiring possession to any property which has been obtained in any manner constituting theft, knowing the property to be so stolen or obtained. One is also guilty of this offense by concealing or aiding to conceal property which has been obtained in any manner constituting theft, knowing the property to be so stolen or obtained.

Mnemonic: **RISK**

A.   **R**eceipt or Concealment
This offense requires either that one have the property in one's possession, through monetary or other acquisition, or that one conceal or aid in concealing the property.

B.   **I**ntent
Some statutes require that one receive or conceal the property for one's own gain or in order to prevent the owner from possessing the property. Other statutes do not require specific intent.

C. Stolen Property
    The property received must have been the object of a theft committed
    by another, such as larceny, embezzlement, false pretenses, extortion,
    or robbery. If it is not possible to show the elements of the underlying
    theft offense, whether or not anyone is actually convicted of such an
    offense, the property cannot be the object of theft. Thus, the property
    must be takable property and the original taker must have had the
    requisite intent.

D. Knowingly
    It must be shown that one knew or should have reasonably known at
    the time of receipt or concealment that the property is the object of
    theft.

IX. FEDERAL THEFTS

A. Interstate Transportation of Stolen Goods
    This offense is defined as the transportation in interstate or foreign
    commerce of any goods, wares, merchandise, securities, or money,
    knowing the same to have been stolen, converted, or taken by fraud.

    1. Transportation
        This requirement is met very easily because interstate commerce
        has been expanded to such an extent that almost any distribution
        of anything is considered to be in interstate commerce.

    2. Goods, Wares, or Money
        This element provides for the application of this statute only in
        regards to tangible personal property. Non-tangible things of value
        such as copyrights are not covered under this offense.

    3. Known to be Stolen
        It must be shown that one knew or reasonably should have known
        that the goods were stolen. Goods are considered stolen if they are
        the object of another person's theft.

B. Wire and Mail Fraud
    These offenses are committed through the transmission by wire or
    mail of false pretenses in furtherance of any scheme to defraud or

obtain property for one's own enrichment. Another feature of this offense is that the scheme does not necessarily have to work and acquisition of property is not required.

1. Transmission by Wire or Mail
   This element has evolved into one of form only. Most courts only require a formal declaration that either phones or the mail was used by the accused in commission of the scheme. Some courts do not require any evidence at all as to their use.

2. False Pretenses
   See, Ch. 9, III.

3. Scheme
   The scheme must have as its object the defrauding of another or the obtaining of property for one's own benefit. This includes all property subject to a theft offense as well as certain non-tangible things, the loss of which directly results in harm to the victim.

C. Extortion under Color of Official Right
   The Hobbs Act proscribes extortion affecting interstate commerce, whether by "wrongful use of actual or threatened force, violence, or fear, or under color of official right." Extortion under color of official right is committed when a public official knowingly engages in wrongful use of his office to obtain money or benefits not due him or his office and thereby affects interstate commerce.

1. Public Official
   A public official is anyone who is publicly elected to office or who works for the government on the federal, state, or local level.

2. Knowingly
   It must be shown that one knew or should reasonably have known that one was wrongfully using the public office and that this induced the victim to give up the money or offer the benefits.

3. Money or Benefits
   The object of this offense is the same as for extortion.

4. Affects Interstate Commerce
This is a threshold element which is not of great importance. It does serve, though, to prevent prosecution for receipt of minor benefits or services.

CASE CLIPS

Commonwealth v. Tluchak (1950) KS

Facts: D sold a farm and some personal property but refused to deliver the personal property to the purchasers.

Issue: Does refusal or failure to deliver goods sold to purchasers constitute larceny?

Rule: Although title passes to a purchaser upon payment of the purchase price, possession and custody do not pass until the seller relinquishes them. Since larceny is a crime of trespass on the right of possession, one in legal possession cannot be guilty of larceny. One can be guilty of fraudulent conversion or larceny by bailee, though.

Topolewski v. State (1906) KS

Facts: D arranged with a meat packer who owed D money to have some meat placed on a loading dock so that D could take the meat as if he were a customer. The meat packer informed the company of D's plan and was instructed to comply.

Issue: Is consent to a taking implied when a victim knows of and aids in the taking?

Rule: When an owner actually or constructively aids in the taking of his property, either by performing or rendering unnecessary a requisite element, there is no trespass with nonconsent and therefore no larceny. It is possible for a victim to set a trap without implying consent if the defendant meets all of the elements through his own doing and not that of the victim.

Nolan v. State (1957) KS

Facts: D worked at a finance company and received payments from customers which he placed in the cash drawer. At the end of the day, D took cash from the drawer.

Issue: Does an owner/employer have possession of property when it is received by her employee and placed where she directed?

Rule: Property which has reached its destination is constructively in the possession of its owner even if she is not the receiver. Thus, a taking by an employee from the owner/employer's possession is larceny and not embezzlement.

Concurrence: This idea of transfer of possession is too subtle and allows criminals to go free. Instead, an indictment under both larceny and embezzlement should be allowed.

Burns v. State (1911) KS

Facts: D, a constable, pursued and apprehended an insane man. D misappropriated a roll of money which the insane man had thrown away while in flight.

Issue: Can one be a bailee for property of another without a contractual basis for the possession?

Rule: A contract between parties is not essential for the existence of a bailment. A constructive bailment exists whenever lawful possession and a duty to account for the property of another are created in any way, even through the finding of property. Taking possession without a coexisting intent to convert establishes a bailment. Subsequent conversion constitutes larceny as bailee.

State v. Riggins (1956) KS, J

Facts: D, owner and operator of a collection agency, was engaged by a merchant to collect her firm's delinquent accounts. D was to collect the money and remit it minus a commission; D collected, but failed to remit.

Issue: Can an independent businessman acting in a fiduciary capacity commit embezzlement as an agent?

Rule: When one acts on the behalf of another by virtue of delegated authority, one is that person's agent whether or not one is directly employed by the delegator or operates his own business. An agent who has the right to collect on another's accounts can fall under the scope of embezzlement statutes.

Dissent: Although a person is a servant of those who employ his services, he is not an agent when he keeps his own offices and is not under the control of his employer. Finding him an agent is too broad an interpretation and is a decision best left to the legislature.

Hufstetler v. State (1953) KS

Facts: D had his gas-tank filled and drove away without paying.

Issue: Does fraud negate transfer of possession?
Rule: If possession is obtained by fraud and is accompanied by the intent to convert, the consent of the owner is voided and possession is not transferred. If the owner only intended to part with possession and not title, the offense is larceny by trick.

Graham v. United States (1950) KS, J
Facts: D, an attorney, convinced an immigrant that D could get the police to drop charges pending against him if he gave D money with which to bribe the police. D kept the money given to him.
Issue: When money is transferred for a special purpose, does title pass immediately?
Rule: Generally, title to money passes with possession of the bills. An exception is when money is given for a special purpose, in which case title does not pass until that special purpose is attained. When title remains with the owner, only possession is transferred. If fraud is used to acquire that possession, possession reverts to the owner and one is guilty of larceny by trick.

People v. Ashley (1954) KS, J
Facts: D, owner of a dating service, obtained loans from two women, promising to secure them with a mortgage or a trust deed. D owned neither of the properties he mentioned and did not secure the loans.
Issue: Is a false promise as to future considerations sufficient for the offense of obtaining property by false pretenses?
Rule: In addition to misrepresentations as to past or present facts, a false promise is adequate misrepresentation for the offense of false pretenses if it is made knowingly and with intent to deceive.
Concurrence in Judgment: False promises should not be acceptable to invoke criminal fraud, because the offense would turn on the subjective issue of intent to deceive, which must depend on uncertain inferences. Only misrepresentations as to existing facts are a reliable basis for criminal fraud and protect debtors from the risk of being accused of false pretenses.

Nelson v. United States (1955) KS, J
Facts: D secured an additional amount of credit as well as his past debt with the equity on his car. He failed to disclose that there was a prior debt on the car. The equity was greater than the additional amount of credit but smaller than his total debt.

Issue: Can intent to defraud be inferred from the making of a misrepresentation?

Rule: Intent to defraud is inferred when a misrepresentation is material. A misrepresentation is material when the victim relies upon it, when it is a wrongful act knowingly or intentionally committed, and when it results in loss or injury. Inducement to act without subsequent loss is insufficient.

Dissent: For false pretenses, it should be necessary to show intent to defraud, not merely intent to misrepresent a material fact.

State v. Harrington (1969) DS, KS, J, MIB

Facts: D, the wife's attorney, wrote to his client's husband stating that if he did not agree to the separation agreement, D would publicize the husband's adulterous conduct.

Issue: Is threat of public exposure sufficient for extortion?

Rule: The threat of public accusation is an extortious threat when it is malicious in that there is an intent to extort payment.

People v. Fichtner (1952) KS

Facts: Ds, manager and assistant manager of a market, confronted Smith and threatened to accuse him of larceny for shoplifting if he failed to sign a paper admitting his thefts and failed to repay the store.

Issue: Is a reasonable belief that a victim is in fact guilty of the crime of which one has threatened to accuse him a defense to extortion?

Rule: A victim's guilt or innocence as to the crime threatened to be exposed is not relevant in extortion. No debt may be collected by use of extortion, even a debt which is the basis for the crime threatened to be exposed.

Dissent: If one acts without malice and in good faith, one should not be guilty of extortion, because there is no criminal intent.

State v. Miller (1951) KS

Facts: D received a guarantee on his debt by falsely stating that he owned a tractor and by issuing a mortgage thereon.

Issue: Is a guarantee on a debt considered personal property for purposes of theft?

Rule: Tangible items with a title which can be possessed and exchanged and which have commercial value are considered personal property; this does not include real property. Since a guarantee on a debt cannot be possessed and has no title or value, it is not property.

United States v. Girard (1969) KS

Facts: D copied information from a DEA computer data base and sold it to a former agent who wanted to smuggle marijuana.

Issue: Is information considered property for the purposes of theft?

Rule: Information can be property, because anything of value, tangible or intangible, is property.

Regina v. Stewart (1988) KS

Facts: Stewart attempted to bribe a hotel security guard to obtain the names and addresses of hotel employees. Stewart was convicted for "counseling" (facilitating) the offense of theft.

Issue: Does criminal law consider information to be property capable of being stolen?

Rule: Confidential information is not property for the purposes of criminal law. Criminal law weighs the interests of society as a whole, not just the interests of the possessor of confidential information, and it may be to the advantage of society to share the information.

United States v. Siegel (1983) KS

Facts: D, officers and directors of a toy company, breached their fiduciary duties by selling clearance and damaged toys "off the books," thereby creating a hidden cash fund used for bribery.

Issue: Is a breach of fiduciary duty sufficient for a conviction of wire fraud?

Rule: Although a breach of fiduciary duty alone does not necessarily constitute wire fraud, when a fiduciary fails to act in the best interest of his company through nondisclosure of material information and this does or could result in harm to his company, he is guilty of wire fraud.

Dissent: This opens too wide the scope of wire fraud and creates a federal law of fiduciary obligations, which Congress has not approved and which allows for a conviction without showing a resulting harm.

McNally v. United States (S.Ct. 1987) KS

Facts: D received funds via a dummy insurance agency pursuant to a scheme with the chairman of the Kentucky Democratic Party.

Issue: Is the right to honest and impartial government an interest protected by the mail fraud statute?

Rule: The purpose of the mail fraud statute is to protect people from schemes to deprive them of money or property. Neither Congress nor the common law has directly indicated that the purpose of the statute extends to non-property rights, such as honest and impartial government.

Dissent: The purpose of this statute should not be read so narrowly. The greater interest is to prevent the mails from being used as instruments of crime, which includes the right to honest and impartial government.

People v. Brown (1894) KS

Facts: D entered a house and took a bicycle in order to get even with its owner for throwing oranges at D. D intended to return the bicycle, but was apprehended before he could do so.

Issue: Is the intent for larceny met when one intends to temporarily deprive an owner of property?

Rule: The required intent for larceny is to permanently deprive an owner of his property. If one intends only temporary deprivation, the intent requirement is not met. Without the required intent, trespass, and not larceny, is committed.

Regina v. Feely (1973) KS

Facts: D, a bookmaker, took money from his employer's safe, intending to return it. At that time, the employer's debts to D were greater than the amount D took.

Issue: Is an intent to repay a defense to larceny?

Rule: An intent to repay negates the required dishonest intent to permanently deprive an owner of property.

People v. Reid (1987) KS

Facts: Ds took some money by force in order to satisfy a debt the victim owed to them.

Issue: Does a claim of right negate the required intent in robbery?

Rule: A good-faith claim of right negates larcenous intent, but not the intent to commit robbery. Claim of right defenses are not allowed in cases where there is a threat of actual or potential force or coercion.

Commonwealth v. Mitchneck (1938) KW, J

Facts: D, owner of a coal mine, was authorized to deduct money from employees' wages for the purpose of paying their bills at a store. D deducted the money, but failed to pay the bills.

Issue: Is a failure to use property for its agreed purpose fraudulent conversion?

Rule: One cannot fraudulently convert that to which one already holds title and ownership; thus, the agreed purpose of the property is not relevant. Fraudulent conversion occurs only when one has legal possession of property belonging to another and then fraudulently withholds, converts, or applies the same to one's own use and benefit.

People v. Davis (1977) KW
Facts: After allegedly entering an unoccupied open office and taking a typewriter, Davis was convicted of burglary. There was no direct evidence linking him to the purported theft.
Issue 1: What are the statutory elements of burglary?
Rule 1: A person may be convicted of burglary when, without authority, he knowingly enters or remains in an area with the intent to commit a felony or theft.
Issue 2: May the elements of burglary be proven circumstantially?
Rule 2: Circumstantial evidence, arising from either evidence of entry or of the criminal's later acts, is sufficient to prove burglary.

People v. Dioguardi (1960) KW
Facts: D made it clear to a store owner that D could end the picketing of the man's store if he retained D's firm and paid a fee.
Issue: Must one create another's fear or threaten to do something in order to be guilty of extortious acquisition of property?
Rule: To commit extortion one does not necessarily have to create a fear, because seizing upon an existing fear so as to gain benefit is adequate. The threat involved can also be one of omission, for a threat to do nothing can be as useful in extortion as a threat to act.

Anon. v. The Sheriff of London (1473) W
Facts: D was to transport bales of woad. Along the way, D broke open the bales, took the goods contained inside, and converted them to his own use.
Issue: Is it larceny to break open a container with which one has been entrusted and to take some or all of the contents and convert them to one's own use?
Rule: There is no trespass in taking when one is already in possession of the property, as in the case of a bailee, so a conviction for larceny is precluded even with a subsequent conversion. However, by opening the container, a bailee trespasses in the taking because she only has possession

of the container and not its contents; thereby making the bailee liable for larceny.

The King v. Bazeley (1799) W

Facts: D, a teller at a banking house, received some money, part of which he placed in his pocket and used for his own purposes.

Issue 1:   Does an employer have constructive possession over money received by an employee which has not yet reached a cash box?

Rule 1: An owner's title to money does not automatically afford constructive possession. Until the money is placed in its allocated place of reception, the employee who first received it retains full possession and cannot be guilty of larceny.

Dissent: Possession in law should follow the right of property, so that an owner would always be in possession.

Issue 2: If an owner has possession and an employee takes possession of the property is he guilty of larceny?

Rule 2: One must have the requisite felonious intent at the time possession is taken. If possession is taken first and the intent to convert comes later, the possession is lawful and larceny will not lie.

People v. Olivo,
People v. Gasparik,
People v. Spatzier (1981) DS, MIB

Facts: In each of the three cases, D acted in a manner that suggested shoplifting, but was apprehended before leaving the store.

Issue: Can one be guilty of larceny for shoplifting without leaving a store?

Rule: Larceny can be complete even before a shoplifter leaves a store. Store owners only consent to a customer's possession of goods for a limited purpose and the requisite taking of property is evidenced by a customer's exercise of control over the goods inconsistent with the owner's continued rights.

State v. Williams (1970) DS

Facts: D leased some hogs for breeding purposes. After the given period the hogs' owner came to retrieve them, but they were no longer in D's possession. D claimed they had already been returned.

Issue: Can conversion in embezzlement be shown by simple receipt, demand, and refusal to return?

Rule: Only in regards to public officials is a showing of receipt, demand, and refusal to return sufficient to establish conversion. In all other cases, fraudulent conversion to defendant's use and an intent to defraud must be proven. Either direct or circumstantial evidence is needed to show actual conversion.

Pollard v. State (1971) DS
Facts: D wrote a check to a used-car dealer which D asked not be deposited until the following week. Later, the check was returned for insufficient funds.

Issue: Is one guilty of false pretenses for the writing of a bad post-dated check?

Rule: False pretenses requires that one receives value (title to property) at the very time the false pretenses are made (delivery of a bad check). Since receipt of title in exchange for a post-dated check is equivalent to a credit-sale, title is legally acquired before any possible false pretense occurs.

State v. Long (1983) DS
Facts: D took money from a locked money box used for purchasing milk. While leaving, D shoved the dairy farmer and drove off.

Issue: Are the elements of robbery satisfied when force is used after the taking of property?

Rule: Robbery requires use of force or threat thereof either preceding or contemporaneous to an act of taking possession of property.

State v. Long (1984) DS
Facts: (Appeal from the lower court.)

Issue: When is a taking of possession complete?

Rule: One takes possession of another's property upon attainment and exercise of complete control over the property. This control is not acquired where a taking is immediately resisted by an owner before the property is removed from the premises or from the owner's presence.

People v. Gauze (1975) DS
Facts: D argued with his house-mate, left their home, returned home with a gun, and shot the house-mate.

Issue: Can one burglarize one's own home?

Rule: It is not possible to burglarize one's own home, because of the absolute right to enter one's own domicile. Thus, even entry for a felonious purpose invades no possessory right of habitation. Since the purpose of burglary statutes is to protect people from the danger of unauthorized entries, it does not apply to entry into one's own home.

State v. Gordon (1974) DS

Facts: After escaping from legal custody, D needed a car. At gun point D took a car from the possession of the owner, saying that D would take care of it and return it as soon as possible. D abandoned the car before being recaptured.

Issue: What is the specific intent required for robbery?

Rule: Robbery is an aggravated form of larceny and requires the same intent as larceny, which is to permanently deprive an owner of property. This intent can be found even if one intends only temporary use, because intent to use temporarily and abandon is equivalent to intent to permanently deprive.

United States v. Adamson (1983) DS

Facts: D, a bank president, approved a loan to a friend's company, which essentially amounted to a personal loan. The loan was greater than allowed by law for personal loans.

Issue: Can the mens rea standard for a willful offense be recklessness?

Rule: Willful indicates that an offense must be committed knowingly. Recklessness is a lower standard than knowledge. When the offense requires willful action, the mens rea must be at least knowingly.

Dissent: When one is under an affirmative duty, intent should be inferable from reckless disregard of the duty.

People v. Robinson (1983) J

Facts: D removed the wheels and tires of a car which had been stolen the night before.

Issue: Can one commit larceny by taking from a stolen possession?

Rule: When asportation has ceased, the original larceny is complete, and a subsequent taking cannot be larceny, but only possession of stolen goods.

Dissent: Intent must be looked at in larceny. If the original thieves' intent is to permanently deprive an owner of part of what they carry away and the accused takes that part, then the larceny is not complete until he takes that part and he can be guilty of larceny.

Commonwealth v. Ryan (1892) J

Facts: D, a liquor-store employee, received money from a sale, placed it in a money drawer, and took the money only minutes later.

Issue: Can one be guilty of embezzlement if the property is constructively in the possession of the owner, even for a very short period?

Rule: Embezzlement involves conversion of another's property that is in one's possession with felonious intent. Although an owner's constructive possession usually precludes a charge of embezzlement, the offense can lie if one's intent is to not relinquish control, because this negates the employer's constructive possession.

United States v. Rogers (1961) J, MIB

Facts: D presented a check at the bank. The teller misread the check and placed too much money on the counter. D left the bank with the extra money.

Issue: Is it larceny to accept and carry away money which one is mistakenly offered?

Rule: Trespass is usually absent when one is offered possession. However, if a unilateral mistake causes the offer, trespass exists when one knows of the mistake and has felonious intent at the time of taking.

People v. Baskerville (1983) J

Facts: D was accused of robbing an Air Force exchange with a towel wrapped around his arm. Soon after the robbery, D bought many things and was found in possession of some of the stolen money.

Issue: Can guilt for robbery be inferred from possession of stolen property?

Rule: Guilt for a higher offense such as robbery can be inferred from the possession of stolen property, but only if no evidence is offered which suggests that the offense was committed by another. In such a case, one can only be convicted for receipt of stolen property.

People v. Blair (1972) J

Facts: D entered a car wash, washed his car, forced open the coin box, and fled.

Issue: What is a "building" for the purposes of burglary?

Rule: A "building" is an edifice designed for the habitation of men or animals or for the shelter of property. It does not need to be completely enclosed and may also be a public place.

State v. Polzin (1939) J

Facts: D agreed to pay a woman's debts for a fee. D then approached her creditors, and they agreed to pay D's agency to collect the woman's debts.

Issue: Can there be a theft when no property is taken from the victim?

Rule: Without a loss of property, there can be no theft. Any mismanagement of property not amounting to loss can only be a civil matter.

People v. Kunkin (1973) J

Facts: A mail clerk for the Attorney General brought D a roster with the aim of having it printed by D's employer, a newspaper. The roster was in D's possession for a period of time, but D did not pay for the roster, although it was printed in the newspaper.

Issue: When is property considered "stolen" for purposes of receipt of stolen property?

Rule: One cannot be guilty of receiving stolen property if the property was not taken with the intent to permanently deprive another of possession.

People v. Talbot (1934) J

Facts: D, a corporate officer, openly used company funds to personally speculate on the stock market, but D intended to repay the monies taken.

Issue: What is the necessary intent for embezzlement?

Rule: Embezzlement requires intent to convert the property of another that is in one's possession. Intent to repay is not a defense to embezzlement, because the harm involved is immediate breach of trust and not necessarily permanent deprivation of possession.

People v. Butler (1967) J

Facts: D went to Anderson's home with the intent to take some money which he believed Anderson owed him. A fight ensued, and D fatally shot Anderson.

Issue: What is the required intent for robbery?

Rule: Robbery is an aggravated form of larceny; therefore, both larceny and robbery require intent to permanently deprive another of property. Any bona fide belief, even a good-faith mistake, negates larcenous intent.

Dissent: A claim of right, mistaken or otherwise, should not negate the intent for robbery, just as it does not for embezzlement.

State v. Burns (1931) J

Facts: D was hired by an employer to determine if any of the employees were embezzling. D confronted an employee and accused him of embezzlement. D told the employee that he would be sent to prison if he did not confess and repay the loss.

Issue: Is it extortion if one's intent is to recover only that amount of money owed and nothing more?

Rule: Intent to recover only that which was actually embezzled negates the felonious intent necessary to a charge of extortion.

People v. Shirley (1961) J

Facts: D received welfare and aid for her needy children. D failed to inform the agency that an unrelated adult was living with D, which would have affected D's welfare checks.

Issue: Can failure to inform be a false representation?

Rule: Failure to report information can be a false representation when coupled with intent to defraud and when property is received in reliance upon the false representation.

United States v. Smith (1982) J

Facts: D taped and reproduced television programs which he copied and distributed in interstate commerce. D was found guilty of copyright infringement.

Issue: Is copyright infringement a form of theft?

Rule: Copyright infringement is not theft. A copyright is an intangible right and is not property which is capable of being taken. Distribution of copied material is not a taking because the tangible property being distributed does not belong to another.

United States v. Lemire (1983) J

Facts: D did not disclose a conflict of interest involving the shipping of employee housing to Saudi Arabia.

Issue: Can one be guilty of wire fraud for deprivation of employee loyalty?

Rule: Schemes to defraud or breaches of duty must intend to deprive another of some benefit from that duty. The duty of employee loyalty is not a benefit in itself, but allows for the existence of benefits, so that a breach of duty of loyalty alone and without more is insufficient for wire fraud.

United States v. O'Grady (1984) J

Facts: D received many trips, meals, and other benefits from the companies with which he dealt in his capacity as a public official.

Issue: Under the Hobbs Act is the mere acceptance of benefits by a public official "extortion under color of official right" if the official knows that the office is the motivation for the benefits?

Rule: The Hobbs Act is targeted at wrongful use of public office, not merely acceptance of benefits. Although accepting gifts is part of the offense, an official must do something to cause or induce the giving of benefits.

Concurrence: Inducement is a necessary element of extortion under color of official right, but it can take many forms. Inducement should be inferable from repeated acceptances of substantial benefits over time.

Concurrence: Instructions can be given that inducement is inferable from a "pattern of receipt."

Concurrence/Dissent: It is simpler to interpret this Act as a form of extortion, which, like extortion, requires criminal intent. This, along with the element of interference with interstate commerce, resolves the problem of conviction for the acceptance of insignificant benefits.

Dissent: A reasonableness standard should be used to determine if benefits were large enough to be extortionary in nature.

Taylor v. United States (S.Ct. 1990) MIB

Facts: Defendant was charged and sentenced under the Career Criminals Amendment Act, which provided tougher sentencing for a defendant with three prior convictions of specified offenses. The defendant argued that one of his convictions, for burglary, should not count for the purposes of this statute because it lacked risk of physical injury to another.

Issue: What is the meaning of the word "burglary" as used in the Career Criminals Amendment Act?

Rule: (Blackmun, J.) The modern generic definition of burglary, which requires an unlawful or unprivileged entry into a building with intent to commit a crime, should be used to convict for the purposes of the Career Criminals Amendment Act. This is necessary in order to avoid disparate results stemming from the variable usage of "burglary" in state statutes.

State v. Howe
State v. Jensen
State v. Walsh (1991) MIB

Facts: All three defendants were charged with burglarizing their parents' homes. The relevant burglary statute required that a person must unlawfully enter a building to be found guilty. The defendants claimed that they were privileged to enter their parents' homes due to their parents' statutory obligation to provide for them.

Issue: May a parent revoke a child's privilege to enter the parents' home?

Rule: A parent may revoke a child's privilege to enter the parent's home, if that intention is clearly and unequivocally conveyed to the child, and alternative means for taking care of the child's necessities (e.g., a foster home) are provided.

People v. Betts (1937) MIB

Facts: D noticed three unfamiliar heifers on his land. They remained there for over a month until D allowed a tenant farmer to sell them and to repay his debt to D with part of the earnings.

Issue: Does finding of lost property with subsequent conversion and without an attempt to return constitute larceny?

Rule: A finder is under no duty to advertise or to make inquiry regarding the identity of the property's owner. If there is no intent to convert when the property is found, there can be no larceny for subsequent conversion, because a subsequent intent to convert does not relate back.

United States v. Parker (1975) MIB

Facts: D rented a car for three days but did not return it. The car was recovered over two months later.

Issue 1: What is the intent required for larceny by bailee?

Rule 1: Larceny by bailee is committed when a bailee has the intent to permanently deprive a bailor of property.

Issue 2: When is it proven that a bailee has failed to return the property and can be guilty of larceny by bailee?

Rule 2: Failure to return by a bailee is established when the bailment is over and the bailee cannot explain the failure to return. Eventual return of the object of the bailment does not negate felonious intent or excuse the delay in return.

Lund v. Commonwealth (1977) MIB

Facts: D, a graduate student, used computer time without proper authorization.

Issue: Is using computer time a taking of property for larceny?

Rule: Computer time, like labor and services, is not property because it is neither tangible nor moveable. Larceny requires a taking and conversion which do not occur through simple use.

Skeeter v. Commonwealth (1977) MIB

Facts: D told an insurance salesman that D's girlfriend could get him three color televisions for $200. He gave D the money but never received the televisions.

Issue: Is direct evidence of felonious intent necessary in larceny?

Rule: Intent to commit larceny is implied when a taking is wrongful. This is allowed because there is usually no direct evidence of intent. A victim's temporary consent to a taking of possession does not negate intent.

State v. Jacquith (1978) MIB

Facts: D stole a pair of prescription sunglasses from a van.

Issue: What test is used to determine value in order to grade an offense as either grand or petit larceny?

Rule: The "fair market value" test is used in grading larceny, unless no market exists, in which case the "replacement value less depreciation" test is used.

Warren v. State (1945) MIB

Facts: D took and sold Prestone from the auto plant where he worked. D had keys to the storage building where the Prestone was kept.

Issue: Does employee access to property constitute constructive possession thereby allowing an indictment for embezzlement?

Rule: Mere access to property does not constitute possession. Possession by an employee exists only when it is accorded though a special trust and confidence with the owner. Without possession, an indictment cannot be for embezzlement.

Hubbard v. Commonwealth (1959) MIB

Facts: D wrote a check to a car dealer in payment for cars, saying that the check would be good by the time it reached the bank. The check was returned. D also asserted that his business was good and that he had a loan to cover the check.

Issue 1: Is one guilty of writing and delivering a bad check if one states that it is not yet good, but will be?

Rule 1: One cannot be guilty of writing and delivering a bad check if one states that it is not good at that time, because no false pretense has been made and intent to defraud cannot be inferred.

Issue 2: Are false promises sufficient to constitute false pretenses?

Rule 2: Unlike false statements as to existing facts or past events, false representations as to future events are not criminal.

People v. Rife (1943) MIB

Facts: D bought a large amount of brass from a boy. Prior to this, a large amount of brass disappeared from a rail yard.

Issue: Can receipt of stolen property be established by circumstantial evidence?

Rule: To be guilty of receipt of stolen property, one must receive property which one *knows* to have been stolen by another, and one must have felonious intent at the time of receipt. Any of these elements can be proven through circumstantial evidence.

Barnes v. United States (S.Ct. 1973) MIB

Facts: D possessed recently stolen checks which were payable to people D did not know.

Issue: Can inference of guilty knowledge be drawn from unexplained possession of stolen goods?

Rule: An inference of guilty knowledge can be drawn from unexplained possession of stolen goods without infringing the right of due process and the privilege against self-incrimination.

Dissent: This inference allows for convictions without proof of wrongdoing, which is contrary to the right to due process.

People v. Patton (1979) MIB

Facts: D grabbed a churchgoer's purse from her fingertips and ran off before she realized what had happened.

Issue: Is snatching property from an unsuspecting person's fingertips sufficient use of force or threat of force to constitute robbery?

Rule: Without any noticeable or material violence to a victim, the taking of property is theft and not robbery.

United States v. Melton (1973)L, MIB

Facts: D broke into another's home during the night, but did not try to flee upon discovery, did not possess any stolen goods, and did not resist arrest.

Issue: Absent an intent to commit a criminal offense, can one be guilty of robbery?

Rule: Some evidence, either direct or circumstantial, of intent to commit an offense is necessary for robbery. Without any evidence, criminal intent cannot be inferred, and one is guilty only of unlawful entry.

Dissent: Criminal intent should be inferred when there is no reasonable explanation for one's presence in another's home.

United States v. Turley (S.Ct. 1957) MIB

Facts: D borrowed a car from another for the purpose of driving mutual friends to their homes. D converted the car to his own use and sold it in another state without the permission of the owner.

Issue: Does the scope of the word "stolen" extend only to those takings which constitute larceny, or does it include embezzlement and other felonious takings?

Rule: Although there is no established common-law meaning, legislative purpose suggests that "stolen" covers embezzlement and other felonious takings as well as larceny.

Dissent: Extending the scope of "stolen" to include all forms of dishonest acquisition is too sweeping a measure and is unwarranted.

TABLE OF CASES

Fox, United States v. 236
Fraley, Ex Parte 156
Francis v. Franklin 156
Frazier, State v. 175
Freeman, United States v. 267
Fulcher v. State 273
Fulcher v. Wyoming 273
G., Joseph, In Re 171
Gallagher, State v. 277
Gamble, United States v. 279
Garcia v. State 225
Garguilo, United States v. 243
Garner v. Memphis
    Police Department 277
Garner, Tennessee v. 258
Garoutte, State v. 260
Gasparik, People v. 302
Gauntlett, People v. 64
Gauze, People v. 303
Gebardi v. United States 225
Gian-Cursio v. State 164
Gibson v. State 168
Gideon v. Wainright 37
Girard, United States v. 299
Girouard v. State 146
Gladman, People v. 159
Gladstone, State v. 219
Goetz, People v. 254
Gooden v. Commonwealth 166
Gooding, Warden v. Wilson 73
Goodman, State v. 160
Goodseal, State v. (1971) 276
Goodseal, State v. (1976) 154
Gordon v. United States 222
Gordon, State v. 100, 304
Gore v. United States 94
Gory, People v. 93
Graham v. United States 297
Grant, People v. 95
Grebe, State v. 229
Green, State v. 265
Gregg v. Georgia 66, 150

Griffin v. California 40
Griffin v. State 235
Grimaud, United States v. 66
Griswold v. Connecticut 70
Grunewald v. United States 228
Guenther, People v. 277
Guest, State v. 97
Guido, State v. 266
Guillett, People v. 282
Guminga, State v. 88
Hamilton, United States v. 195
Hampton v. United States 279
Harmelin v. Michigan 58
Harrington, State v. 298
Harris, People v. (1956) 167
Harris, People v. (1978) 191
Hatch, State v. 98
Hayes, State v. 220
Hays v. United States 70
Heinlein, United States v. 163
Henderson v. Kibbe 171
Henley, Commonwealth v. 198
Hernandez, People v. 104
Hickman, People v. 160
Hicks v. United States 218
Hillsman, United States v. 260
Hilton Hotels Corp.,
    United States v. 221
Hodges, State v. 256, 270
Hoffman Estates, Village of v.
    Flipside Hoffman Estates, Inc. 73
Holland v. State 232
Holloway v. United States 283
Holmes v. Director of
    Public Prosecutions 167
Holmes, United States v. 62
Hood, People v. 103, 264
Hopkins v. State 98
Horton, State v. 174
Howe, State v. 309
Hubbard v. Commonwealth 310

MacDonald & Watson Waste
Oil Co., United States v. 222
Magliato, People v. 164
Magness, United States v. 232
Maher v. People 146
Maik, State v. 271
Majewski, Director of Public
Prosecutions v. 270
Malloy v. Hogan 40
Malone, Commonwealth v. 148
Mandujano, United States v. 193
Marley, Ex Parte 104, 234
Marrero, People v. 88
Marshall v. Garrison 65
Marshall, People v. 174, 229
Martin Dyos, Regina v. 194
Martin v. Ohio 275
Martin v. State 84
Martin, Commonwealth v. 256
Mathews v. United States 279
Mayes v. The People 157
Mazza, Commonwealth v. 163
McCleskey v. Kemp 150
McDonald v. United States 241
McFadden, State v. 187
McIlwain School Bus Lines,
Commonwealth v. 155, 244
McNally v. United States 299
McQuirter v. State 189
McVey, State v. 219
Melton, United States v. 90, 312
Mercer, State v. 98
Merrell v. United States 241
Michael M. v. Superior Court of
Sonoma County 74
Michelena-Orovio, United
States v. 227
Midgett v. State 158
Migliore, People v. 198
Miller, State v. 298
Mitchneck, Commonwealth v. 300
Monahan, State v. 282

Moore, United States v. 269
Moretti, State v. 243
Morgan, Director of Public
Prosecutions v. 92, 122
Morgan, Regina v. 122
Morissette v. United States 87
Muench v. Israel 220
Mullaney v. Wilbur 39, 151
Murphy, United States v. 280
Murray, People v. 195
Myers v. Commonwealth 37
M'Naghten's Case 265
M'Naghten's Case, Daniel 265
Nash v. United States 59
Neapolitan, United States v. 236
Nelson v. United States 297
Nelson, People v. 128
Nelson, State v. 272
New York Central & Hudson River
Railroad Co. v. United States 221
Newton, People v. (1970) 84
Newton, People v. (1973) 95
Nix v. Whiteside 35
Nolan v. State 295
Noren, State v. 166
Norman, State v. 255
Northington v. State 168
O'Brien, State v. 154
O'Grady, United States v. 308
Ochoa, State v. 233
Odom, State v. 90
Olivo, People v. 302
Olsen, People v. 86, 127
Olshefski, Commonwealth v. 103
Onofre, People v. 278
Onufrejczyk, Regina v. 36, 172
Orndorff, People v. 192
Ostrosky v. State 101
Ott, State v. 166
Pace v. State 233
Palendrano, State v. 60
Paluch, People v. 198

THE BEST WAY TO
LAND A LEGAL JOB:
AN INTERNSHIP

Internships are the hottest way to get job experience, learn about the legal profession, and showcase your talents before potential employers. *The Experienced Hand* is a wonderful guide that will show you how to find an internship and do your best while there. The book contains worksheets to help you evaluate and accomplish your goals, advice on how to enlist faculty support for academic credit for your internship, a sample learning contract, a sample evaluation form, actual case histories, journals, sample letters and resumes. *The Experienced Hand* is a valuable resource if you are considering work experience as part of your legal education.

THE EXPERIENCED HAND: A Student Manual for Making the Most of an Internship
by Timothy Stanton and Kamil Ali, $11.99

BLOND'S® LAW GUIDES

SULZBURGER & GRAHAM PUBLISHING
505 Eighth Avenue
New York, NY 10018

800-366-7086

ORDER FORM

Name: _____   Phone: _____

Shipping address: _____   Law School: _____
(No PO Boxes)
_____   Graduation: _____

City/State/Zip: _____

Credit Card #: _____   Expiration: _____

Signature: _____

BLOND'S LAW GUIDES $15.99

___ Torts
___ Torts, Prosser Ed.
___ Torts, Henderson Ed.
___ Property
___ Property, Dukeminier Ed.
___ Evidence
___ Contracts
___ Contracts, Farnsworth Ed.
___ Family Law
___ Income Tax
___ Corporations
___ Criminal Law
___ Civil Procedure
___ Civil Procedure, Yeazell Ed.

___ International Law
___ Constitutional Law
___ Administrative Law
___ Commercial Law
___ Criminal Procedure

BLOND'S ESSAY SERIES $21.99

___ Torts
___ Contracts

BLOND'S MULTIPLE CHOICE $29.99

___ Multistate Questions

BAR EXAM ESSAY $24.99

___ Scoring High On Bar Exam Essays

Shipping Information

)UPS Ground: $3.00 per order
)
)Second Day Air (3 day if ordered late):
)$7.00 first book, $1.00 each additional book

)Next Day Air:
)$10.00 first two books, $3.00 each
)additional book
)Saturday delivery an additional $10.00

Delivery time will vary, based on distance from New York City. Washington/Boston corridor can expect delivery 2 working days after shipment. West Coast should allow 6 working days, unless Second Day or Next Day Air is specified when ordering.

PLEASE MAKE CHECKS AND MONEY ORDERS PAYABLE TO: SULZBURGER & GRAHAM PUBLISHING